SAMUEL AJAYI CROWTHER

Bishop of the Niger

TOKUNBO OTESANYA

WESTBOW
PRESS®
A DIVISION OF THOMAS NELSON
& ZONDERVAN

WestBow Press books may be ordered through booksellers or by contacting:

WestBow Press
A Division of Thomas Nelson & Zondervan
1663 Liberty Drive
Bloomington, IN 47403
www.westbowpress.com
844-714-3454

Scripture quotations are taken from the Holy Bible, King James Version.

ISBN: 979-8-3850-0916-9 (sc)
ISBN: 979-8-3850-0917-6 (e)

Library of Congress Control Number: 2023919011

Print information available on the last page.

WestBow Press rev. date: 11/06/2023

Samuel Ajayi Crowther

SLAVERY AND LIBERATION

Alafin Abiodun, the king of Oyo empire who ascended the throne at about 1770, was the maternal great-great-grandfather of Bishop Samuel Ajayi Crowther. Alafin's daughter Osu became the mother of Olaminigbin, meaning "all my joys, honour, and glory are laid low". Olaminigbin was the father of Ibisomi, who is the mother of Bishop Samuel Ajayi Crowther. Ibisomi was a priestess of the deity called Obatala. She was also known as Afala, signifying the princess or priestess of Obatala, or "Lord of the White Cloth,". The god Obatala was to bring order and beauty out of chaos, and his habitation is supposed to be a sphere of absolute and dazzling purity. The distinctive honour of Afala was that she was responsible to keep pure and clean the snowy raiment and immaculate curtains of this deity.

On his father's side he belonged to the clan "Edu" and his grandfather was the Bale or Duke of Awaiye-Petu, from Ketu. His grandfather was a successful weaver of a fabric, specially designed for the use of the King of Erin, and this "aso Elerin" became the recognized production of the family looms.

Ajayi's ancestors, founded the settlement called Osogun, literally meaning "It is not unlike medicine," the native explanation of which is that " wisdom being the gift of the gods, unlike medicine, is freely imparted from man to man." In Africa, names of persons and places have distinctive meanings. It was in this little town (in today's Iseyin Local Government, Oyo State, Nigeria), at a date which cannot be precisely determined, but was probably in the year 1806, that Ajayi was born. The name Ajayi is only given to a child born with his face to the ground. Yoruba tradition believes such child would have a remarkable future. His parents according to Yoruba custom, went to the shrine of Ifa, the god of divination, whose priest, called babalawo, i.e., "father who has a secret" to inquire of the oracle concerning his future.

The Ifa priest sometimes use a whitened board, upon which strange figures were drawn and calculations were made. The priest could also use the carved wooden

Ifa bowl, in which thirty split palm nuts were shuffled and the decision of the god announced after counting the whites and the browns. The priest declared for Ajayi, that on no account was he to be a devotee of any idol worship, for he was destined to be an Aluja, that is, one celebrated and distinguished, to serve the great and highest God and no idol whatever. By this he implied the principal deity, spoken of as Olorun, the maker of heaven and earth.

His parents were puzzled with this prophecy and decided to keep a close watch on the little boy. Ajayi's father continued the family trade of weaving and was prosperous. He was also one of the elders or councillors in the community. Because of his responsibilities in the town, he handed over his farm to the care of Bola, his elder son. At a young age of about eight years, Ajayi was a successful breeder of poultry having a market to sell his birds and possessing a head of cowrie shells worth sixpence. At this young age Ajayi got for himself a piece of land near his father's farm. He was trained to farm by his senior brother Bola and became quite good in the cultivation of yams, the staple food of the people. Every morning Ajayi goes to work in his farm seven miles from Osogun. It was the custom of the people to teach early in life the young ones the spirit of industry. The youths of Osogun form themselves into little clubs to help each other in their small farms in case of need. Ajayi was made captain of such a club having forty members. Ajayi grew up taking leadership role among his peers in Osogun.

Dispersion and Emancipation

The young Ajayi grew up in times of insecurity in Yoruba land. The fall of the old Yoruba empire of Oyo, and the effect of the great Islamic jihads, which were establishing a new Fulani empire to the north, meant instability for the Yoruba states. Warfare and slave raiding became widespread with war destroying peaceful existence of towns, villages, and other settlements in much of the Yoruba country. It was the time when the major commerce of the day was selling and buying people as slaves. Many women and children were taken captive as slaves and men that surrendered. The enemies who carried on these wars devastating the land carried out the wars principally for slave raiding. They had no other employment but selling slaves to the Spaniards and Portuguese on the coast. They were mainly Yoruba and Fulani Muslims and their armed slaves. The slave raids with its trauma of divided families and disrupted socio-economic life of several communities provided market for European traders at the coast. These maintained a trade in slaves, though declared illegal by the British Colonial government but still richly profitable, across the Atlantic.

During this period at about 1821, the boy Ajayi was enjoying parental care and love from his family and peace in the community. But fate was preparing him for the future evangelism of his race just as Joseph was sold as slave in Egypt to save his family from famine. Ajayi was to be torn apart and separated from family and relations and experience being in slavery. Fate had marked him out for a journey from the land of idol worship and superstition to a place where His Gospel is preached.

It was a quiet morning when Osogun was attacked by slave raiders and caught unprepared to ward off the attackers. The ill-fated inhabitants had no warning and had risen as usual at daybreak to be engaged in their daily activities on the fateful morning. In the various dwellings could be heard the sounds of the women and children engaged in domestic chores and the men preparing for their occupation. All seemed to be peaceful. This fateful day Osogun was to have its turn of sorrowful fate of desolation and deprivation caused by the inhuman act of slave traders and their agents. At about 9 a.m. the enemies approached Osogun and not long after, had surrounded the town to prevent any escape of the inhabitants. Just then the alarm was raised that the enemies were on them and in an instant, there was confusion.

Osogun had a wooden fence about four miles in circumference defended by a deep moat. There were about twelve thousand inhabitants and of this were three thousand fighting men. Some of the able-bodied men were not at home and those who were had about six gates to defend, and many other weak places about the fence round Osogun. The men available seized their weapons and were mustered to defend the walls, but their efforts were not enough to hold so long a line of defence and prevent the enemy gaining ground. For three or four hours they maintained a brave resistance, but while holding the enemy in check at one point, another party forced their way into the town through the weakest link in their defence. The defenders engaged the attackers in fierce hand-to-hand fighting in the streets while in the confusion calling to their women to flee to the forest. In one of the huts at this supreme moment rushed Ajayi's father to tell his family to flee to safety; and then, he hurried back to the front to continue fighting in their defence. His wife, like the others, hastened to the bush with her little niece and three children; one an infant of ten months, and the eldest a boy of twelve years and a half, who, child as he was, valiantly seized his bow and arrows to protect them. This little fellow was Ajayi, the future Bishop of the Niger.

Terrified women caught up their little ones, and bidding the elder children to follow, tried to escape in the bush. The women and children, with infants on back of mothers, ran as fast as they could through the shrubs to escape and avoid being captured. The panic-stricken women abandoned their loads and tried to save themselves and their children. It was a big struggle running and trying to escape from the slave raiders for those who had many children to care for. The women and children were overtaken and caught by the slave raiders who threw a rope noose over the neck of every individual, to be led like goats tied together. Many families experienced being divided between three or four enemies and family members led away to see each other no more.

Ajayi was caught with his mother, two sisters, one infant about ten weeks old, and a cousin, while they were trying to escape. Ajayi's load consisted of just his bow and five arrows in the quiver. He however lost the bow in the shrub while trying to escape and could not use it to protect his mother and sisters against the attackers. They too were captured, tied together with ropes, and led out of the burning town. The last time he saw his father was when he came from the fight to give the family the signal to flee and Ajayi never saw him again. His father was later killed in another battle.

The slave raiders were mainly Yoruba and some Fulani Muslims, who led them away from the town. Before they got half-way through the town some Fulani among the attackers separated Ajayi's cousin from their midst. His cousin's mother was living in another village. The huts in the Osogun were set on fire and was rapidly spreading and the flames were very high. As they passed along the blazing streets, they saw many wounded and dying men lying helpless, where they had been struck down. In a few minutes afterwards they left the town to the mercy of the flames. He was never to see Osogun the place of his birth anymore. It was farewell to Osogun where he would have lived and raise his family and be buried peacefully in old age.

They were taken to a town called Iseyin, the rendezvous of the enemies, about twenty miles away. On the way he saw his grandmother in the crowd at a distance, with about three or four other cousins taken with her, for a few minutes, then he saw her no more. Several other captives shared same experience and were held in the same manner as Ajayi's family—grandmothers, mothers, children, and cousins all taken captives. It was a sorrowful sight. The aged women and the infirmed that were not able to walk as fast as the younger ones were often threatened with being put to death on the spot, to get rid of them. The captors were wicked and showed no compassion to the pitiful state of the captives.

The tragedy of Osogun was one of common occurrence in West Africa of those days. During their march to Iseyin they passed several towns and villages raided and left as heaps of burning ruins; many human beings lay dead among the debris, and many more led away into cruel slavery by slave raiders. By evening they were tired from the long walk after the day's sorrowful event of being violently separated from their families. Coming to a spring of water they all drank a great quantity because of their thirst, and this served them for the first meal of the day, with a little dry corn and dried meat, previously prepared by the slave raiders for themselves. It was almost midnight before they reached Iseyin, where they passed the first night in bondage.

The next morning, the cords round their necks was taken off giving them a little relief. They were brought to the chief of the slave raiders as trophies at his feet. Other chiefs were present at the meeting where the captives were to be shared as slaves and spoil of war to his warriors. That is, one half were claimed by the chief, and the other half by the soldiers. Ajayi and his sister fell to the share of the chief of the slave raiders while his mother and the infant to the victors. The captured slaves dared not show sign of their grief as they were being separated from their loved ones. His mother, with the infant, was led away, comforted with the promise that she should see her son and daughter again when they leave Iseyin for Dahdah, the town of the chief slave raider. Hence for the first time, Ajayi and his mother were separated and great of course was his sorrow. A few hours after it was soon agreed upon that Ajayi should be bartered for a horse in Iseyin that very day. In the space of twenty-four hours of being captured and deprived of liberty and all other comforts, Ajayi was made the property of three different persons. After about two months, when the chief was to leave Iseyin for his own town, the horse which was then only taken on trial, not being approved of, Ajayi was restored to the chief, who took him to Dahdah. In Dahdah, Ajayi was very happy to meet his mother and infant sister again, with great joy.

Ajayi lived for three months in Dahdah going for grass for horses with fellow-captives. He was able to visit his mother and sister from his new master's house without any fear or thoughts of being separated any more. One evening he was sent with a man to get some money from a neighbour's house. Ajayi went, but with some fear for which he could not explain, and to his great surprise in a few minutes he was added to the number of many other captives, tied, to be led to the market town early next morning. He became restless and could not sleep. Ajayi spent most of the whole night in thinking of his hopeless situation with tears and fear of being separated again from his mother and sister. There was another boy in the same situation with him; his mother was in Dahdah. Being unable to sleep, he heard the first cockcrow, and when the signal was given the traders arose, loaded the men slaves with baggage, and with one hand chained to the neck they left the town. Ajayi's little companion in affliction cried and begged much to be permitted to see his mother but was soon silenced by punishment. Seeing this, Ajayi was too scared to ask to see his mother. Thus, he was separated from his mother and sister who were then his only comfort in this world of misery. After a few days' travel they came to the market town of Ijaiye. At Ijaiye he came across many who had escaped from Osogun, his native town to this place, or who were in search of their relations, to set at liberty as many as they had the means of redeeming. Their captors kept close watch over them because there were many persons in search of their relations, and through that some had escaped from their owners. In a few days Ajayi was sold to a Mohammedan woman, with whom he travelled and passed many towns on their way to Popo country on the coast, where the Portuguese buy slaves. When they left Ijaiye, after many stopovers, they came to a town called Toko. From Ijaye to Toko all spoke Ewe dialect, but his mistress Oyo, his own dialect. Here he was a stranger, having left the Oyo part of Yoruba land far behind.

Ajayi lived in Toko, his new home for about three months, and walked about with his owner's son with some degree of freedom. His new owner considered this to be safe because Ajayi was not familiar with his new environment and could not possibly run away. There are many destroyed towns and villages to pass through and the danger is high of becoming a prey to some others, who could seize him as a slave. Now and then Ajayi's mistress would send him and her son to the Popo country to buy tobacco and other things to sell at their return. Ajayi saw these errands as a sign that he would be sold to the Portuguese. He heard several stories about them during these journeys to Popo country. Being aware of this, he was afraid and lost his appetite. In a few weeks he caught dysentery. He made up his mind not to go to the Popo country again, but to kill himself one way or other. Several nights out of frustration and how life has turned out for him, Ajayi attempted to strangle himself with his band, but had not courage enough to close the noose tight. His attempts were not effective. He prayed later in life when he became a Christian and asked God to forgive this sin of attempted suicide. When his owner perceived the great change in his mood, she sold Ajayi to another person. Thus, the good Lord, while Ajayi knew Him not, led him not into temptation and delivered him from the evil. After his price had been agreed and counted before his eyes, he was delivered up to his new owner. Ajayi was filled with great sorrow, not knowing where he was now being led.

About the first cockcrowing, which was the usual time to set out with slaves to prevent their being much acquainted with the way, for fear an escape should be made, they set out for Elabbo, the third dialect from his. After having arrived at Ikkekuyere, another town, they stopped. It was not long before he was bartered for tobacco, rum, and other articles. He remained here bound alone for some time before his owner could get as many slaves as he wanted.

After about two months, Ajayi was brought to a slave market called Ikosi, towards the coast, on the bank of a large river, close to Lagos. He was so much terrified at the sight of the river. He had never seen so much water like it in his life. The people on the opposite bank are called Eko. Before sunset, he was bartered again for tobacco and Ajayi became another man's slave. He was now scared with the thought of going into another world and in deep sorrow. He became frightened of crossing this extensive water in a canoe, and was so cautious in every step he took, as if the next would bring him to the bottom. His motion was very awkward indeed. Night coming on, and the men having little time to spare, soon lifted him physically into the canoe and placed him amongst the corn bags and gave Ajayi an Abalah (a cake of Indian corn) for his dinner. Through these fearful hours poor little Ajayi expected every minute would be his last. He was very alarmed at the sound of the waves as they dashed against the sides of the canoe. He had no more desire to end his life, as he had planned, by casting himself overboard. He remained in this same position with the Abalah in his hand, quite confused in thoughts. He waited for his arrival with others at the new world, which they did not reach till about four in the morning. Having now entered Eko, Ajayi was permitted to go anywhere he pleased, as there was no way of escape on account of the extensive river. After landing he was then employed as storekeeper at his master's house at Lagos.

Ajayi had a fortunate meeting with two of his relations in Eko, belonging to different masters. One part of Eko was occupied by the Portuguese and Spaniards, who had come to buy slaves. It was more than three months in Eko before Ajayi saw a white man one evening in a company of six and they came to the street in which he was living. He could not summon enough courage to look at them as he was always suspicious that they had come to take him away. A few days after, just as he feared, he became the eighth in number of the slaves of the Portuguese slave-traders along with other unhappy captives for the transatlantic market. When this happened, Ajayi lost hope of ever seeing his country again and patiently took whatever came his way. It was with a great fear and trembling that he felt for the first time the touch of a white man, who examined him whether he was physically fit or not, as he would inspect a horse. He was kept with a number of other unhappy captives, in the old barracoon or slave shed in which slaves from the interior used to be kept until shipment. The barracoon was suffocating with heat, and on the slightest provocation slaves were beaten with long whips. Upon the site now stands St. Paul's Church Breadfruit station. Men and boys were at first chained together with a chain of about six fathoms (a unit of length equal to 6 feet or 1.8 metres, chiefly used in reference to depth of water) in length, thrust through an iron fetter on the neck of each individual, very heavy and fastened at both ends with padlocks. It was extremely distressing to bear for the slaves and the boys suffered the most. The men, sometimes when they are angry or uncomfortable, would pull the chain forcefully to ease themselves of the weight and this often result in bruises on the necks of the boys or almost suffocating or bruised to death, in a room with one door which was locked as soon as they entered. Very often at night, when two or three individuals quarrelled or fought, the whole group suffered severe discomfort. At last the boys were happy to be separated from the men, when their number increased and no more chain to spare. Boys were now tied with rope together. They were always tied together whether they were going in or out, bathing together and so on. The condition of the females was not much better. They were like this for nearly four months. The very thing Ajayi so much dreaded was ordained by Him who is all knowing to be the means of using him far beyond his wildest imaginations in the Lord's vineyard.

About this time intelligence was received that the British men-of-war were cruising along the shores of the Gulf of Guinea. They belonged to the patrol squadron charged with the suppression of slave running. This became a subject of sorrow to the slaves—who thought that there must be wars on the sea as well as on the land—a thing never heard of before nor imagined practicable. This delayed their embarkation. In the meantime, more slaves were brought into Eko to join them. Among the number was Joseph Bartholomew, who later served the Lord with Ajayi in the service of the Church Missionary Society. After a few weeks delay the one hundred and eighty-seven slaves were embarked at night in canoes from Eko to Victoria Beach just beside the entrance to the lagoon. The following morning, they were taken onboard the vessel (a Portuguese ship called the (ESPERANZA FELIX), which immediately sailed away. The crew being busy in embarking the slaves had no time to give them either breakfast or supper. The slaves were unaccustomed to the motion of the vessel, and they suffered with seasickness, which rendered most of them not fit to take any food whatever throughout the day. But in the midst of this helplessness and hopelessness came the providence of God. That evening, As Her Majesty Ship (H.M.S.) *MYRMIDON* and *IPHIGENIA* cruised slowly along the coast, the officers of the watch detected a suspicious-looking vessel. Instantly the course of the warships was set in that direction, and all doubt as to the cargo and mission of the strange vessel was soon removed. The slave ship ESPERANZA FELIX on sighting the men-of-war, changed her course, and fled in the direction from which she had come. Unable to escape to the open sea, she sought in the twilight to evade her pursuers by entering the Lagos lagoon. But the keen eye of Captain H. G. Leeke detected this manoeuvre; throughout the night his ships kept watch off the bar, and at daybreak he entered the lagoon and the slave vessel ESPERANZA FELIX was arrested by two English men-of-war (warships). By morning of 7 April 1822, Ajayi and other slaves found themselves in the hands of English sailors, whom at first the slaves very much dreaded, because they were armed with long swords. The slaves were called up from the compartment below the deck and were surprised to find themselves between two very large men-of-war and several brigs (a two-masted square-rigged ship, typically having an additional lower fore-and-aft sail on the gaff and a boom to the main mast). The men-of-war were HMS MYRMIDON having Captain H. G. Leeke, and HMS IPHIGENIA having Captain Sir Robert Mends, who captured the Portuguese ship. The Portuguese captain was bound, with his sailors, except the cook, who was preparing breakfast for everyone. The liberated slaves, not realising that they were in friendly hands, stood on the British decks looking on with surprise, mingled with fear. They did not realize the significance of what had happened and, in their ignorance, thought they exchanged one set of masters for another. Hunger later rendered them bold and not being threatened took liberty to get some fruits from the stern (stern is naval term for rear of a ship or boat). In a short time, they went about the vessel in search of plunder of every kind.

After breakfast they were divided into several of the vessels around. This caused new fears, not knowing where their misery would end. The Portuguese had told them that the English only seize slave ships to use the blood of negroes to dye their scarlet cloth and their flesh as baits for cowrie fishing. The slaves had formed a bond as one family, and now being separated as they began to take leave of one another into other vessels, not knowing what would become of them. About this time six of the slaves had become intimate friends—among them were Ajayi and Joseph Bartholomew—kept close together that they might be carried away at the same time. It was not long before the six were conveyed into the MYRMIDON, in which they discovered no trace of those who were shared before them. Ajayi and his mates soon concluded what had become of them when they saw part of a hog hung up to dry and the skin was white—a thing they never seen before, as a hog was always roasted on fire to clear it of the hair in Yoruba country. They supposed that a number of cannon balls ranged along the deck to be the heads of their countrymen. Ajayi and his friends thought what they saw was supposed to be the flesh of the individuals who had been killed for meat. But they soon discovered this not to be so by a close examination of the flesh, with cloven feet, which resembled those of a hog, and by a cautious approach to the cannon balls that they were iron and not human heads. After a few days, the captives were quite at home on the man-of-war and slowly discovered that they were free. Being only six in number, the rescued slaves were soon selected by the sailors as their boys and were soon supplied with dress. The Portuguese owner and his son were brought over in the same vessel, bound in fetters, and Ajayi full of liberty, stepped up to strike him on the head while he was standing by his son. Years later Ajayi thought of this act as very wicked and unkind in its nature and of course repented of it.

Leaving Lagos with the freed slaves, Captain Leeke sailed away and Ajayi spent two months and a half onboard while the man-of-war continued her cruise looking for slaves to set free. Ajayi had time enough to get familiar to his new friends. and became a great favourite with the sailors as a youth of outstanding intelligence. On 17 June 1822 they reached Sierra Leone and set foot again on African soil as liberated slaves and were distributed among the villages in Sierra Leone. During this period, the colony of Sierra Leone had been founded by a coalition of anti-slavery interests who were mostly evangelical Christian and belonged to the circle associated with William Wilberforce and the "Clapham Sect". They were evangelical Christians, prominent in England from about 1790 to 1830, who campaigned for the abolition of slavery and promoted missionary work at home and abroad. After the abolition of the slave trade by the British Parliament in 1807 and the subsequent treaties with other nations to outlaw the traffic, Sierra Leone achieved a new importance. Sierra Leone was intended from the beginning as a Christian settlement, free from slavery and the slave trade. The first permanent element in the population was a group of former slaves from the New World. It was also a base for the naval squadron that searched vessels to find if they were carrying slaves. The slaves were brought to Sierra Leone if any were found aboard.

The West Coast of Africa was still supplying the plantations of the New World with slave labour. These slaves were carried in the ships of those nations, such as Portugal, Spain, France, the United States and Brazil, who had not yet put an end to the traffic. The Evangelicals, the Humanitarians and the British Government soon realized that mere legal prohibition of the traffic was not enough. A way had to be found to put an end to the illegitimate trade in slaves and it must be replaced by legitimate trade in the raw materials from Africa. By this means the manpower of Africa, instead of being exhausted to cultivate the New World and the Indies, could be turned to agricultural production on Africa continent. Only through cultivating habits of industry and preaching the Gospel of Christ could the illegal trade in human be stopped and Africa regenerated.

To all appearances the whole way of life of Sierra Leone - clothing, buildings, language, education, religion, even names closely followed Western models. These were people of diverse origins whose cohesion and original identity were now beyond recall. They accepted the combination of Christian faith and Western lifestyle which Sierra Leone offered. Such was the setting in which young Ajayi now found himself.

Shortly afterwards Ajayi and the other slaves were sent from Freetown to Bathurst and returned for a short time in order to give evidence against their former Portuguese owners; then, coming back, they were placed under wise and kindly care. Ajayi was sent to the family of Mr and Mrs Davey a missionary schoolmaster at Bathurst, a small town a few miles from Freetown. In the loving care of Mr Davey's family, he regained his health and strength. It was in this family that he received divine grace that prepared him for his future destiny as a servant of God Almighty. A native boy who had been there before him gave Ajayi his first lesson in the English. After his first day at school Ajayi was so delighted with his new taste of knowledge that he ran down into the town, begged a halfpenny from one of his countrymen, and with it bought for himself an alphabet card. Within six months from the day of his landing Ajayi was able to read the New Testament. Little Ajayi exhibited a proficiency for study, and under the care of the Mission schoolmaster made good progress. Those early days he would sit with his books in the evening, a candle burning in the middle of the table, at the head of which sat the schoolmaster's worthy wife, and by his side another little able scholar named Asano (i.e. Hassana; she was formerly Muslim) —a Yoruba girl who had also been rescued from slavery. Ajayi Crowther passionately devoted himself to study and reading.

Ajayi learnt carpentry under the care of another schoolmaster, Mr Weeks, and from his wife he increased his steps of reading. As a carpenter he soon showed a proficiency in the use of the chisel and plane, and years later this ability to work for himself and for others became useful to him. Naturally studious and intellectual, he desired after more knowledge. He became in time a monitor and received for that official position sevenpence-halfpenny a month.

The greatest incident of his life, and of any life, was when he met Jesus Christ and worshipped Him, saying, "My Lord and my God." It was the beginning of a new page of unique history of life and mission for Ajayi. He was baptized on 11 December 1825, by the Reverend John Raban, of the (Anglican) Church Missionary Society, and received as his new name Samuel Ajayi Crowther, after a member of that society's home committee, a venerable clergyman, the Rev. Samuel Crowther, Vicar of Christ Church, Newgate Street, London. It was a name by which he became known throughout the world, "Samuel Ajayi Crowther".

One could not have imagined that with this humble beginning, the little boy Ajayi would rise in life and one day be known as Bishop of the Niger and would direct the see of Sierra Leone!

CALL TO MISSION WORK

On 16 August 1826, about four years after arriving Sierra Leone and the year after his baptism, Samuel Ajayi Crowther was taken to Britain by his guardians, Mr and Mrs Davey. The short visit to London broadened Samuel Ajayi Crowther's knowledge of English history which he had developed interest in through his reading books. It was Samuel Ajayi Crowther desire to remain in London to be trained and qualified as a teacher. During his stay of about eight months in London, he became a pupil in the Parochial School Liverpool Road, Islington.

On his return to Sierra Leone, he was appointed as schoolmaster by the Colonial Government in one of the villages at a salary of £1 per month. Though his salary was not much, it was the first income he earned since forcefully taken away as slave from his old home at Osogun. A schoolmaster was an evangelist and in Sierra Leone, Church and school were inseparable.

On Christmas Day, 1827, Samuel Ajayi Crowther was admitted as a student of the Fourah Bay College and the first name of the half-dozen native youths who are entered on its roll of students. The College was established to provide higher level education than the colony's modest schools had given. Also because of the high deathrate of European missionaries sent to the West Coast of Africa, the Committee of the Church Missionary Society felt that if Africa was to be evangelized it must be through her own sons who have better immunity against malaria than the white missionaries. It was therefore necessary that native evangelists should be trained, intellectually and spiritually, for this high vocation specifically to prepare them to go into the hinterland. Some members of Church Missionary Society abroad never trusted in the capacity of an African to discharge the functions of a responsible ministry. They believed the experiment would fail. At this point the Society sent out the Rev. Charles Haensel, a young Lutheran to start the Institution. He was a young missionary, of German birth, from the Basle Seminary. Fourah Bay College did much to prove that the African was quite able, if only he had equal opportunity, to hold his own with the European. The site selected for the College, which provided the first university education in tropical Africa (the college was in 1876 affiliated with the University of Durham, so that its students could qualify for English degrees without leaving Africa) was an old disused slave house, with extensive grounds overlooking Fourah Bay. It was far enough away from the surrounding villages and provides a conducive learning environment that ensure privacy and quiet for students. The building was an ordinary dwelling-house, where students were boarded and lodged on the ground floor, the principal and his wife occupying the floor above. The verandah served for classroom and lecture hall. It was a simple and modest beginning. Mr. Haensel the principal of the school from 1834 to 18840, was a strict administrator whose responsibility was to prepare intelligent and pious natives with education required for becoming Christian teachers among their countrymen.

PICTURE OF FOURAH BAY COLLEGE - Wikipedia

Samuel Ajayi Crowther was the first student to enter the doors of Fourah Bay College. He made some sacrifice leaving his present position as a schoolmaster, to become a scholar again. The pioneering students mostly brought with them scanty possessions —a couple of shirts, a pair of trousers, a hat and perhaps a jacket, with a book of Common Prayer, and in some instances a Bible, which constitute their entire possessions. Mr Haensel, where necessary, added a Bible to their stock, a pair of trousers, and a shirt after a little while, a jacket, if necessary, after a month or two, and another pair of trousers. This for their full dress on Sunday and other particular occasions. At school they always go barefooted. Even Samuel Crowther does so at school, though his visit to England has raised him to the height of white stockings, a suit of blue cloth, a waistcoat, and a beaver hat on Sundays. Samuel Ajayi Crowther brought with him a mattress with which he had been presented when in England, but the principal considered this too great a luxury and at once asked him to return it back home, to which he readily consented.

Their food consists of boiled rice and yams, with some meat or fish occasionally and palm oil, which they eat out of tin pans. The students do their chores; they sweep and scrub the schoolroom and sleeping room, clean the table, and wash their clothes.

At Fourah Bay College, there were four of them who were promoted to the position of monitors and this gave them opportunity to wear shoes. Four strong, stout shoes with very thick soles were procured and given to them from the soldiers' barracks; they were called " Blucher shoes." On a Saturday afternoon they were called, presented with a pair each, and told to put them on every Sunday to Church at St. George's Cathedral, a distance of about three miles. Never having had shoes on before, they began practising in their dormitory that evening. None of them could move a step after lacing up on their feet these bulky items, and consequently they were objects of laughter by their pupils. An idea struck Crowther at once, which he put into execution. Crawling to a corner of the room, he first knelt down, then holding on to the wall for support he stood up, and still being supported by the wall, he stepped round the room many times, the others following his example, till they were able to leave the wall, stand alone, or move about without support. It can be imagined what a burden this was to them, and after losing sight of the college they sat on the grass, took off the shoes, walked barefoot, and only put them on at the porch of the church. They did the same on returning to college. After some months' practice they were able to move better in them but complained how they hurt their feet so and would rather be without them. Much later they invested in the purchase of boots themselves and were careful to buy those that made noise and creaked as they stepped with them, to their great delight and the admiration of their pupils.

Ajayi Crowther began to make tremendous progress in this college. In a letter written a few months after Crowther came into the Institution, Mr. Haensel spoke well of his pupil and observed in him special ability.

"He is a very clever lad," he writes, " and it is a real pleasure to instruct him. He advances steadily in knowledge." Later, he writes: " He is a lad of uncommon ability, steady conduct, a thirst for knowledge, and indefatigable industry."

The climate to Europeans gave urgency to this effort to train others, who did not suffer from the same physical danger to labour in this field. It was high time that something should be done. The Gold Coast had earned an awful name, and its fever-stricken shores became a graveyard of the Europeans.

Very graciously God blessed the new venture, and it produced graduates that went forth, full of faith and zeal, to preach the unsearchable riches of the Gospel to their brethren. Crowther made progress, and became an assistant teacher in the College, and this mark of confidence and respect was quite a turning point in his career.

Crowther was already on the threshold of manhood, and he found a companion in a girl called Asano, who learnt her letters at his side. She too, was a rescued slave, having been captured by HMS BANN, Captain Charles Phillips, on 31 October 1822, and was landed at Sierra Leone in the same year as Crowther. She was at this time acting as schoolmistress and had changed her name at baptism to Susan Thompson.

They were wedded and happily married for over half a century until his wife's death at Lagos in 1881, leaving three sons, one being the Venerable Archdeacon Dandeson Coates Crowther; two were laymen, and the three daughters all married African clergymen. She was spared to see her children's children to the third generation.

In the year 1830 Crowther was appointed from the College to the care of a school at Regents Town, and his wife was officially associated with him as school mistress. Two years after they were promoted to still more important duties at Wellington; and finally, he came back to the College in 1834 on the installation of the Rev. G. A. Kissling as the new principal. Here for some years was Crowther's sphere of work and several of his students were afterwards ordained and appointed as government chaplains at important stations on the coast.

Crowther has a natural aptitude for languages and in his work at the College and elsewhere he showed how great an advantage he possessed in dealing with the chiefs and headmen of the district. This marked him out for notice at a critical moment in his future career.

Though appointed tutor and as a parish assistant under the Rev. G. A. Kissling, who had succeeded the Rev. C. L. F. Haensel as principal, he worked hard at his Greek and Latin during his leisure hours. The conducive learning environment of The College enabled Crowther to improve greatly on his private study with Rev G.A Kissling assistance. He also did useful work with two other students who were under instruction by him, named George Nicol and Thomas Maxwell, who both afterwards became Government chaplains, and the former the husband of one of Crowther's daughters. A Sunday-school in the care of Crowther, was held in an old building called Gibraltar Chapel. With his study of the Greek language which he learned through the aid of Mr. Schlenker, Crowther was soon able to understand the Word of God in that language, in which it was first written by the evangelists and apostles.

The education of the natives in Sierra Leone and their Christian teaching was not an easy task. The challenge Crowther faced like other missionaries was the temperament of the natives, their emotionalism, superstition and ignorance which had to be drastically dealt with. Despite this situation, the Gospel preached to the natives in Sierra Leone brought wonderful change and gave great hope of future progress.

The natives through the labours of the servants of the Church Missionary Society were freed from their superstition to serve God, becoming a new person in Christ. The number of Christians amongst them increased and now fill the Sunday-schools, able to read for themselves the wonderful works of God. There were some few, who pretend to be interested and attended the evening school merely to please their missionary, who was also their manager. The students often play truancy, for when school was opened with a hundred or more students, not more than fifty remain at end of the class. Many of the students under pretence of going out, slipped away to their homes. Some openly expressed their displeasure at school and think that it was only useful for the youths. These were the inhabitants of Wellington who after a while willingly contributed and built a chapel which later was too small to accommodate members during public worship on Sunday mornings and for the Sunday school.

There were some others who gave a greater part of their time to drumming and dancing. At that time this was a favourite amusement, which they do not want to part with. These conducts might have caused great discouragement to the missionaries as it would seem all their work in Africa was to no purpose. But the perseverance of Christian missionaries always bear fruit with success to crown their efforts.

The Anglican missions were often successful in converting 'Liberated Africans', who in turn began to see it as their mission to spread the word in neighbouring parts of Africa. Sierra Leonean 'Liberated Africans' or 'Krios' were an influential diaspora along the coast of West Africa from at least the 1850s.

Thus far, Samuel Ajayi Crowther had accomplished three things in his life: liberation from slavery, salvation from sin, and freedom from ignorance. He had become a free man, a Christian and an educated person. All this took place within the first thirty years of his life. It was in appreciation of all what He had achieved thus far that he determined in his heart that, as God would give him opportunity and ability, he would work among his own people, teaching them as he had been taught, and leading them also to the Saviour who had manifested Himself to him.

FIRST NIGER MISSION

The River Niger is an obvious means of communication and a highway into the very heart of the country. In 1841 the British Government commissioned three iron steamships, the ALBERT, WILBERFORCE and SOUDAN, under Fowell Buxton's idea and Prince Consort Albert's support to explore and chart the Rivers Niger and Benue to open new field for British commerce. This investigative mission was intended to spread commerce, teach agricultural techniques, spread Christianity, and help destroy slave trade at the root and introduce legitimate commerce in its place taking advantage of the trading instincts of negro peoples. The spread of Christianity among the people would achieve moral results and all these would bring permanent peace and prosperity to the Niger nationalities. The leaders of the Niger Mission were to negotiate in the Queen's name with important local chiefs and powers, treaties for the abolition of the slave trade. They were to establish instead, a friendly commercial intercourse between Her Majesty's subjects and African chiefs within whose territories internal slave trade is carried on and the external slave-trade supplied with its victims. The mission was to ascend River Niger by steamboats as far as the meeting points of some of the principal rivers falling into it from the eastward. At these, or at any other points which may be found favourable for the promotion of a legitimate commerce, it was proposed to establish British factories. Through the establishment, the natives may be taught that there are methods of employing the population more profitable to those to whom they are subject than that of converting them into slaves and selling them for exportation to the slave traders. The command of these vessels was placed in the hands of Captain Trotter *(ALBERT)*, Captain William Allen *(WILBERFORCE)*, and Captain Bird Allen *(SOUDAN)* and these three were appointed Her Majesty's Commissioners for the control of the undertaking. These Commissioners and most, if not all the officers, were Christian men. The crews, too, were chosen for their moral character as well as for their seamanship.

The Church Missionary Society (CMS) saw this as an opportunity to reach the Niger with Gospel. They proposed to send two representatives along with the Government officials. When the Government agreed to this, they appointed the Rev. James Schon and Samuel Ajayi Crowther to go with the expedition to ascertain what facilities there might be for the introduction of the Gospel among the nations of the interior of Africa and to report on the disposition of the African chiefs to receive missionaries. James Schon was a German missionary who had spent ten years in Sierra Leone as a missionary of the Society. He had thus become intimately acquainted with the African character and had acquired some knowledge of the native languages like Hausa and Igbo from liberated Africans in Sierra Leone. He was an able linguist with a desire to preach the gospel in the Niger territories. It was a call to duty for Samuel Ajayi Crowther, a lay teacher. The expedition had a great influence in shaping his future career and provided an opportunity to partake in establishing a Christian mission among the natives of the Niger district. God had called him to a wider and more important field of planting Christian Mission in the hinterland of the Niger District. Crowther had a burning desire to preach the Word of Life, at any sacrifice, among his own people in the far-off interior. The great waterways will become highways of salvation, along which the message of peace and goodwill should travel into the interior. In this and subsequent Niger expeditions missionary, commercial and the anti-slavery cause were intricately linked. Four thousand pounds was raised in England for the establishment of a model agricultural farm at the confluence of the Niger and the Benue, a practical demonstration of Buxton's unity of "Bible and Plough". When the tidings came to Messrs. Schon and Crowther that they were to accompany the expedition, they gladly prepared themselves for a trip, which was not without fear of danger to themselves.

The prospect of preaching the Gospel to those who had never heard of the love of Christ was a sufficient incentive to put aside all fears. For Messrs. Schon and Crowther, a separation from wife and home was naturally a painful event, but their families bravely accepted it. Mrs. Schon was only just recovering from a serious illness, and it was not until Rev. James Schon had prayed long and earnestly for Divine help that he ventured to break the news to her of his immediate departure. His wife gladly approved of the journey. With Crowther the parting was not less a painful event. He had to leave his College work, home, and those dear to him.

On 14 April 1841, the three vessels sailed from England and in about ten weeks reached Sierra Leone. The residents of the colony in Sierra Leone had long known of the proposed expedition and great was the excitement when the long-looked-for squadron cast anchor in harbour. The expedition relied heavily on Sierra Leone for interpreters and other helpers whose mother-tongues were those of the Niger ethnic nationalities or surrounding nations, Igbo, Yoruba, Eggarra, Kakanda, Hausa, Borno, Laruba, and Fula. Many of the Sierra Leoneans were eager to accompany the expedition as seamen, labourers, or anything else, and a number were chosen. This expedition brought Samuel Ajayi Crowther into a life-long friendship with Rev Schon.

ALBERT, first vessel of the long-expected Expedition, arrived on 24 June 1841. Members of the expedition had a long time waiting for the arrival of the vessels and in consequence of the delay, were better prepared, by prayer to God for His direction, for the undertaking. While preparations were made to join ALBERT, the "WILBERFORCE" and the " SOUDAN" also arrived. The steamers composing the Expedition, while lying at anchor, graced the harbour of Freetown. They also excited a very great interest among the inhabitants, and were visited, from curiosity, by many persons. Special services were held in Freetown Churches, and a prayer meeting in the principal Church was attended and addressed by the captains of the fleet. At about 5 o'clock Crowther took leave of his wife, children and friend to go onboard SOUDAN where he was quartered in the engineers' mess and Rev James Schon was on the WILBERFORCE. The expedition sailed on 2 July 1841.

Bearing no arms of war; equipped for no devastating conflict with the natives, but carrying a message of peace and goodwill, these three vessels set sail for Niger. In saying good-bye to their wives and children, the brave men who stood full of hope on the decks of the vessels little thought how disastrous would prove their venture, and how many valuable lives would be sacrificed.

For Crowther, this expedition unconsciously prepared him for the administration of a huge diocese in the future. The tears of separation from Mrs. Crowther and rest of his family are still upon his cheeks as his vessel SOUDAN at about eleven o'clock got under way for the Niger, the highway into hinterland of the Niger country. SOUDAN was soon followed by the WILBERFORCE, which took her in tow to save fuel. Ajayi looked back on the colony in which he had spent nineteen years—the happiest part of his life, because there he met with and experienced the saving knowledge of Jesus Christ. He left his wife and four children behind for a while for the mission. He prayed as he left them behind that the Lord, who has been his guide from youth up till now, keep them and him, and make him neither barren nor unfruitful in His service.

He begins to work on his vocabulary of African languages, but gives it up, as seasickness made him feel so ill; but he was down in the steerage (bottom deck of the ship), joining in a Bible-class. He soon meets with a little misadventure which might have been serious.

On 10 July while they were at dinner the glass called "the bull's eye" fell from its fastening on Samuel Ajayi Crowther's head and then on two plates in which he was taking his dinner and broke to pieces. Fortunately, this heavy glass, weighing about five pounds, did not fall perpendicularly on him. At night also his hammock (a wide strip of canvas or rope mesh suspended by two ends, used as a bed), in consequence of its not being properly fastened, gave way at the foot, when he fell and got a slight stroke on the head. Had the lash given way from the head of the hammock he should have suffered seriously. In these circumstances, insignificant as it seems, without God's watchful care over them how soon many misfortunes would have visited them.

By 15 July at about 9 o'clock in the morning the ship was off Cape Coast Castle. They went ashore and met the Wesleyan missionary the Rev. Thomas Birch Freeman, who received Samuel Ajayi Crowther with noticeable kindness, took him into his library, telling him that he might use what books he liked. While wandering among the monuments in the graveyard of the Castle, Samuel Ajayi Crowther made a note of the tablet erected to the Rev. Philip Quaque, a native who was sent to England by the Society for the Propagation of the Gospel in 1754, baptized at St. Mary's, Islington, 7 January 1759, and returned fully ordained as chaplain to the factory, and died, after many trials and disappointments, in 1816. This tablet was naturally of fascinating interest to Crowther. He never knew anything of him before, except from this monument. What attracted his attention was that he was a native of that place — sent to England for education, received Holy Orders, and was employed in his own country upwards of fifty years. During the time they were lying at Cape Coast, which was about two weeks, Crowther got ready his Yoruba Translations, which Captain Allen sent off from this place, by a vessel bound direct for England.

On 25 July Lord's Day in the afternoon, Crowther had the opportunity of going to Rev. Freeman's Meeting, at this place. It was interesting experience to him, as it was the first time, he heard a Sermon preached through an interpreter. The service was conducted according to the Order of the Church of England. After Prayers were read, the Minister went into the pulpit; when he gave out a hymn, before Sermon; and while the last verse was being sung, the interpreter joined him in the pulpit. The Minister read his text in English, and sat down; then the interpreter rose, and read the same in the Fanti, or Cape-Coast Language. The Minister then stood up and preached in English for about ten minutes, and sat down; when the interpreter rose, and spoke to the same effect to the people.

Frequently, the interpreter occupied more time than the Minister. This resulted in the Sermon taking much time, and consequently must be tiresome to English hearers. The attention of a great part of the congregation was encouraging, while others were there merely from curiosity. He had the opportunity of comparing preaching through the medium of an interpreter with that of preaching direct in the language of the people. Much of the meaning is lost by the interruption unless the interpreter is a well-qualified person. To act as interpreter in preaching, is no easy task. Though the preacher may not be able to deliver so long Sermon as he might wish in the language of the people, yet there is this satisfaction, that the spirit of his short discourse is not liable to be lost, as we may have reason to fear may be the case through the medium of an interpreter. The plan of studying the language of the people, and translating the Scriptures into it, ought to be immediately adopted by every Missionary sent into the world. Although this is a tedious and difficult work, as it takes years to bring it to perfection, yet, when once the foundation is laid, it is easy to build on it till the work is completed, to the great benefit of the people and succeeding missionaries. It was very amusing to see the different dresses in which the natives came to the Meeting, especially the women. Some were in English dresses, and others merely with their country cloths thrown across their shoulders or tied around their loins. Most of them had their heads shaven, leaving bits of hair, in the form of a circle, on the crown of the head, for ornament.

On 1 August, the Lord's Day Crowther was unwell in the evening, being attacked with fits of cold and fever. He was very much revived by the next day when he received a letter from his son, brought by the PLUTO from Sierra Leone. In the evening of 4 August, they were underway for the mouth of the Niger, to complete their cargo from the HARRIET. By 9 August, they were at the mouth of River Niger and dropped anchor outside the bar to take in a full supply of stores. A few days after on 13 August, they crossed the bar of River Nun, the most important mouth of the Niger with its dangerous shallow water, the sailors cheering and found the other two vessels awaiting their arrival.

The last preparations were made, pilots taken on board, and on 20 August, the ships weighed anchor and headed up stream, but not before special prayer had, by order of the Commander of the expedition, been offered on each vessel. One prayer (composed for the occasion by the chaplain) contained these words: -

"Give success to our endeavours to introduce civilization and Christianity into this benighted country. Thou hast promised, Ethiopia shall soon stretch out her hands unto God: make us, we pray Thee, instruments in fulfilling this Thy promise."

The time for proceeding up the Niger had been carefully chosen so that the river would be in flood, and therefore there would be less risk of sandbanks and other obstacles. It was also believed that would be the least trying time for Europeans from the point of view of health.

By 21 August, the three vessels slowly steamed up the principal channel of the river. Everybody seemed pleased that the navigation of the river had begun, some could not help also remarking that they believed they were going to their graves. They left the mangroves and started seeing forest of palm and bamboo trees on both sides of the river with other trees of beautiful foliage. All hands were invited on deck to see this new scenery, and the day was spent with great interest at this novel appearance. They saw on both sides of the river several plantations of bananas, plantains, sugar cane, cocoa, and now and then some huts with natives in them. Occasionally the ships stopped at a village and an interpreter tried to get into conversation with the people. The natives were so frightened that several times pulled their canoes ashore and ran away into the bush and glanced at the steamer with fear and great shock. It was not easy to convince them that the English were their friends, the only white men known in those places being the Portuguese slave traders. The slave traders often pursue their victims through the mangrove swamp. Some of the riverside chiefs were in the habit of carrying out raids upon their neighbours and sending their captives downstream to the coast for shipment. The vessels got opposite a village containing about seven or eight huts, where the inhabitants armed themselves with sticks and country machetes and ran along the bank to a neighbouring village, to warn the villagers of the frightful approach of the steamer. These villagers also followed the example of their informers, having armed themselves in like manner, they went to the next village to bring them same tidings. When they were urged to come onboard, it was difficult to find any person willing to do so. Those who ventured to come near took care not to go further from shore than the distance of a leap from their canoe in case there should be cause for it. The captain, perceiving some of them encouraged to come off, stopped the engine and convinced them to come near the vessel. In the meantime, they had come opposite to a large village, into which all the former villagers had gathered.

There was a little boy who acted as their interpreter because he understood two English words, " Yes " and " Tabac," which he had picked up at some place. The villagers told him something to tell the visitors, but he could not say anything else besides his " Yes " and " Tabac." After much hesitation, a large canoe came off with no less than forty-three persons in it. Samuel Ajayi Crowther expectation was greatly raised when he found among them a Yoruba boy of about thirteen years of age, from whom he thought they could get some information about the people; but the poor little fellow had almost lost his native language through his lonely situation among them. Crowther could not get much information from the boy.

As they proceeded up the stream they met with other natives from another village that came in their canoes, laden with fruits to exchange for rum, for which they frantically called " Vlolo ! Vlolo ! " and applying their hands to their mouths to show they wanted something to drink. As the Captain Allen would not comply with their demand they paddled back again in deep resentment and the vessel could buy not many things from them.

After a week on 28 August, Samuel Ajayi Crowther had the opportunity of seeing

Mr. Schon onboard the ALBERT early in the morning, where the treaty was made with Obi a native monarch at Aboh a hundred miles up the river. King Obi sent one of his sons to welcome the strangers. He was a very fine-looking young man, about twenty years of age. Both himself and his companions attended the morning devotions, after which they were told about the Bible from which Crowther had read a portion. They were surprised and could not well understand how it was possible that Christians should have no object in view to worship. When Crowther told one that slave trade was a bad thing, and that white people wished to put an end to it altogether, he responded that, if white people give up buying, black people will give up selling slaves.

The native interpreter on board the WILBERFORCE was Simon Jonas, one of the liberated slaves; and when he came amongst people who had known him, they were surprised that he is still alive and well. The natives believed that slaves purchased by the white people were killed and eaten, and their blood used to dye red cloth. Though many years had elapsed since Simon Jonas was sold, and the other had in the meantime become an old man, they instantly recognised each other. It cannot be described the shock displayed by the Igbo man at seeing one whom he very much believed had long since been killed and eaten by white people. To see Simon Jonas return after an interval of years, dressed and living as white men, was almost beyond belief. "If God Himself had told me this, I could not have believed it. But now I see it with my own eyes," said one. The interpreter then found out that Anya was the very place to which he had been first sold as a slave, and at which he had spent nine years of his early life. The very person with whom he was speaking had been his doctor and nurse in a severe illness, on which account he had retained a thankful remembrance of him. The Igbo man was kindly treated by the captain, and his request to be allowed to accompany them to Obi was instantly granted.

The monarch is a middle-sized man and between the age of forty and fifty, his countenance is soft, and he appears calm. The monarch was dressed in calico (a type of plain white or unbleached cotton cloth) trousers of a country make, and an English-made jacket of the same stuff. He had on his neck three strings of pipe coral, as large as a man's small finger, two of which were short and close to the neck, while the third extended to the navel. The monarch had his feet about the ankles ornamented with eight strings of coral, an old brass button closing each string, and two leopard's teeth attached to the strings of coral at each foot. He had on a red cap, over which was a marine's cap decorated with brass scales and other pieces of coloured cords. The very idea of white men who were not engaged in the slave trade was new to many of the riverside people. The missionaries explained the purpose of the visit and the message of the Gospel. When this monarch heard of the suppression of slavery, he found it hard to believe saying: "This is a hard thing". Before the treaty was formally signed, it was explained to the chief that it was the custom of Christians to ask the blessing of God before doing anything of importance, and the whole company knelt in prayer. The Obi did as he saw the others doing, but as he knelt there and heard strange words uttered with passionate feelings, he became alarmed, supposing that the white men were using incantations against him and his people. Perspiration rolled down his face, and trembling violently from fear, he called loudly for his charms. Only with difficulty was his peace of mind restored. At the end they presented Obi Ossai with two Bibles, one in English and the other in Arabic. King Obi could neither read nor write but the missionaries asked Simon Jonas to read and translate in Igbo the Sermon on the Mount from St Matthew Gospel to the King. He was amazed with this and squeezed Jonas's hand most heartily, saying: "You must stop with me; you must teach me and my people; the white people can go up the river without you. They must leave you here till they come back." That a white man could read and write was a matter of course; but that a black man-an Igbo man-should know these wonderful things was more than he could ever have anticipated. Obi insisted that Simon Jonas be left behind at Aboh where he remained to preach the Gospel and explain the mysteries of the written word. It was arranged that, as soon as the ALBERT had passed beyond the Igbo country, Jonas, being no longer needed as interpreter, should be sent back to Aboh and remain there till the return of the expedition. He thus had the honour of being the first worker of the C.M.S. (or any other mission) to be stationed on the Niger.

His Majesty was happy with the expedition and consented to the treaty and made a proclamation the same day among his people for abolition of slave trade and human sacrifices, and for promotion of lawful commerce in his country. About 3 o'clock they got underway; the three steamers being beautifully dressed in flags, which gave them a respectable and splendid appearance, while King Obi was saluted with several guns from them all. All hands well and cheerful onboard their ship looking forward to the Attah's territory.

As the expedition proceeded to Iddah, important information was collected touching the condition and capabilities of the country; and Schon gathered much linguistic material which afterwards proved valuable. The beauty of natural scenery of the Niger with villages under the palms and mangrove trees as the vessel made its way up the river always appealed to Samuel Ajayi Crowther. But the gross ignorance and spiritual darkness of the people weighed heavily on his mind. On 6 September, the expedition sustained a severe loss in the accidental death of their Igalla interpreter, upon whose services they depend on in communicating with the Igallas. He had fallen overboard and was carried away by the stream and drowned before any help could come. This sad event, coupled with the sickness which began to prevail, had naturally a depressing effect upon the crew, and Crowther did his best to inspire the sinking spirits of his fellow-travellers.

On 9 September in his presence the steward of the ship breathed his last breath. In the forenoon the poor fellow was buried on a small island in the river. Day by day their troubles were increasing, and whenever they got a chance of exchanging notes with the other vessels it was to tell each other a rather sad tale.

In the morning on 10 September ALBERT and WILBERFORCE came alongside SOUDAN where the crew were getting wood. Captain B. Allen went with Mr. Sidney, one of the officers, to a village on top of the hill, below which they were cutting woods. These villagers are refugees from the town of Addu Kuddu, on the right side of the river at the confluence, having been driven away by the Fulatahs. From the top of the hill three other villages were visible at the foot. The four villages had an estimated population of eight hundred people. The people are Kakandas. Samuel Ajayi Crowther explained to them the purpose of the expedition and they were happy. He asked them whether they would like him to stay among them and teach them about God. They all answered in the affirmative.

The chief of this village, an old man about sixty, had been sacrificing a fowl to his idol this morning. He sprinkled blood on his forehead, to which were attached a few of the fowl's feathers. His idol was a mixture of some sort of grass or palm leaves, clay, and broken pieces of calabashes, to which feathers of fowls were fastened by means of blood. Samuel Ajayi Crowther shook his head, indicating that it was not good, at the same time pointing his finger to heaven, directing him to worship the only true God. The chief did not pay much attention. They all took fright at Mr. Sidney's instrument to take the distance, but their fears soon subsided. Their huts are built in a circular form, and they are so low and close to each other that if a fire should break out in one, the whole village of about sixty huts would be consumed within a short time.

The expedition got their supply of fuel of wood for the ships from natives living on the banks of the river and were paid in cowries, the current means of money and payment that time. The logs were kept in the stokehole (a space in front of a furnace) of the ships. Because of the circumstances of so much illness afflicting them on board, Crowther had to take these tasks in his charge. Samuel Ajayi Crowther attributed the terrible loss of life on board, in this particular expedition, to the practice of storing green wood in the hold of the vessels, which in progress of rapid decomposition contributed to the state of sickness on the ships. Crowther suggested for future expeditions that a supply of dry wood for the engines should be towed after the ships in barges to prevent a recurrence of ship's crew falling sick onboard.

The natives were honest in their dealing with the expedition but smart at getting a good bargain for articles sold or bought. They love to give presents because they expect to receive twice as much. They were very fond of mirrors.

On the Lord's Day, 12 September another death onboard the ALBERT was recorded previous night, and several persons still terribly ill in each of the vessels. There is no knowing what another day may bring forth. They had a solemn service and Crowther administered the sacrament for the first time onboard the WILBERFORCE. The service was held on the quarter-deck; behind him was the lifeless corpse of the sailor who died previous night. Before him was an attentive audience of as many as could be spared from their work. On deck were the carpenters making a coffin; on the forecastle of the vessel were seven persons dangerously ill of fever; and at a few yards from them was ALBERT, lying with the usual sign of mourning, a lowered flag. Crowther spoke on the right state of mind which ought to possess all at the approach of death. His text was taken from Acts VII., the last two verses. The sailor was buried by Crowther at Addu Kuddu same evening. One of the men said to Crowther that he hoped by God's mercy to be spared and permitted to see his wife and child once more.

One of the most serious aspects of this fever was that the medical men attached to the expedition were beginning to suffer themselves; and one of them, Dr. Nightingale, the surgeon on the ALBERT, was mortally struck down. He was a young and particularly healthy man, with a prospect of being very useful. One of the two missionaries was with him in his dying moments and was led to believe from his last words that the Saviour of sinners was precious to him. Fifty-five persons were now lying helpless on the decks of the ship, and from time to time they were added to the number of the dead. Where they had hoped to bring the blessing of Christian teaching, they found only a grave, and a piece of land was purchased from the king of Attah as a burial ground, where Dr. Nightingale and others were interred. A deep solemnity rested on the crews, and the morning and evening prayers became times of striking feeling. As the shadows drew on and night closed in, they sang with heart-breaking emotion and yet a reviving faith,

At this point, forty-two white men out of one hundred and fifty died within two months. The vessels were like hospital ships with their quarter-deck, forecastle and cabins full of patients with Captain William Allen lying prostrate. In spite of all the medical officer and his helper could do, the sickness increased and situation so serious that on 18 September, it was resolved that the SOUDAN should carry them back to the sea. To the intense disappointment of everyone she sailed on 19 September and began her journey downstream. On September 20, it was concluded that the WILBERFORCE should return to the sea with the fresh patients. The whole day was spent in making necessary arrangements to that effect. Death passed among the suffering, and again and again they had to consign their bodies to the deep; while many of those who lived on rant and rave in hallucination, and in one or two cases flung themselves from the ships in the madness of fever. The WILDERFORCE followed on the homeward track shortly afterwards, a moving hospital, with scarcely enough strength on board to direct its passage down the river. Captain Trotter and Captain B Allen were in the ALBERT with fewer hands having enough strength to work the ship and were to push on a little further. Crowther had the opportunity to join Mr. Schon on ALBERT, to their mutual satisfaction.

The following day September 21 Brother Thomas King left ALBERT to remain at the Model Farm till their return. About 6 o'clock the vessel got underway for the Kworra. The renewal of the journey brought new hope to everyone. After the changes, all was lively, and everything went on satisfactorily; for Captain Trotter, Captain B. Allen, and many other officers, prefer ascending the river as far as they can, to returning to the sea. They passed many villages buried under water. As the building of these huts costs the natives very little labour, it seems they do not care much on what spot they build, if they can but inhabit them only for a short time. About 5 o'clock they came to a town called Muye, on the right side of the river, a great part of which was completely under water: the inhabitants had to wade from one house to another; and some were seen in canoes, which served them for bridges in moving from one place to another. They had time to collect a few words and sentences in Hausa Language, from the interpreter. The vessel anchored this evening a little above Muye, as the natives were to bring them some wood. Two inhabitants of this town came onboard to show them the villages. They place a very great confidence in the white men and were quite free on the ship.

On September 22 they reached a place called Gori and went ashore. At Gori market the trade of dyeing and blue is carried on here: plenty of country-cloths and raw cotton were seen in the market. The blacksmith was busy at his anvil, and the grinders of the Guinea-corn at the stones. In a word, this people are provided with their necessities and could be better off, if they have the techniques to produce in quantity and better qualities. They were led to the house of the chief, where the gentlemen of the expedition were seated on mats in the courtyard, about twelve feet by eight and formed by five huts in the shape of casks placed in an oval form.

The chief is about seventy years of age. He appeared to have been so frightened at the sudden appearance of white men. He had a speaker who spoke on his behalf and answered with great reserve every question put to him, especially such as related to slave trade. He denied knowing the number of slaves brought to market that day, or that they were the Attah's subjects. The meeting was rowdy and the noise so great.

Negotiations under such circumstances were not easy, and disorderly especially when almost all the visitors are ignorant of the language. Rev. Schon was, of course, a good linguist, and during the expedition was able to reduce to writing and grammatical form some of the dialects of the Niger ethnic nationalities; but it is evident that Crowther had to be the principal spokesman, and his kinship as a negro no doubt gave the people a certain confidence in listening to him.

On September 23, the Chief of Gori came onboard and met the Attah's son who also was onboard. The Chief acknowledged that he was the Attah's subject. Notwithstanding the proclamation of the law which was made by the Prince among his father's subjects, the Chief acknowledged that there were five slaves sold in the market the day before. An opportunity was offered of showing the people, by example, the true design of the expedition. A canoe, owned by a native of Muye, came alongside from Egga, with three slaves and three colts onboard. According to his statement, at one time he had been absent from home about twenty-one days, and at another time about three months; and that he did not have an opportunity of hearing the law, as his father, whose was the canoe with the property, did not send a message to him about it. After a fair trial before the Prince, the Chief of Gori, and many others, the three slaves were liberated; and the canoe with the cargo, was left to him, to excuse his ignorance of the law; or otherwise, the whole would have been forfeited. In the presence of the Prince, the Chief of Gori and the owner of the slaves, a new suit of clothes was given to each of the slaves, when their dirty and threadworm-out clothes were taken from them, and for as many as might see them, the benevolent intention of the Queen of Great Britain in sending out this expedition. The poor slaves fell on their knees, in token of gratitude for their liberation. Two of the slaves are Yagba women: the Yagba is a dialect of Yoruba. They calculated their country to be about nine days' journey to this place from the interior. The young man is a Bunu: the dialect between Nun and Kakanda. One of the women was asked whether she would prefer returning to her country, if there was an opportunity to do so. " No," said she; " there is no more safety in my home than it was before I was liberated." She was first sold by her husband, through jealousy, three years ago, as it appears from her own statement; and since that time, had been sold four times. She prefers remaining in the English settlement. The other two were kidnapped.

On 24 September at about 6 o'clock in the morning they got underway and dropped anchor for a short time at a village called Bezzani, on the left side of the river, to buy wood. Crowther went ashore with Rev. Schon and Dr. Stanger. This village also was flooded, on account of which it was very muddy. Some of the houses had fallen in; others were ready to fall. The inhabitants, about 150, are in a miserable condition and are greatly impoverished by the Fulatahs, to whom they pay a monthly tax. When they cannot afford to pay it, they must run away into the bush, to prevent their being taken away to be sold. They considered themselves already as slaves of the Fulatahs because they are entirely under their power. They pointed out a village not far from theirs, on the right side of the river, where they said the Fulatahs lived.

After collecting wood for fuel, the following day, it was proposed by Captain Trotter that Crowther go to Egga, about four or five miles from Kinami, to tell the Chief of their approach to his town, and to invite him onboard, as well as to collect every information he could. At one o'clock, having two interpreters with him, one a Fulatah, the other a Nufi, Crowther left the steamer, with the hope of getting to Egga in two or three hours, as they had to stem the current.

Contrary to expectation, when they got to Kinami, the village of the canoe men, they refused to go any further—their heart failed them. They consulted the Chief; but he could not sanction their taking Crowther to Egga, till he had also consulted two other Chiefs; one living near Egga, and the other on the opposite side of the river. The fears of this people plainly showed in what state of oppression they are under to the Fulatahs. The Chief said that he was quite sure that the men who were to take Crowther and others to Egga would not return; that he considered them already as slaves; and that his town would be burnt by the Fulatahs, and his people taken in slavery, as soon as the steamer leaves the river. He believes the Fulatahs would surely consider them as betraying Egga into the hands of the White Men. Notwithstanding all persuasions given to them, that the team was not going to Egga as enemies, but as friends and that the expedition was sent out on purpose to persuade all the Chiefs of Africa to do away with war and slave-trade; their fear of the Fulatahs was so great, and the apprehensions of what would follow were so strong.

It was about two hours before the messengers returned from the Chief near Egga. He wished first to see Crowther, before he gave his opinion about taking them to Egga. As they had been in the village already three hours, spending the time in nothing else but in persuasion, Crowther briefed Captain Trotter of the development, before proceeding any further. The attempt to go to Egga was given up for the day.

On September 27 they succeeded in getting a canoe to take them to Egga, the highest point reached some 350 miles from the sea by the expedition. As their dresses were different from those of the natives, they soon attracted their attention as the canoe approached the town and became objects of curiosity to the spectators ashore. On landing, many youngsters ran away, being afraid of them. The Fulatah Interpreter was left with the canoe, to keep watch over things and the Nufi Interpreter followed them. They were led to the palace and introduced to Rogang the Chief, a person of great authority. After a long walk through narrow and crooked streets, to the palace they waited for about half an hour before the Chief made his appearance. After a hearty salutation, by shaking of hands in the name of the King of the ship and telling him the reasons why the ship could not then come near, Crowther explained the purpose of the expedition from a commercial and religious standpoint. He explained that the Queen of the country called Great Britain has sent the king of the ship to all the chiefs of Africa to make treaties with them to give up war and the slave trade; take to cultivation of the soil and commerce; and to listen to the missionaries as they wish to teach them about Christianity. Crowther added likewise that there are many Nupe, Hausa, and Yoruba in the white man's country who have been liberated from the Portuguese and Spanish slave ships, that they like white men pray to God and learn His Book. These men now are living a happier life than when they were in their own country, and much better off than their country people are at present. To this many of them said that they could judge of their happy state merely by Crowther's appearance. Crowther added, moreover, that our country people in White Man's country are ready to return if they give up war and the slave trade; and if they consented to the Queen's proposals on anti-slavery and trade. The ships are now here; the King of Igbo, and the Attah, king of Igalla, had consented to all that the Queen of Great Britain sent the King of the ship to say to them. If all the other Chiefs would consent to do the same, they would soon see their people, whom they had lost for many years and supposed to have been dead. Some of the freed men from their countries might do legitimate trade with them, as they do in the White-Men's country.

Rogang was favourably impressed by the purpose of the expedition but he took Crowther aside and confided to him that nothing final could be arranged, as he himself was subordinate to Sumo Zaki, the Fulatah King of Rabbah, who must be consulted. After further discussions Crowther, with much diplomacy, gathered useful information on the importation of strong drink into Africa, a practice which has been such an unspeakable evil on the population. Crowther found the natives were not only being drugged with vile stuff but were cruelly deceived by those who traded upon the alcoholic craze they had created.

The following day, 28 September two Arabs came from Ilorin where they live to trade. They visited Crowther in the morning and their slave, a Yoruba man, who speaks Hausa, was the interpreter, as Crowther and the team also speak Hausa. When they heard that the expedition was against the slave trade, they showed a very great indifference. The report of the three slaves who were liberated at Gori market had reached here some days before; and those who earned their living by this trade are biased against them. Their Yoruba slave informed Crowther, on inquiry, that the Arabs very often carry away many slaves from there and Rabbah, across the Desert; some owning forty, fifty, and some a hundred, each one according to his circumstances.

The fever now began to claim its victims onboard with sickness and death overshadowing the expedition. They had hoped that the sickness would disappear after leaving the unhealthy delta behind. It was not to be so. The dangers to health were not understood, nor were the safeguards known. No one thought of attributing malaria to the mosquito. On 3 October, Captain Trotter was sick in his cabin, and Captain B. Allen lying down critically ill. The only officer left to navigate the ship was Mr. Willie, the mate. Dr. Stanger has had to take charge of the engines. Four days after on 7 October at ten o'clock in the night the captain's clerk who had been raving for some days took advantage of the darkness to fling himself overboard in his delirium from a porthole in the Captain's cabin. Fortunately, he was caught by a black sailor, who immediately jumped overboard in pursuit of him. A boat was soon sent after them; and they were brought back safely. He was roped down in his hammock; this precaution has also now to be taken with the second engineer, who is fast losing his wits. This took place a little below Muye where they anchored. Next morning, after they got underway, the engineer, who was this morning relieved of his yesterday's confinement, sought for an opportunity, when no notice was taken of him, and jumped overboard: two boats, which were examining the soundings, went immediately in search of him; but he had gone down, and could not be found. This having twice occurred, it increased the distressful state of the ship, and cast gloom upon the brightest chance of the expedition.

Day by day men were dying as the death-stricken vessel slowly found her way between mudbanks and shoals, until on 9 October coming from Egga they reached the model farm at the confluence that had been purchased in such high hopes less than a month before. The three workers left behind at the Model Farm were all taken ill almost the same week they left them. Captain Allen, for whose recovery they have been entertaining cheering hopes, was so low, that, according to human judgment, there was no hope of his living till the next hour. That day, Captain Trotter and Captain Allen were so ill that they said good-bye to one another, expecting to die. Crowther kept up with him till 12 o'clock at night. Dr. McWilliam has had charge of the ship the last day or two while Mr. Willie being laid up with fever.

October the 10th on the Lord's Day Captain Allen was still alive against all expectations Necessary arrangements having been made with the coloured men who were left at the Model Farm—Thomas King a Sierra Leone schoolmaster being put in charge to carry on the good work he had commenced —the three, sick gentlemen were taken on board; when they got underway at half past 10 o'clock a.m. for Iddah and dropped anchor there for the night.

The following day no message was sent to the Attah at this time, on account of his majesty's custom of detaining messengers, for the present state of the ship could not admit an unnecessary delay. Crowther was very anxious to know what the Attah thought of the three slaves who were taken from his people at Gori market, as such he was looking out for the coming of his messengers since morning. Just about ten minutes before they got underway, the Prince and a Mallam came. When Dr. McWilliam asked the Prince if his father approved of their proceedings in liberating the three slaves, he declared his approval. The Mallam promised to take a bullock and some vegetables to the men at the model farm when he goes to Keri market.

On October 12 at about 5 o'clock in the evening the vessel anchored off Aboh. Rev. Schon, Mr. Brown, and Crowther went ashore. It was getting dark when they arrived at Aboh and not much of the town could be seen as visibility was poor. The water has risen here a good deal since they left, while it has very much fallen in the upper part. Many houses which were then in mud at Aboh are now nearly under water. The Natives had to make a kind of scaffold attached to the outside of their huts, on which they sit to enjoy themselves in the evening or expose for sale their fruits to the buyers who wade thither; or, if the water be too deep, they come in their canoes. They were kindly received by king Obi. The Interpreter Mr Simon Jonas who was left here by the "SOUDAN," on her way to the sea, was very well treated by him. Obi is very anxious that the White Men should come and build the house for which they asked him a place, as he has found a good spot of land which they can use for the purpose. He wished also that a large trading ship should be sent to deal with his people and desires also to have teachers among them. Before the Steamer lay at anchor, about thirty canoes had come off to meet her, to sell their fruits and country cloths and other products.

The following day 13 October Mr Kingdom, one of the gentlemen taken onboard from the Model Farm, having died on Tuesday night, was buried this morning by Rev J.F Schon by the marshy bankside. King Obi got all the things that were wanted, with readiness. He himself came onboard to see his honourable friends, Captain Trotter and Captain B. Allen, who were both very sick, and he was sorry to see them in such a state. He brought one of his Chukwus with him. When Captain Trotter was told that that was one of his gods, he gave Obi a Bible instead of it, and told the king that his god was of no use. Obi asked for one of Captain Trotter's chairs, which was given him.

They got underway at about 10 o'clock and Dr. McWilliam, in this emergency, takes control of the vessel. By this time only one white sailor remained in health and able to help Dr. McWilliam in navigating the ship. They were still a hundred miles from the mouth of the river and were expecting on reaching it to encounter a very serious difficulty of crossing the bar because of lack of trained and experienced sailors left onboard. But help was forthcoming. ALBERT then drifted dangerously down the river. Crowther was untouched by the fever while many were stricken by it and are dying or dead. He kept his head as well as his health through it all, working anywhere, and at anything to save the situation onboard ALBERT. The vessel was running almost unguided down the swift current of the Niger with the overworked doctor managing the engines from a book on machinery he finds in the captain's room. The doctor while managing the ship had to attend to the sick, some who were screaming in confusion. The whole company thrilled with the news that a ship was in sight. It was the ETHIOPE coming to their aid. They met ETHIOPE, with Captain Beecroft, about 3 o'clock. He was coming to see after the ALBERT. Painful news was brought by him of the deaths of eight of the sick friends who were sent to the sea; among whom were Dr. Marshall, Dr. Coleman, the Assistant Surgeon, and Mr. Waters, the purser of the SOUDAN. The homeward voyage was a tragedy. Rev. Schon was not spared of the fever. There was pain of body, distress of mind, weakness, sobbing and crying everywhere onboard. The few that were healthy, are more like walking shadows without any endurance.

On 14 October after the first engineer of ETHIOPE boarded ALBERT they started from their anchorage at 7 o'clock in the morning and reached the mouth of the river at 6 o'clock in the evening. The men were very happy at seeing the salt-water again; and many of the sick seemed revived in their hammocks merely at the sight. Surely the Lord has been with us, and delivered us from many dangers, both seen and unseen. When they left the Confluence, they had many rocks, which were partially covered with water, to avoid, and from Iddah to Aboh many shallow parts of the river to shun; and Mr. Brown, a Native of Cape-Coast Castle, who has some knowledge of this river, assisted Dr. McWilliam in piloting the ship with safety.

The following day the rigging of the ship was put to rights, to fit her for the sea while the men were cutting wood.

On 16 October Captain Beecroft himself came onboard ALBERT when they got underway about 6 o'clock in the morning, and crossed the Bar in calm water safely, and the Steamer was making her way to Fernando Po at a good rate. The SOUDAN, commanded by Lieut. Strange, was met at the Bar, going up the Niger to meet the ALBERT. She returned to Fernando Po with them. This night a marine, called Cole, died; and Mr. Willie, the only officer who had held out longer than the rest is now dangerously ill.

October 17, the Lord's Day at half past 7 o'clock in the morning the body of Cole, the marine, was committed to the deep by the Rev. J. F. Schon, till the sea shall give up the dead which are in it. The vessels anchored off Fernando Po about 4 o'clock in the afternoon.

All the sick were landed on 18 October, and lodged in different private houses hoping, by the blessing of God, the change may prove beneficial to their recovery. While Captain Trotter has been improving since last Saturday 16 October, Mr Willie died the night they landed and was buried the following day by Rev. Schon. The Purser's Steward also died a few days after.

Captain B Allen breathed his last at 10 o'clock in the morning of 25 October when Captain Trotter, with tears, closed the eyes of his departed friend. In him he lost an active companion. The Captain was buried in the evening, by the Rev. J. F. Schon. His corpse was followed to the graveyard by all the ship's company who were able, the Agent and many of the inhabitants of Fernando Po. Since the death of Captain B. Allen, to the 7 November, three officers and a marine were buried.

When the hopes of great commercial gains were not realised, the sponsors of the expedition lost their enthusiasm for the development of trade with the Niger basin to the great disappointment of the native population. For the natives, the expedition had held out highly cherished hopes of their national improvement and prosperity, by having opportunities of trading with their natural resources with the outside. The abandonment of the expedition was a heavy blow to the country. It appeared as if the Niger waters was destined to float down only human cargoes, aggravating the miseries of the country' and her people; — as if, instead of becoming a highway through which to convey light, life, and liberty into the heart of the country.

The expedition failed to a considerable extent to achieve the object for which it was sent out. Out of a complement of one hundred and fifty Europeans, the expedition lost forty-two within two months. The news of the disaster came as a shock to people in England. Its enemies sneered and The Times newspaper was triumphant. It is not surprising that public opinion would not risk a repetition of the attempt for twelve years.

Despite this setback and heavy loss of human life the expedition had not been a total failure that contemporaries judged it to be. Though, the high mortality obscured its achievements, but those achievements were nonetheless real. The expedition had paved the way as lessons learnt for other pioneers to put to good use in future expeditions. The river proved to be a great highway, navigable for hundreds of miles. The ethnic nationalities by the riverside were found to be friendly, and there was obviously great opportunity if only the deadly climate could be overcome. Rev. Schon was able to compile a valuable vocabulary of the different tongues, and it added some fresh geographical knowledge of one of the waterways of the world. The experience had an immense influence on the life and character of Crowther, who was destined to bear such heavy burdens of evangelism of the Niger hinterland.

Treaties for the abolition of the slave trade were negotiated with the rulers of Aboh and Iddah, who also granted permission for the entry of missionaries. The interview with Obi Ossai of Aboh conducted by the Rev. Schon demonstrates the warm reception accorded the Christian message by some of the Igbo rulers.

Though for the moment discouraged, the promoters of the expedition believed that the failure was not final, and they had not thought of giving up the effort, least of all the C.M.S. On receiving reports from Schon and Crowther, the Committee felt that it had a call from God to minister to the ethnic nationalities around the Niger, and they resolved to go forward when it should please God to open the door. Not only were the great chiefs found ready to listen to the message of Christ but were also equally willing to be taught by black men, and the Committee recognized this new factor.

But as always in history during times of failure and reaction there are men who see beyond the happenings of the present to the possibilities of the future. These men clung tenaciously to Buxton's idea in the missionary circles. It was during this period that the Rev. Henry Venn, became Honorary Secretary of the C.M.S. from 1841 till 1872. His period of office coincided with the foundation of the Niger Mission. With his faith in the African, and unflinching support, Samuel Ajayi Crowther, achieved the greatness he did in the Niger Mission.

Nevertheless, as far as the C.M.S. was concerned the interval was used to plan the work along more practical lines. The reports of Schon and Crowther greatly assisted them in formulating a sounder policy for a future expedition on the Niger territories. Schon's recommendations may be briefly summarised. He stated emphatically that the West African climate and lack of regular communications in the Niger Districts would make a mission run by Europeans a physical impossibility. The high mortality of the 1841 expedition, he said, "not only demonstrates to us, that the designs for which the expedition has been chiefly undertaken will, in the course of events, be carried out by natives (of Africa);" he went on to stress that the inhabitants of the African interior "acknowledge the superiority over themselves of their own country people who had received instruction" at the white man's hands. These educated Africans, Schon pleaded, mainly resident in Sierra Leone, should be sent back as missionaries to their own countrymen. "In Sierra Leone," he claimed, "there is a general desire among the liberated Africans to return to their own countries. This was unheard of a few years ago." Schon discerned the Hand of God in the reciprocity of feeling between the educated Africans abroad and the ethnic nationalities who desired their services at this critical hour in African history. He therefore called upon the Home Committee of the C.M.S. to adopt the measures he advocated. "Everything," he said, "tends to confirm my opinion of Sierra Leone and its destiny, that from thence the Gospel will proceed to numerous benighted tribes of Africa." He ended his appeal to the C.M.S. Committee with this question: "Are the natives of Africa then, to become missionaries to their own country people?" "Yes," he answered--"for this the Church of God has been longing and praying."

Schon was strongly supported by Crowther in this view. Writing to the C.M.S. Secretary from Fernando Po on 2 November 1841 the latter declared: "As regards missionary labours on the banks of the Niger and in the interior of Africa--very little can be done by European missionaries... On the other hand, it would be practicable to employ native converts from Sierra Leone who are willing to return and teach their fellow countrymen." In order to implement this proposal, Schon strongly recommended that the C.M.S. should expand educational facilities in Sierra Leone in order to prepare its people adequately for missionary enterprise. He suggested the reorganization of Fourah Bay Institution "on such a footing that the students might receive superior education, with a special view to prepare them for the missionary work." He urged that the languages spoken in the Niger should be reduced to writing and that portions of the scriptures should be translated into these languages. He stressed that "the work of translating should be made a distinct branch of the operations of the Mission." Perhaps Schon's greatest service to the Niger Mission was his clear grasp of the practical difficulties in the field and his convincing presentation of these to the C.M.S. authorities in England. The Home Committee agreed with Schon that Africa should be saved not only by European efforts but largely through the agency of her own children who had come into touch with Western civilization in Sierra Leone and the West Indies. The Niger Mission therefore began, particularly with regard to its personnel, as a predominantly African Mission, drawing no doubt much guidance and financial support from the C.M.S. Fourah Bay College was developed along the lines he suggested, as a training institution "for a Native Ministry..."

It was clear from Schon's recommendations that the man intended to lead the team of native missionaries into the Niger Valley was Samuel Ajayi Crowther. The C.M.S. was impressed by Crowther's ability and later invited him to England for training and ordination.

YORUBA MISSION FIELD

The Church Missionary Society (C.M.S.) used the lessons learnt from the first expedition up the Niger to plan for subsequent ones to the Niger. Rev. J.F. Schon in his report to the C.M.S. on the expedition recommended native ministry and stated its importance in evangelising mission in West Africa. He strongly recommended in his report that the C.M.S should send Crowther to England for ordination. Rev. Schon had known him intimately, and his experience of his character and capacities under the trying ordeal of this expedition supplied sufficient evidence to justify his strong recommendation. Rev J.F Schon in his letters to CMS on 26 June 1841, observed the interest of Samuel Crowther in the service of the mission and that he was of great assistance to him.

Rev. J. F. Schon raised the point of ordaining Samuel Crowther in another letter, addressed to the Secretaries in London on 10 September 1841:

"I have thought much about the propriety of Samuel Crowther's returning to England with me and receiving ordination and should be happy to learn what opinion the Parent Committee may form of this plan on my return to Sierra Leone. Of his decided piety I have no doubt; his studious habits and anxiety to improve himself would, after a few weeks' attention, qualify him in other respects. He is highly esteemed by all who know him, and his love to his country and for his people would prevail on him to lay himself out for their good. The committee in Sierra Leone was ever in favour of the measure, and his excellent conduct in this expedition can only raise our opinion of him."

The head of CMS at this time, Henry Venn, needed little convincing. He believed that overseas Churches should be self-supporting, self-governing, and self-extending, and therefore wanted African priests and bishops to oversee the African Churches. Samuel Ajayi Crowther was an ideal candidate. In response to these high testimonies to Samuel Ajayi Crowther's life and struck by the intelligence of his journal of the Niger expedition, the CMS committee summoned him to England, the following year, 1842 and he travelled on 3 September 1842. He devoted himself to working on the grammar and vocabulary of the Yoruba language for the work of translations during his leisure hours onboard on his way to England. While in England, he finished his first published literary work, *Yoruba Vocabulary*, in 1843 and a Yoruba version of the Anglican *Book of Common Prayer* followed later making it the first such work by a native speaker of an African language. He also began codifying other languages. After several interviews, the Committee placed him at the Islington Church College for a few months' preparation under the direction of the Rev. C. F. Childe. He worked hard and excelled during training and is listed as one of the brightest in its roll of honoured names inscribed upon its walls. The annual examination at the Islington Church College was conducted by the Rev. James Schofield, Professor of Greek at Cambridge University. Rev Schofield had often discussed with others, having the belief that the mental capacity of a negro is deficient as regards the logical faculty. But after conducting the examination on Paley's " Evidences of Christianity," he made the following significant remark to the principal of the College:

"I should like, with your permission, to take young Crowther's answers to those Paley questions back with me to Cambridge, and there read a few of them in the Combination Room to certain of my old Trinity friends. If, after hearing that young African's answers, they still contend that he does not possess a logical faculty, they will tempt us to question whether they do not lack certain other faculties of at least equal importance, such as common fairness of judgment and Christian candour."

In a few months he was qualified for presentation to the Bishop of London as a candidate for ordination. On Trinity Sunday, 11 June 1843, twenty-one years (less one week) after the poor frightened Ajayi was landed by H.M.S. MYRMIDON at Sierra Leone, he received his deacon's orders and was duly admitted to the ministry of the Church. He was invited, with another candidate, Prebendary Newell, to breakfast at Fulham Palace, and to the latter the Bishop remarked, directing attention to Crowther: "That man is no mean scholar; his examination papers were capital, and his Latin remarkably good." On October 1st in the same year, the same Bishop ordained him as a presbyter of the Church in full orders. This occasion, when the first African was to be so ordained in connection with the CMS, was looked upon as one of the events of the year. An interesting incident happened at the ordination. "When the candidates for deacon's orders were to go up to the Bishop, an awkward pause occurred. The Englishmen, by a sudden and simultaneous instinct, waited for the negro to go first; while he was sitting with his eyes on the ground, unconscious of the precedence they wished to accord him. At last, suddenly seeing that all eyes were fixed on him, he quietly arose, went forward, and knelt before the Bishop. When Bishop Blomfield preached the anniversary sermon he referred to this when he said:

"What cause for thanksgiving to Him who hath made of one blood all nations of men is to be found in the thought that He has not only blessed the labourers of the Society, by bringing many of those neglected and persecuted people to a knowledge of a Saviour, but that from among a race who were despised as incapable of intellectual exertion and acquirement He has raised up men well qualified, even in point of knowledge, to communicate to others the saving truths which they have themselves embraced, and to become preachers of the Gospel to their brethren according to the flesh".

Soon after his ordination Samuel Ajayi Crowther returned to Africa full of many thoughts and expectations as he was to commence his ministry amongst his countrymen. He was happy with the prospect of working in the Lord's Vineyard amongst his own people. Back at home the natives were excited at his home coming as their African minister. Crowther was one of the first three negro clergy men in connection with the Society to have been educated in England and ordained by the Bishop of London. The others were George Nicol, and Thomas Maxwell who had received deacon's and priest's orders in the year following the Jubilee.

Crowther was instructed by the Parent Committee to preach in Yoruba language in the Mission Church at Freetown for the benefit of the large section of the population whose vernacular it was. He thus began making some translations during the return voyage. He translated the first three chapters of St. Luke's Gospel with less difficulty than he had at first anticipated. He left what appeared to be difficult to translate until further revisions, when new words and thoughts would present themselves. This is generally the case in revising translations. He also translated the first two chapters of the Acts of the Apostles to see how that also would go, and it answers equally well. Thus, he prepared himself with some portions of the Holy Scriptures, although some verses require greater consideration before the sense is fixed, that he might not be without some sort of provision for his countrymen.

On Saturday 2 December he arrived at Freetown and was cheerfully welcomed by groups of friends some who, like himself, had once been slaves but now were free. The missionaries were delighted to grasp his hand and wish him God-speed, and afterwards to hear all the news and to receive messages from London. The natives were, of course, full of joy, and one, an old catechist, exclaimed in the spirit of ancient Simeon:

"Happy am I to see that the saving knowledge of the truth, as it is in Jesus, is spreading far and wide in the world, that even Africans, who were bowing down to images, are receiving the sacred scriptures as the very Word of God. Truly may one say that the Lord is now opening a way into the interior of Africa by choosing an African, the Rev. S. Crowther, to be a minister to bear his name among his countrymen. Now many of the sons of fallen man will hear the glad sounds of a Saviour's Name! May the Lord give His blessing to His servant, that he may be useful in turning many souls to glory! May the Lord raise up many more after him to become faithful ministers of His Gospel to the world!"

Crowther preached his first sermon in Africa the following day which was a Sunday to a large congregation of natives in the mission Church at Freetown. His sermon was delivered in the English language the lingua Franca of the colony which was taught in the schools as well as used in the Churches. The text for the sermon was taken from Luke XIV. 22: " Lord, it is done as Thou hast commanded, and yet there is room."

It was Sacramental Sunday, and the congregation was excited to see a native clergyman performing Divine Service. After service, he assisted the Rev. E. Jones to administer the Lord's Supper. In the evening Crowther preached to a large and attentive congregation from 2 Cor. X., parts of 15th and 16th verses. At the end of each service, after the Benediction had been pronounced, the whole Church rang with the cry of " Ki o se" " So let it be." Crowther was welcomed as a messenger of Christ in the colony wherever he went.

Back in Freetown, he began a diligent visitation of his countrymen in the district, and he had his first visit to a Muslim, who has shown a great desire to see the black minister from oversea. Crowther always took a deep and intelligent interest in the followers of Islam.

On 17 December, Lord's Day morning the head of Muslims in the neighbourhood of Fourah Bay sent four men to Bathurst, about seven miles distance, to ask after Crowther's health and to learn for certainty whether he was going to the Yoruba country. The following day, Crowther saw him. He is a strict Muslim and has a great influence over those who profess Islam. He speaks Hausa like a native. Crowther told him and his people who were present, in Yoruba language, of the influence of Christianity on the people of England and remarked that it was the religion of Christ which taught them to love all men and to do them all the good they could. He told them of the importance of yielding to Christianity, because it led to the sure way of happiness, that the Bible had already been translated into many languages and also into the Arabic, a copy of which Crowther gave him some years ago. He further told him that he was instructed to translate the same into the Yoruba language, that the people may read the Bible for themselves in their own tongue; and that he (Crowther) should open a service in the Mission Church, where he should read and preach to the people from the Holy Scriptures in Yoruba language. Crowther did not raise any objections to Islam nor attack it but endeavoured to show them the great blessings Christianity bestowed on mankind wherever it was embraced. To Crowther's great surprise they gloried at one of their countrymen being the first clergyman of the Church of England among the liberated Africans in the Colony of Sierra Leone.

Rev Samuel Ajayi Crowther requested Rev. H. Rhodes to notify the Church on Sunday, the 7 January that he would commence services and ministrations in his native tongue to his own people in their native Yoruba on Tuesday 9 January at half-past four in the afternoon. After the morning service on the 7 January, he visited the people in their houses, especially those who never attended Divine Service, and invited them to the Yoruba Service on Tuesday afternoon.

On Monday 8 January 1844, Crowther was visited by the headman of the Yoruba Muslims, who is living in the neighbourhood of Fourah Bay. In their conversation Crowther told him, among many other things, that he would commence a Yoruba service on the 9th and would be very glad to see him and his people there. On the afternoon of 9 January at half-past four o'clock Crowther opened the Yoruba Service in the Mission Church in Freetown. The novelty of a service in an English Church conducted in a native language brought many people together—Yoruba, Igbo, Calabar, etc. Although the language is Yoruba, with which Crowther is well acquainted, yet on this occasion it appeared as if he were a child just learning to utter his mother tongue. Everything seemed strange and new to him as he stood before the congregation. But the Lord supported him. Crowther opened the Service in English, when he read those of the prayers which were not translated and a portion of St. Luke's Gospel in Yoruba. This, it may be presumed, was the first Christian Service ever in Africa in Yoruba tongue. In the congregation he observed three of his young Muslim friends, sent by their headman to attend the Service, according to promise. The text from which he preached was taken from the lesson he had read to them—Luke 1. 35. Crowther was glad to hear the people express their satisfaction at his feeble attempt to express this doctrine. After service, the Muslims followed him to his house and expressed their satisfaction at what they had heard. They apologized for the non-attendance of their leader who could not come as earlier promised as he had a visitor to attend to. They wished God to help Crowther in this important work he had commenced.

The attendance of three of his young Muslim friends, sent by their headman encouraged Rev Crowther and shows that his tactful treatment of these Muslims had met with a measure of success. He was deeply moved at the sight of the heathenism around and even in Freetown, where the Gospel had been preached for so long. So many were idolaters and his visits to their homes made some to be uncomfortable. Generally, they received him with great respect, and always acknowledged the worship of the only true God as superior to any other; but they cannot resolve to give up their gods, whom they believe were created by the great God for the good of mankind and ought therefore to be worshipped. Crowther told them that none of these things are true but are the devices of Satan to keep man from God and in darkness and superstition.

Crowther's first missionary tour took him to the town of Abeokuta. The devastating raids of the Fulanis, Foulah or Fellatah tribes had depopulated vast areas of the country, and Crowther's town of Osogun had been rebuilt and again destroyed. It is difficult now to identify the site of the place. The Alafin of Oyo moved his capital and retreated to the town of Ago-Oja with diminished authority. The old Oyo having been destroyed by the enemy, his junior chiefs had thrown off their allegiance to the fallen sovereign, each fighting for his own survival.

At that time the whole Yoruba Country was at war and turmoil. Many of the scattered natives, ran from slave hunters and settled round a high isolated rock called Olumo, near the River Ogun, in the south-western district of their country. It was a primitive fortress, that initially provided a hiding-place for a band of robbers. It was here in 1825 a few poor frightened fellow-countrymen of Crowther's, finding the robbers departed, were glad to take up their abode. Others joined them, sharing their hardships as well as their safety. These refugees from at least one hundred and thirty towns which had been destroyed by the slave raiders, found a safe abode at the bottom of the rocky hill. In a few years a large community was built, comprising a number of sub-ethnic groups and clans, each with its own war captain, judge, and code of laws. Many little villages developed and, in many cases, named after the town of their better days now destroyed. The settlement prospered as it became a secured place, and soon they gave their new dwelling-place the name of Abeokuta, i.e. Under the Stone. These people belonged to the Egba sub-ethnic group of the Yoruba. They were all under the government of a brave and enlightened chief named Sodeke, who arranged for each to have its civil governors or mayors called Ogbonis, and war chiefs or generals, called Baloguns. Then they had a sort of general council or parliament, of all these at Ake under the personal leadership of Shodeke. This unity of interests against a common peril and ties of common blood gave great strength to the new settlement, and they were able to defend themselves successfully against several serious attacks from their enemies.

The new settlement of Abeokuta received news from liberated Africans at Sierra Leone, of English ships with big guns cruising on the sea off the coast and capturing slave vessels. In Sierra Leone, which is under the British flag, many of their kin were living and slowly settling down to their new life. On both sides arose burning desires to meet again after been torn apart so ruthlessly by slave raiders. To those in Sierra Leone it seemed as though the Promised Land of a restored nation was before them at Abeokuta. Sierra Leone was now a prosperous settlement. Many of the liberated slaves had become flourishing traders along the coast. They were determined to start trade relations with Abeokuta. In 1839, a few of the most enterprising, who belonged to the Yoruba nation, purchased from Government a small slave-ship which had been captured, named her the WILBERFORCE. The vessel, freighted with English goods likely to attract buyers, set sail for what was then known as the Slave Coast, a thousand miles to the east of Sierra Leone, and the gate into their own Yoruba country. Lagos being in the hands of a hostile and slave-kidnapping people, they landed at Badagry, the nearest port to their destination quickly disposed of their cargo, filled their little vessel with the produce of the country, and returned to Sierra Leone. A brisk trade speedily sprang up. Other spirited adventurers landed at Lagos, at the mouth of the Ogun river. The inhabitants of Lagos were deeply into slave trade and only welcomed the emigrants with their goods. They set upon them, robbed them of all they had, and taunted them that they should be thankful that they were allowed to proceed at all. The unfortunate visitors were sent into the interior without food or guidance to perish by the way. They would have been re-enslaved had it not been that they had become British subjects with official passports and the slave traders were afraid to touch them. So, a new route to Abeokuta had to be found, and from that time the emigrants landed at Badagry, a town on the lagoon some forty miles west of Lagos, and established a new centre there where they were known locally as Saro. Soon a more or less regular stream of Sierra Leonians was passing from Badagry to Abeokuta. Between 1839 and 1844, over 800 ex-slaves had arrived in Yoruba territory, predominantly in Abeokuta, Lagos and Badagry. Groups in Sierra Leone raised money, and four boats were purchased by Liberated Africans—the QUEEN VICTORIA, the WILBERFORCE, the FREE GRACE and the WONDERFUL—in order to bring more emigrants from Sierra Leone to Yoruba territory. They were also encouraged by the Wesleyan missionaries who disliked the prospect of losing much of the civilized West African population to the West Indies.

Those who settled at Badagry fared better and their chief, Wawa, was friendly and helped the newcomers. Some who belonged to the Egba sub-ethnic of the Yoruba people, emigrated to Abeokuta, and their return had many touching incidents. After their arrival at Badagry they would travel for many miles through a flat alluvial country, here and there swampy or covered with thick jungle. During the travel from Badagry to Abeokuta they would common across the blackened ruins of towns which the enemy had destroyed. In one day's, journey they would pass no less than twenty of these sad scenes of meaningless destruction. And now as they approached Abeokuta, they would notice signs of cultivation and industry, farms with poultry, and men busy everywhere and happy. Then following River Ogun along its beautiful banks of luxuriant foliage they caught sight of the glorious city Abeokuta. With great joy they soon passed its gates and eagerly inquire for their relatives and friends; they clasped each other with kisses of recognition, and each had a wonderful story to tell of suffering and escape to the sheltering rock of Olumo, of the kindness of the English at Sierra Leone, and the strange marvels of civilization there. Amongst other things the visitors were not slow to tell of the missionaries who had taught them the Bible, the book of God, and preached how Jesus Christ came to seek and to save those that were lost.

The return of many freed slaves of Nigerian origin from Sierra Leone to their old homes in Nigeria gave the missionaries some fears that without guidance and restraints of Christian life, living in a wholly heathen country, they might possibly fall back again into dark practices of their old traditional religion. It was felt that despite promises to continue in the good way, the new situation was filled with danger. It was because of the fears that a petition was sent to the C.M.S in London, asking for teachers and pastors to accompany them to provide Christian ministrations and teaching. In response to the petition, Mr. Henry Townsend, a very promising young missionary from Exeter, was dispatched on a visit of inquiry to Abeokuta to find the best possible way to deal with the situation. He travelled onboard WILBERFORCE and on 17 December 1842, landed on the coastal strip opposite Badagry after nearly five weeks at sea with some African catechists.

Badagry itself does not stand upon the seashore, but on the farther side of the great lagoon that lies behind the actual coast. This lagoon is part of a series that run for more than a hundred miles, more or less parallel with the seashore, and separated from it by a narrow strip of sandy land usually about a mile or so in width. Badagry was a place long known as a stronghold of fetishism and human sacrifice, and it was also an important slave market. The hostile intent from the slavers of Lagos, and a friendship with the rising power of Abeokuta made the inhabitants to be friendly to the Sierra Leonian emigrants passing through their town or even settling there, as some of them did for purposes of trade, a fact that caused one section of the place to become known as " Englishtown."

On Christmas Eve, Rev. T.B. Freeman returned to Badagry from Abeokuta, and the two pioneers met to discuss their plans for "planting the banner of the Cross" (a familiar phrase of Freeman's) in the very heart of the country long ravaged by the slave raiders. Christmas Day was spent in united worship, the missionaries joined in conducting services for their travelling companions and Sierra Leonians that were then living in Badagry. Thus, began that happy fellowship and spirit of co-operation that has always characterized the two Missions in their efforts to evangelize Nigeria. Townsend took useful counsel from Rev. T. B. Freeman.

After a few days together they parted, Freeman to visit the great King of Dahomey and Townsend to proceed on his journey to Abeokuta. Leaving Badagry on December

29, Townsend was carried forward in a travelling basket, the shape of a coffin, made of basketwork and carried on the heads of two strong men. The traveller lay full length, his head on a pillow, and was carried feet foremost along the narrow bush paths. Townsend found it uncomfortable and impossible to look about much, his head being too low, and in the more open country the heat and bright light of the sun upon his face hurting him severely. The journey took six days. At Abeokuta, Townsend was warmly received by the principal Chief of the town, Chief Shodeke. The Chief allowed him to hold Services in his palace yard, and promised that if more missionaries were sent to live there, he would give them places of worship and his full support. Townsend was the first white man to enter Abeokuta. The visit was intended to be a reconnaissance, and after a week's stay, Townsend took leave of Shodeke and his chiefs and returned to Badagry en route for Sierra Leone and came to England in 1843. He reported to the Committee in London the results of his investigations and the remarkable opportunities for a new mission a thousand miles away from Sierra Leone, in the very country ravaged by slave trade. The Committee of the C.M.S. felt that only one course was open to them. The hand of God was beckoning to Abeokuta, and for the moment there was no opportunity of carrying out the earlier project of a mission on the Niger. Every possible circumstance pointed to the Egba capital as strategic base for the new venture. Several of the teachers and catechists in Freetown, being Yoruba, were keen to work among their kin. Townsend stayed back in England, where he was ordained by Bishop Blomfield on Trinity Sunday, 1844, just a year after Crowther and sent again to establish a mission at Abeokuta together with Crowther and a young German missionary, the Rev. C. A. Gollmer, in the Yoruba country.

This proposal created great interest in Sierra Leone and many willingly offered money and other resources. Many Yoruba ex-slaves especially of Egba sub-ethnic group volunteered to accompany the missionaries as carpenters or labourers. Mr. Fergusson, the Governor of the Colony, was fully in sympathy with the undertaking, and invited Townsend and his fellow-missionaries to breakfast with him on the morning when the expedition was to start. All the missionaries within reach gathered to say good-bye; they sang: Guide me, O Thou Great Jehovah, and Rev Schon, with many memories of the Niger expedition, committed them to the safe keeping of God in prayer. Thus, on 18 December 1844 the Yoruba Mission was begun as the party embarked from Freetown amid scenes of deep emotion and excitement. Crowds gathered at the wharf to see them off.

There had been no opportunity to train an African mission team foreseen by Schon and Crowther in their report on the Niger Expedition, but at least in Crowther there was one ordained Yoruba missionary available. The missionary party was a large one, for it was felt that in such a place as Abeokuta a beginning must be made on a scale that would give reasonable hope of success. There were four Europeans: The Rev. and Mrs. C. A. Gollmer, and the Rev. and Mrs. Henry Townsend. The Rev. Samuel Ajayi Crowther was accompanied by Mrs. Crowther and their two children. The other African workers were: Mr. Marsh (a catechist) with his wife and two children; Mr. Phillips (a schoolmaster); Mr. Mark Willoughby (the interpreter) with his wife and three children; four carpenters, three labourers, and two servants. They took with them, in addition to the usual equipment for such a journey, windows and doors and other fittings for the houses they were to build in Abeokuta. The mission headed by Rev Henry Townsend was to demonstrate a whole new way of life, of which the Church and the school were all a part. They were to establish Sierra Leone in Yorubaland. The Sierra Leone trader-immigrants, the people who had first brought Abeokuta to the attention of the mission, became the nucleus of the new Christian community. They sailed on 18 December 1844, spent Christmas Day at Monrovia, and reached Badagry on 17 January 1845 after a month journey.

At Badagry, they were very kindly entertained by Rev and Mrs W Annear, the resident Wesleyan missionary and received the sad news that Shodeke, the friendly chief of Abeokuta, was dead. They had built great expectations on the promises of this strong and wise leader. Messengers arrived soon afterwards with welcoming words from the chiefs at Abeokuta. They were warned against going to Abeokuta, especially as the roads were overrun with robbers and local wars. They had, therefore, no alternative but to stay in Badagry for a time until the journey to Abeokuta could be safely undertaken. Their present situation, indeed, offered plenty of opportunity for mission work. The natives were Popos and were deep in their traditional religion and superstition, and in addition utterly demoralized by the vile rum which the slave ships had been in the habit of supplying in exchange for the captives. Human sacrifices were common, and it was no strange thing for some poor woman, suspected of witchcraft, to be dragged through the streets by her feet until death terminated her sufferings, and her body was thrown into the fetish grave. Just after the party had arrived, Kosoko the nephew of King Akintoye of Lagos, had conspired against him, and fled to Badagry. He was a merciless slave dealer, who was responsible for many massacres, tried to gain possession of the town, and threatened Abeokuta. But these troubles did not affect the purpose and conviction of these brave missionaries in their work. They were prepared for suffering in their Master's cause. and had been in Badagry scarcely three months when Mrs. Gollmer passed away suddenly in April. They laid her body to rest with much solemnity and mourning.

This is the first Christian funeral that has ever been publicly performed in this country. Many of the natives out of curiosity attended the funeral service in the Church and accompanied the missionaries to the burial ground, to witness the burial of a Christian. About 150 persons were at the burial ceremony. The chiefs having been informed of the mournful bereavement, sent their messengers to express their sympathy with the missionaries.

Mr. Townsend took the opportunity of acquiring more perfectly the Yoruba language, while Crowther and the bereaved Gollmer visited the people, and from time to time preached the Gospel under the shade of an ancient tree, between the two busy markets. As Badagry would have to be the port of entrance for the future, they secured their position by acquiring a site as the Wesleyans had done. The site was the shade where they preach and within seven weeks of landing, they opened for worship the first C.M.S. Church in the new field. On the following morning, a day school was opened.

While in this place, Crowther and Gollmer paid a visit to chief Ogunbona's house. They met him with his daughter about ten years old sitting close to him at the entrance on a mat spread on the ground. He soon obtained a chair and two empty powder kegs for Crowther and Gollmer as their seats. As the drums continued beating and the horns blowing, the noise was so great that they could scarcely hear themselves. Many of the chiefs came and were introduced to the two gentlemen by Ogunbona. As the noise was still very great, he took them to the square and into his room, where they were lodged. Ogunbona asked whether they had brought their house (tent) with them; they answered in the negative on account of our haste in leaving Badagry. Ogunbona not being accustomed to providing lodging for white men, was at a loss what to do on this occasion, but they soon made him easy by ordering one of their men to assist in boiling a fowl and some yams for dinner and supper. Before supper was ready, they passed the time in conversation, lying on a leopard skin, which was sometimes used for a chair and at other times for a sofa, as they wished to change their position. Supper being ready, after a blessing had been asked, everyone took his plate on his lap or placed it on the leopard skin, as it suited him best. The two men asked Ogubonna to partake with them, but he declined because he did not know how to eat as white men eat. They took some tea without milk and asked Ogubonna to take a cup, to which he consented. To make it agreeable to his taste Mr. Gollmer sweetened it well with sugar, and the chief enjoyed it very much.

When it was about nine o'clock Crowther and Gollmer expressed their desire to have family prayer and said they should be glad if Ogunbona and his household would join them. Ogunbona instantly ordered all in the square to assemble when Crowther read Acts XVII. 16-31, and explained it to them and prayed in Yoruba, their native tongue. After prayers they told Ogunbona that it was their custom to read a portion of Scripture every morning and evening and to pray to God with our people, and that not only had they been taught in the white man's country thus to read the Word of God, but many also of freed slaves in Sierra Leone. To prove this Mr. Thomas Puddicomb, a liberated African of the Yoruba nation, who is the head carpenter of the missionary team, and Mr. Mark Willoughby, Mr. Gollmer's interpreter, were each requested to read a portion of Scripture and to translate it to the chief, and Mr. Willoughby read the miracle of the widow's son at Nain, which they both translated to the astonishment of Ogunbonna. Mr. Willoughby was liberated at the same time with Crowther, and Mr. Puddicomb at the same time with Crowther's wife. They were all taught to read the Word of God at Bathurst school, superintended at that time by Mrs. Weeks.

The Services held by Crowther and Gollmer under the umbrella tree were a great success, and the formation of a Sunday-school of forty children, the first ever seen in Badagry, became an immensely popular feature of their work. Crowther had always a tender place in his heart for the children and could hold their attention. On 13 April, Crowther preached to a congregation of sixty-three adults and forty children. The children seemed to be peculiarly delighted with the service, and were heard distinctly joining in the Confession, the Lord's Prayer, the Creed, and the responses to the Ten Commandments in the Yoruba language. This day he brought with him a few letters of the alphabet, thinking they might amuse them and that thus they could at the same time be taught, though but slowly, into reading and understanding the Bible in their own language. The simple-hearted children were quite pleased with this new art. The children surrounded Rev Crowther to see him point to the moonlike O and the serpent-like S. Although the men and women were at liberty to go away after Service, yet they remained to see these wonderful letters.

During their enforced stay in Badagry, they worked hard among the people. Crowther made great progress in his translation of the Scriptures in Yoruba language, and had also translated the Liturgy, so that the congregation could now join intelligently in the service. This work was of permanent value to the mission, and with the new accomplishment of learning to read, the natives were filled with delight. The Chief was surprised that Christians pray to Olorun (God) for everything, for all people, for their enemies even. This is unheard of before.

The journey to Abeokuta, so long delayed for about a year and a half because of safety concerns, was fortunately expedited by the interference of an enemy. Jose Martino Domingo, a notorious Portuguese slave dealer of Porto Novo, had sent £200 in presents to Sagbua at Abeokuta, promising to clear the roads of robbers if he would allow a traffic in slaves to be established; but the missionaries at Badagry had managed to send a private appeal to Sagbua, of their intention to come to Abeokuta and commence missionary work among the people. Ignorant of this, Domingo had taken the precaution to give a scandalous report of the missionaries. He knew that if Christianity became strong in Abeokuta, his slave trade would suffer. When the messengers arrived and had given Domingo's account, Sagbua replied that Egbas know who their best friends are - those who rescue our children from captivity and send them freely back home to them and not those who bring goods to purchase them for perpetual slavery and misery. He warned Domingo of the consequence if any harm is done to the missionaries. They started the journey on 27 July 1846, in the rainy season, fearing that any delay might give Domingo a chance of blocking the way. Gollmer, however, remained in charge at Badagry. It proved to be a difficult journey, but faith kept them going despite the opposing elements.

The weather was very bad for travelling and the narrow bush paths were flooded for it rained throughout the day. The Townsends and Mr. Crowther rode on ponies, but Mrs. Crowther preferred a hammock, while the children were carried, African fashion, tied to the backs of carriers. They travelled about twenty-five miles first day of the journey to Abeokuta with an escort of twenty-five men from Badagry to accompany them till they had passed the most dangerous part of the route. They rested in their tent, which they pitched, after clearing away the bush, in the middle of a large forest on the bank of a stream. At night, the only shelter was a tent pitched on the wet ground, with a fire to dry their clothes. The missionaries had provided for crossing the river by taking with them a bathing tub to use as a boat. The next morning it served the purpose as it was unsafe to delay proceeding to Abeokuta.

They crossed the stream safely, navigated by two men as they waded to the middle in the water, the bottom of which was full of roots of trees which grow in it. The second day's journey was more difficult than previous day because the road was so affected by rain with fallen trees blocking the way. Often the horses struggled with the water up to their knees or sank deep in a swamp; at best the ground was so slippery that they could hardly keep their footing. In other places the path, long neglected through the months of war, was so overgrown as to be almost impassable and the horses' feet got entangled in briars, while overhanging branches or creepers caught the heads of the riders. Drenched with frequent showers and with torn clothes and bruised limbs, they plodded on. Mrs. Townsend had difficulty in keeping her seat. The path twisted so sharply between the trunks of trees that frequently there was not room to turn the hammock pole. Mrs. Crowther's carriers slipped and fell so often on account of the slippery nature of the path that she was obliged to walk most of the way to Abeokuta which was so tiring for her. The children, Juliana and Dandeson, were carried on the back and it was not a nice experience for them travelling in the dark forest, besides which they were beaten by rain. The path followed did not allow the use of an umbrella. When they rested in the forest the second day, they were obliged to catch rainwater for their use, there being no water near where they could pass the night with safety. For the two nights their rest was still further disturbed by invasions of columns of the terrible driver ants.

A few days later they were glad to meet some messengers from the chiefs to welcome them to the town. Townsend and Crowther with others entered Abeokuta the great Egba town on 3 August 1846 at last in pouring rain, wet to the skin, amid joyous reception from chiefs and people. They were made by their enthusiastic friends to go all round the town to see the sights before being introduced to Sagbua, the principal chief of the town. The day previously the town-crier, dressed in striped garments of bright colours, with a head-dress of monkey skin, a bell in one hand and a suspicious-looking axe in the other, warned all and sundry of the consequences of interfering with the safety and comfort of Sagbua's guests.

Mrs. Townsend attracted general attention, she being the first white woman most of the people had seen. Moreover, the Egbas were intensely proud that Abeokuta had been chosen as the first town for the great English people to reside in, and it was on every tongue that the news of their arrival "would fly from Lagos to Ilorin and excite the envy of all the chiefs." There had been eager discussion as to which chief and township should have the honour of entertaining the visitors; but eventually it was settled that it should go to Sagbua as premier chief. In the public council house of the Council of the Nation, and surrounded by the chiefs, he accorded to them a splendid welcome, and at the very first interview showed his wisdom in a remarkable way.

When the missionaries were in due time introduced to Sagbua, they presented him with a large mirror from the C.M.S. brought from England for the purpose, which had miraculously survived this travelling. Lest so rare a present should stir up jealousy among his brother chiefs he caused it to be hung, not in his own palace, but in the council house, that it might be public property. A public meeting was summoned under the presidency of Sagbua, and Crowther gave a speech in Yoruba, explained fully the object of their coming and the purposes of the mission (their future labour). Contributions were made towards the new premises required for the work, everybody gave at least one thousand cowries, equal to two shillings and sixpence English (which would have broken the record in any missionary meeting in the white man's land), and Sagbua, with a chairman's generosity, gave 20,000 cowries and a sheep into the bargain. Some of the chiefs had liberated relatives of their own, sitting by them at the very time.

The first few days were spent in visiting in turn each chief in charge of the major sections of Abeokuta. In every case the missionaries were received by the local ogboni with his balogun and full council of local elders, and Crowther, was the spokesman, explaining so that all might hear in their own tongue the object of their corning. Thus, the national and municipal organizations of the city were utilized for giving publicity to the mission and making clear to all the motives that had brought them.

The next thing was to acquire a site on which to build a mission house, a Church, and a school. A piece of land three acres in extent was at once given to the missionaries by the chiefs, and as Ake was the "royal township," in which the great Shodeke had lived, and where the council always met, it was decided that the mission centre should be there also. The house was to be built of mud, like all the houses in Abeokuta. The missionaries began to enlist their friends in the task of building the house. Women fetched the clay with which to make the walls and were paid three pence each. So many offers of assistance came that the missionaries reduced the pay to two pence, but nearly four hundred applied. To further reduce the number of helpers the rate was again reduced to one penny, when six hundred and seventy offered, and even then, more hands were willing but unemployed. People stood all day watching in admiration at the way the industrious women worked. They were able to build respectable church with glass windows and smooth boards for flooring. It was good finishing with high quality work considering it was native handiwork. Townsend and Crowther did not wait for the completion of the buildings before entering upon their true mission. Regular Services were held from the very first, even though there was no place to hold them save the veranda formed by the overhanging thatch in one of the compounds, with part of the congregation under cover and the rest sitting or standing in the open. The people listened attentively to the Christian message, especially when Crowther spoke to them. Each Sunday the congregations increased; and weekday preaching services were held in the markets and in the compounds of the chiefs' houses. Sometimes as many as 500 people were present and great interest was aroused throughout the town. The Yoruba Mission quickly took a foremost place in the interest and sympathies of the Society's circle of friends; and for some years no Mission was watched more eagerly or prayed for more fervently.

After the first Church had been opened -2 March 1847- capable of seating a couple of hundred people in Ake, the royal township, other chiefs gave permission for the building of simple little places for worship in their townships. By the close of the year no less than four were in use. They were situated in the districts of Igbein, Owu, Itoku, and Ikaja. The chief of the last-mentioned township was particularly friendly, choosing for the Church a site opposite his own dwelling and superintending the measuring of the ground; when the Church was opened, he was the first to enter.

Before Crowther had been three weeks in Abeokuta, he received intelligence that his mother was still alive with his sisters at the neighbouring town of Abake. He therefore lost no time in sending for them, but the news seemed so incredible that the sisters refused to act on it. But the old mother's heart had more faith, and in the company of one of Crowther's half-brothers she started for Abeokuta.

It was on 21 August that the meeting of mother and son occurred; and Crowther noticed that the text that day in the Christian Almanack was, "Thou art the helper

51

of the fatherless." After about twenty-five years of being forcefully separated from his family when the slave raiders took them, Rev Samuel Ajayi Crowther reunited with his mother. When she saw him, she shivered and could not believe her own eyes. They grabbed one another, looking at each other in silence with great surprise, while the big tears rolled down her shrunken cheeks. She trembled as she held her son by the hand and called him by the affectionate names which he was called by his grandmother, who has since died in slavery. They could not say much, but sat still, casting many a loving look towards each other. Love and affection of mother and son towards each other, which years of violent separation had long checked, but could not extinguish. His two sisters, who were captured with him, and their children were all living with his mother. He had given up all hope of ever seeing them again, and now, after a separation of twenty-five years, without any plan or device of his, they were brought together again. His feelings and joy were beyond description.

The story she had to tell her son was full of very sorrowful remembrance. After he had been taken to the coast, she and her daughters regained their liberty, and went to live with the half-brother, who had redeemed them. They could hear nothing of the lost Ajayi. The sisters married, and after a time of peace and safety, one day when the mother and her eldest daughter were going to market, they were kidnapped, and the daughter had to be ransomed by her husband. But the poor old mother was dragged from place to place, exposed for sale in the marketplace and being so aged was made a domestic slave. She was sent by her mistress to Abeokuta, and, again captured on the road, sold into hard and bitter bondage, until her daughter collected cowries sufficient and bought her back for £4 10s.

Rev Samuel Ajayi Crowther asked her to live with him, which she accepted but he was sad that she was still without knowledge of the true God and still a traditional religion worshipper. His mother attributed this happy event of meeting her son once more to the influence of his deceased father in the unseen world and proposed to offer a special sacrifice to her gods in gratitude for the discovery of her long-lost son; but was assured that it was to the Christians' God that she owed this great mercy. On one bright day she accepted Christ as her Saviour. Her change of heart was in part due to an illness, and it was an abounding joy to Crowther when she quietly told him, "Had I been left alone I should have attributed my sickness to this or that deity, and should have made sacrifices accordingly; but now I have seen the folly of so doing, all my hopes are in the Lord Jesus Christ, whom now I serve." She became her son's first convert in Abeokuta and received Christian instruction with gladness, for she recognized that it was the Christian God Who had wrought such wonders for her son. On 6 February 1848, when the first six new converts of Abeokuta were admitted to baptism, Afala herself was one of them, receiving, as the mother of "Samuel," the appropriate Christian name of Hannah. Thus Samuel Crowther, the ex-slave, had the joy of baptizing his own mother into the Church of Christ. He had translated the baptismal service into Yoruba for the occasion. Another of that first company of converts was a priestess of Ifa, and four of Crowther's own nieces were baptized at the same time. Month by month, the work now expanded and prospered, notwithstanding frequent severe persecution from some. Mr. Marsh, the catechist, likewise found his mother in Abeokuta. By 3 August 1849, when the mission was three years old, it had 500 constant attendants on the means of grace, 80 Communicants, and 200 candidates for baptism in that short period.

But amid many encouragements, the old customs and practices of the people still caused the missionaries deep pain. Though the people vaguely recognized a supreme God, whom they called Olorun, and to whom the enlightened Shodeke had built a small temple, the worship of the city centred round such deities as Ifa (the god of secrets), Ogun (the god of iron and war), Shango (the god of thunder), and perhaps most of all a powerful spirit believed to dwell in the Olumo rock and worshipped in the largest of its caves. Sacrifices were constantly offered, and the people held the gods in awe. Though loving freedom for themselves, the Egbas had no thought for other people. They did not scruple to hold slaves or to trade in them, and on occasion to engage in a war upon some neighbouring town or village, a war that was in reality a slave raid. Very soon after Crowther found his long-lost relatives, he was thrown into great anxiety, for a strong force of Egbas laid siege to Abake, the town where his two sisters were living. After four months siege, Abake people were compelled to surrender and were brought to Abeokuta as slaves. Another town full of life and activity swept off the face of the earth and now all is silent and desolate. As the captives from Abake were led into the Egba capital, Crowther, in his anxiety, kept watch for his dear ones and found his brother, two sisters, and their children among the number, all of whom he was able to ransom.

A month after the baptism of Crowther's mother, a new missionary reached Abeokuta, the Rev. J. C. Muller. He had landed at Badagry earlier in the year, and within a month had laid his wife in the grave beside Mrs. Gollmer. Rev. J.C. Muller travelled to Abeokuta at once to relieve Mr. and Mrs. Townsend who greatly needed a short vacation on account of his wife's ill-health. Meanwhile, the Yoruba chiefs and people were beginning to see the value of lawful commerce with the outer world and desired to trade with England. At the port of Badagry, some of the Sierra Leone merchants had settled, and they were ready to buy the palm-oil, nuts, indigo, cotton and other produce from Yoruba country. The great obstacle to this objective was the fact that the shortest and most convenient way from Abeokuta to the sea was through Lagos and this route had been long closed to them by the slave-raiding fraternity.

The ruler in Lagos was a slave trading king and they could only obtain English ironware and other articles from Portuguese slave-traders, who would only take slaves in exchange. The Egbas were also anxious to strengthen their friendship with the British. When, therefore, the chiefs learned that Henry Townsend was about to visit his native homeland in 1848, the chiefs took the opportunity to send by him a letter to Queen Victoria, not doubting that she could interfere, and "open the road" to Lagos. Sagbua himself dictated it in full council and is worth quoting:

"The words which Sagbua, and other chiefs of Abeokuta, send to the Queen of England. "May God preserve the Queen in life forever! Shodeke, who communicated with the Queen before, is no more. It will be four or five years before another takes his office. "We have seen your servants the missionaries, whom you have sent to us in this country. What they have done is agreeable to us. They have built a House of God. They have taught the people the Word of God, and our children beside. We begin to understand them. "There is a matter of great importance that troubles us: what must we do that it may be removed away? We do not understand the doings of the people of Lagos, and other people on the coast. They are not pleased that you should deliver our country-people from slavery. They wish that the road may be closed, that we may never have any intercourse with you. What shall we do that the road may be opened, that we may navigate the River Osa to the River Ogun? The laws that you have in your country we wish to follow in the track of the same—the slave-trade, that it may be abolished. We wish it to be so. The Lagos people will not permit: they are supporting the slave-traders. We wish for lawful traders to trade with us. We want, also, those who will teach our children mechanical arts, agriculture, and how things are prepared, as tobacco, rum, and sugar. If such a teacher should come to us, do not permit it to be known, because the Lagos people, and other people on the coast, are not pleased at the friendship you are showing to us."

In due time this letter was presented to Her Majesty, and she commanded the Earl of Chichester to send a reply on her behalf. Sagbua and his chiefs had, with their letter, sent the Queen a present of cloth finely woven on the looms of Abeokuta.

Fourteen months elapsed between the sending of Sagbua's letter and the receipt of the reply from Queen Victoria. During that period things moved rapidly in Abeokuta. There were, on the one hand, great encouragements, and on the other, very serious opposition.

Meanwhile, Crowther was steadily building up the work in his section of the town. He had built for his growing flock a mud and thatch Church similar to the one in Ake, his old friends in Sierra Leone providing the money for it and Egba Christians doing most of the work. He was busy, too, with the all-important work of translation and sent home for press St. Luke's Gospel, Acts, Romans, and a catechism. Great was the joy among his scholars when a supply of Yoruba primers arrived. Crowther himself established a school for boys, and Mrs. Crowther, who had been a teacher in Freetown, took charge of one for girls.

All missionary experience has shown that such work never goes on long without opposition for the old priests see danger ahead and do all in their power to frustrate the progress of Christianity. It was so in Abeokuta. The Churches at Ake and Igbein were filled to overflowing. The smaller Churches were attended by hundreds, and the number of candidates for baptism was steadily increasing.

The inevitable trouble began over difficulties created in family affairs by the conversion of some young men who were shortly to be married. Urged on by jealous priests, the fathers of the betrothed girls refused to give them to their prospective husbands, on the grounds that, having become Christians, the men would not worship the household gods. The young men stood firm and banded themselves not to marry any girl who would not join them in reading God's Book. Attempts were made to poison some of these resolute youths, and Christian girls also were threatened with the mysterious terrors of the Oro that for ages had filled with fear the heart of every Yoruba woman. Things grew more serious. Christian men and women were seized and thrown into prison, and some were put into stocks. One man was in the stocks for five days till his legs and feet were swollen with pain.

In Igbore the storm broke out with redoubled fury. Everything was done to make the situation terrifying to the converts. The dreaded Oro was called out, and with a furious beating of drums, an excited crowd, armed with whips, clubs, and cutlasses, chased the Christians through the streets, and, when caught, dragged them to the council house of that township. There both men and women were mercilessly scourged, and the feet of the men were pushed through holes in the wall and made fast on the outside. Some of these holes were two feet above the ground on which the sufferers were forced to lie.

For five days and nights those people lay there, exposed alternately to the scorching tropical sun and rain. They were not fed but were pestered to forsake their new faith. Some might have died had it not been that on the council there were men who opposed the action of their colleagues and secretly fed and comforted the poor victims. Meanwhile, the dwellings of the prisoners were attacked and plundered of everything worth carrying away; even the doors were taken off their hinges and stolen. As so often happens, the persecutors overshot their mark, and the constancy of the Christians made a deep impression. There grew a general feeling of sympathy with the people who could suffer so bravely for their faith. Even the persecutors were puzzled, and asked: "What is it that the white man gives you to eat that makes your hearts so strong?"

In the Igbein, Itori, and lmo quarters of the town similar persecutions broke out.

But in the other townships the chiefs, notably Sagbua, refused to permit it, stood by the Christians, protected them to the limit of their power, and in the end secured the liberation of the prisoners in those places where the councils had persecuted them.

In response to their appeal in the letter sent to the Queen of England, Lord Palmerston, as foreign secretary sent Captain Beecroft as Consul to Abeokuta. The Consul arrived there at the beginning of 1851 and found Abeokuta in the midst of a new danger. The various slave-trading chiefs and countries were combining to destroy Abeokuta which they perceived was a standing block to their slave trading, and to drive all Englishmen out of the country. At the head of this confederacy were Kosoko, king of Lagos, and Gezo, the bloodthirsty tyrant reigning over the neighbouring warlike kingdom of Dahomey. Commander Forbes, who had visited Dahomey just before, gave a most shocking account of the barbarities prevailing in Dahomey. There was a large army of trained warriors, men and women, the "Amazons" being especially famous for their courage and cruelty. This army had devastated most of the neighbouring countries. The women and children were taken into slavery, and the men put to the sword. Abomey, the capital, was a city of human skulls. "They are stored up in thousands, and brought forth on state occasions, the heads of kings in large brass pans. Skulls form the heads of walking sticks and distaffs, ornament drums and umbrellas, surmount standards, decorate doorways, are built into walls, crown the ramparts of the palace, form the footstool of the king's state chair. The very drinking-cups which the ladies of the royal harem carry at their girdles are polished skulls."" Had Gezo succeeded in destroying Abeokuta, the future Bishop Crowther's skull would probably have adorned the palace at Abomey.

Fortunately, the news of the coming attack reached the Egbas in good time. As early as January, 1851, Beecroft, the British consul, warned them of Gezo's intentions, and Sagbua with some of the more energetic chiefs at once began to make preparations. Some miles of the city wall were repaired, and all possible was done to repel the enemy. On Saturday, 1 March, came news that the Dahomian army was approaching, estimated at 16,000 strong (10,000 men and 6,000 Amazons) and this soon plunged the city into panic. Everybody, including the missionaries, knew that it would be a life and death struggle against this well trained and disciplined army. The King of Dahomey had determined to totally destroy Abeokuta, which stood so much in his way as a slave trader.

The attack by the Dahomian on Abeokuta, took place on Monday 3 March 1851. On the previous Sunday night special prayer-meetings had been held by the Christians in their churches and cried to God for deliverance from their cruel foe. Their cry: "Give peace in our time, O Lord, because there is none other that fighteth for us, but only Thou, O God." The missionaries at Ake, Crowther at Igbein, and Smith at Ikija, sought to strengthen and advise their people. On Monday morning, the men among them joined the defending army on the low mud walls and at the gates. All day long scouts brought in reports of the enemy's approach, and early on Monday morning, the Dahomians crossed the Ogun. At the outset the Egbas failed to hold back the enemy at the ford, and retreating, waited on the walls to repel the assault and stood before the walls. At first it seemed as though Abeokuta was helpless and at the mercy of the enemy, and that the city built up with such patriotism and patience, and the mission work with its peaceful success, were to be wiped out amid a wholesale slaughter of the inhabitants.

Fortunately, the Dahomians had been misled by the people of lsaga (who were secretly aiding the Egbas) and delivered their attack on the south side, where the defences were strongest. Had they carried out their original intention of approaching from the north (where the walls were in ruins) nothing, humanly speaking, could have saved the town. For a long time both sides exchanged musketry fire, much to the advantage of the defenders, who were partly sheltered behind the walls and the conflict was a fierce one. The Dahomians flung themselves against the defences with ferocious recklessness; and the Egbas resisted each attack with desperate courage. The din was terrible; the shouts of the enemy as they came on time after time in well-ordered ranks, were answered by the heavy fire of musketry from the walls. The Egba women, and even the children, showed great courage and stood behind their menfolk to reload the guns and carry water to quench their thirst, for all knew they were fighting for life and liberty.

Then the Dahomians extended their lines; but the Egbas saw the manreuvre and met it by lengthening their own line of defence. Over a battle front of a mile the conflict raged. There were moments when the issue trembled in the balance. At one point, after almost superhuman efforts, the enemy succeeded in making a breach in the wall and pressed through in triumph. For a moment the Egbas wavered. Had they given way the day would have been lost and thousands of their heads would have been carried to Abomey. But at that moment, when the issue hung by a thread, someone gave a cry of surprise, the Dahomians who had breached the wall were not men but women. Instantly the wavering Egbas rallied. They were not going to be beaten by women, and with a tremendous effort they stemmed the tide.

The fight had now raged for six hours without a pause. From the top of a high rock, behind the Ake mission house, the missionaries, with intense anxiety, watched the struggle, praying all the time that God would deliver the city they loved so well. Then as the sun was sinking towards the west, they detected a new development: the Egbas were outflanking their foes. The Dahomians wavered, and the defenders poured out from the gates to press their advantage. To baffle their enemies, they set fire to the dry grass that stood ten and twelve feet high, and swiftly the flames and smoke added confusion to the scene. Before those fierce onslaughts, the Dahomians fell back, leaving hundreds of their dead upon the field. But their discipline and valour prevented the defeat from becoming a rout, and all through the night they fought rearguard actions.

At dawn, the Egbas pressed forward in force to drive their beaten foe from the country. At Isaga, another decisive battle was fought, if anything more deadly than that before the walls of Abeokuta, and again the Egbas were victorious. The proud Dahomians' armies were now in full retreat, and their losses were estimated at more than 3000 slain and 1000 taken prisoners. Some of the famous Amazons (female warriors) were captured, but many of the enemy died in battle. The war through the goodness of God resulted in the total defeat of the Dahomians. It was a glorious victory, and a merciful deliverance for Abeokuta.

On the day following Crowther picked his way over the battlefield and was saddened to observe that almost as many women were killed as men on the Dahomian side. The Egba chiefs, heathen as they were, openly ascribed the victory to the God whom their Christian subjects worshipped; and the result was a motivation to the whole work of the Mission. They realized, too, that had not the white men warned them of their peril, the Dahomians would have caught them unprepared and their fate would have been sealed. The Egbas saw in the missionaries and Saro settlers a new ally in defeating their regional rival, the kingdom of Dahomey. The King of Dahomey, Ghezo, regularly disrupted Yoruba trade with the port at Lagos by conducting slave raids in the region. In the period between 1840 and 1851, over 51,000 slaves had been embarked in the region of the Bight of Benin, with over half these embarkations taking place at Lagos.

On the Sunday that followed that eventful week the Services were crowded, and with grateful hearts the Christians sang: "God is our refuge and strength, a very present help in trouble." But sorrow was mixed with joy, for some Christians had fallen in the battle and some missing, were in fact carried off by the enemy to an unknown fate.

The missionaries were not a little anxious lest the triumph should be marred by cruelty to the prisoners who had fallen into the hands of the conquerors. With people still bitter, revenge would have been natural; and the possibility of it was increased by the violent behaviour of some of the captives. Two captured Amazons, for instance, killed the people who took them food. Yet the Egbas did not act with cruelly towards their prisoners.

Soon after the Dahomian army was defeated in March 1851 Crowther came on his third visit to England, reaching London on 13 August of that year. Before going, he had the opportunity of reading and translating to the chiefs and people a very gracious message which had arrived from the Queen of England. This was in answer to a letter which they, on their own initiative, had sent to her through Mr. Townsend.

The gracious reply of Her Majesty, sent through the Earl of Chichester, was delivered at a great gathering of chiefs, and at the same time Sagbua was presented with some gifts which accompanied it, two beautifully bound Bibles one in English and the other in Arabic, there being no Yoruba version at that time and a steel corn mill from Prince Albert. Crowther explained the letter to the chiefs that the Queen and people of England are very glad to hear that Sagbua and the chiefs are interested in commerce, and that they so kindly received the missionaries, who carry with them the Word of God, which many of the people are willing to listen to it.

The reading of this message created a deep feeling upon the King and his great warriors as they sat in the outer court of the Council House at Ake. Crowther then took the opportunity of reminding Sagbua that in reading the Bible he would see that King David, Jehoshaphat, Hezekiah, and Josiah had prosperous and glorious reigns because they feared God and led the people in His worship and service. On the other hand, he pointed out that when Israel rejected God and turned to idolatry and sin, they were punished with severe judgments.

After this Crowther brought forward the steel mill which Prince Albert had sent to Egbas for their use. The whole crowd watched with eager eyes full of curiosity, and when some Indian corn was put in, the handle turned, and fine flour poured forth, their delight knew no bounds. An incident a few days later showed that Sagbua, however impressed by the words of the missionaries and the message of the Queen, was still deep in idol worship. Crowther was talking to him when he seriously asked whether he ought not to offer some sacrifice to the beautiful things which he had received. Astonished, Crowther asked, "What things? The corn mill or the Bibles? " "The Bibles," was the prompt reply. After reading from Scripture some passages about idolatry, it was explained to the chief how such an offering would be at conflict with its teaching.

During Samuel Ajayi Crowther's brief visit to Britain in 1851 organized by Henry Venn, the CMS Secretary, he spoke to various assemblies in London—including an audience with Queen Victoria and Prince Albert—urging military intervention to put down the slave-trading kingdom of Dahomey in support of settler missions in Abeokuta.

While in Britain, one day, when Crowther was sitting in the Church Mission House a gentleman walked in. Crowther sprang to his feet, rushed at him, and embraced him, much to the visitor's suprise. It was Sir Henry Leeke, who had been captain of the ship that rescued the slave-boy Ajayi thirty years before; and Crowther had never seen him since. Sir Henry invited him to his country house in Kent, and in the parish Church there the negro clergyman preached in the presence of his deliverer on the liberty wherewith Christ makes His people free.

On 18 November 1851, at 4.30 p.m., Lord Wriothesley Russell took Rev Samuel Ajayi Crowther to the Palace at Windsor. While they were waiting in a drawing-room to see Prince Albert, Crowther could not help looking round at the magnificence of the room glittering with gold, the carpet, chairs, etc., all brilliant. Soon they were invited to an upper drawing-room, more richly furnished than the first. Here they met Prince Albert standing by a writing-table. Lord Russell made obeisance and introduced Crowther, and he made obeisance. They discussed West Africa, and Abeokuta in particular. The Prince asked whether he could be shown Abeokuta on any map, or thereabouts. Crowther then showed the position in the large map from the Blue Book and brought out from his pocket the small one his eldest son had made on the section of slave trade influence, with the different towns and seaports legibly shown. During the conversation, a lady came in, simply dressed, and the Prince looking behind him, introduced her to Lord Russell, but in so quick a way that he could not catch the sound. This lady and the Prince turned towards the map to find out Abeokuta and Sierra Leone. All this time he was unaware of the Great Majesty before whom he stood, was conversing freely, and answering every question put to him about the way slaves are entrapped in their homes or caught as captives in war. On inquiry he gave them the history of how he was caught and sold, to which all of them listened with spellbound attention. It was getting dark, a lamp was got, and the Prince was anxious to find and define the relative positions of the different places on the map, especially Lagos, which was the principal seaport from which Yoruba slaves were shipped. When the Prince wanted to open the Blue Book map wider, it blew the lamp out altogether, and there was a burst of laughter from the Prince, the lady, and Lord Russell. The Prince then said, "Will your Majesty kindly bring us a candle from the mantelpiece?" On hearing this Samuel Ajayi Crowther became aware of the person before whom he was all the time. He trembled from head to foot and could not answer the questions that followed.

Lord Russell and the Prince told him not to be frightened, and the smiles on the face of the good Queen assured him that she was not angry at the liberty he took in speaking so freely before her, and so his fears subsided. He pointed out Lagos, the particular object of inquiry, and told them that he with others were shipped from there. He then showed the facility which the port has, beyond all the other ports, as a depot, being much nearer, and the port of the highway to the interior Yoruba countries. The Queen was highly pleased to hear this information from him. Lord Russell then mentioned his translations into the Yoruba language, and he repeated, by request, the Lord's Prayer in the Yoruba, which the Queen said was a soft and melodious language. Lord Russell informed the Queen of his having seen Sir H. Leeke, who rescued Crowther and others from the slave ship many years ago. This interested her very much. She was told that Mrs. Crowther was recaptured in the same way that he was. She asked after Sally Forbes Bonetta, the Yoruba African young girl rescued from Dahomey. After these questions she withdrew with a marked farewell gesture.

During the brief stay in England Rev Crowther had an interview with Lord Palmerston, to explain to the Foreign Secretary the political position on the West Coast, and especially Abeokuta, and how Ghezo, the King of Dahomey was not only a ruthless slave trader but was injuring the interests of commerce and civilization on the coast.

Before he returned to his native land Crowther addressed a large audience composed of students of the University of Cambridge, and appealed to them with sincerity for missionaries, who would preach the Gospel to his people on the West Coast of Africa. His closing words were "St. Paul saw in a vision a man of Macedonia, who prayed him to come over to his assistance. But it is no vision that you see now; it is a real man of Africa that stands before you and on behalf of his countrymen invites you to come over into Africa and help us".

On 5 December 1851, at the old schoolroom in Church Street, Islington, Crowther and his wife, with another missionary, at a meeting said goodbye on their leaving for West Africa. The Earl of Chichester, the President of the Church Missionary Society, presided, and amongst many well-known friends of the cause was the Rev. Daniel Wilson, the Vicar of Islington. The speeches were not many, but the reply of Crowther, who with his wife attracted the greatest attention, sitting there with their bright eyes filled with emotion.

The Secretary of Church Mission Society arose, and thanked God for all that had been done since the Yoruba mission eight years ago, and how very merciful He had been in delivering Abeokuta from the hordes of the King of Dahomey. He then advised outgoing missionaries that they might be " harmless as doves " in the midst of people. He congratulated Crowther upon his tactful dealing with the chiefs and urged him to be careful in dealing with their enemies, slave traders, Mohammedans and native priests. He further advised the missionaries to remember that the future character of the Christian Church in West Africa was at stake, and their policy and individual action would influence it. In the Niger they would have not only to spread Christianity, but fix its character, organize a native Church, create a Christian literature, and lay plans for days to come.

He asked them to aim at self-government and self-support, to put the Bible in the hands of the people and said how much they were already indebted to Crowther for his translation into Yoruba of a great portion of the Holy Scripture and the Liturgy. They were recommended also to start an educational institution at Abeokuta for young men and women. He then turned to Mrs. Crowther and told her how heartily England welcomed her as the helpmeet of her husband, and how important they all felt her position was as the first Christian mother in Abeokuta, and they rejoiced that her own children were also an example to others.

When Crowther spoke in response, he reminded the audience that eight years ago, with much fear and trembling he first received his commission. He feared because he had a doubt in his own mind whether it was possible to obtain an entrance into a country which slave trade had rendered so difficult of access; but the promise of Him who said, "Lo, I am with you always, even unto the end of the world," had been fulfilled. He drew attention to the importance of the work on translation, so that the Word of God, at any rate a part of it, was now in the hands of their converts. The converts are now able to make the Word a topic of conversation in their homes and on their farms, and its influence had also been felt in the war camp. With a fervent optimism he spoke hopefully of his nation. They were an industrious people, anxious for trade and commerce. They were tired of the slave traffic and desired to be relieved from it. This was their great enemy, and when this was removed there was nothing to disappoint the expectation that Christianity would extend rapidly over the Niger territories.

Crowther told them that the natives are quite ready for employment in the cultivation of cotton in the country, of which he has hopes that a real trade will one day be established. The Christian natives of Abeokuta do not wish to keep the Gospel to themselves. Already they have promised that teachers should be sent to other towns; nor do they fail, wherever they go, to speak of what they know. Crowther told the gathering that he was going back to his own land with great hope in his heart, feeling much blessed and encouraged, and have only to ask that his many kind friends in England will continue to pray for him and for the salvation of his people.

At the close of this meeting many crowded round Crowther and his wife to wish them God-speed, and a few days afterwards they had set sail, and were once more on their way to their native land.

Samuel Ajayi Crowther was not just a missionary and preacher of the gospel; he was also a social activist as well as economist. He used his position and connection to advocate for the social welfare of the people he was preaching to. He was not only concerned about their salvation but also with their socialization. Ajayi Crowther was a practical friend and helper of his people. He taught them handicrafts, and encouraged them in the cultivation of cotton, for which there seemed a wonderful opening in the way of trade. He was also passionate for the total abolition of slave trade which was still rearing its ugly head in Lagos and around Abeokuta.

SECOND NIGER MISSION

When Crowther arrived at Sierra Leone he was well received by many old friends. He had fond memories of his growing up here where he first received the blessing of Christian love and as a student and afterwards tutor at Fourah Bay College. It was in Sierra Leone he met and married his wife who was a schoolmistress at Bathurst.

While in Sierra Leone he preached in the Churches and the congregation were eager to listen to him. In some cases, he preached in English, but the people were always eager to hear him in his native tongue. Afterwards he would often give them a little conversation in Yoruba language to their pleasure and profit. In some cases when preaching in English, and there occurred any text of special difficulty, he would explain in his native tongue, so that his countrymen would have a better understanding. Before leaving Sierra Leone for Abeokuta his final destination, he attended a missionary meeting where he told them how converts in Abeokuta withstood the serious persecution, and what a grand future appeared to be in store for this famous city, the rallying-point of his scattered nation.

He left Sierra Leone with his family and on 14 June 1852 they reached Lagos. He was able to point out to Mrs. Crowther the very spot from which, in 1822, he had been forcefully shipped as a slave boy in Lagos. He remembered the events so well, his trembling at the strange sight of wide expanse of water, and his simple and unfounded fears when on the safe deck of the English warship. Walking over the old places again, he stopped to take off his hat and reverently thank God on the very bit of shore where he with others was chained to the slave hut.

He could recollect many places he knew during his captivity, so he went over the spots where slave barracoons (an enclosure in which black slaves were temporarily confined) used to be. Some of the spots are now converted into plantations of maize or cassava, and sheds built on others are filled with casks of palm oil and other merchandise, instead of slaves in chains and irons, in agony and despair. Crowther's personal history is a testimony of God's great mercy. One of the reasons for his thankfulness was the sight of so much change and improvement and civilization showing itself everywhere. Crowther loved his country and was happy to see peaceful pursuit of trade and industry everywhere instead of degrading and depressing effect of slavery.

When Crowther reached Abeokuta, many Christian natives and missionaries came to welcome him and were glad to have him back again. He found the work advancing, and during his next two or three years he was able to make progress with translating the early books of the New Testament. During the work on translation, he found many of the laws and customs of his own nation in harmony with those given to ancient Israel. He noted that many Yoruba words were related to the Hebrew and his countrymen are intelligent people in many respects.

One day in a discussion with an Ifa priest on Christianity, the priest advised Crowther to exercise patience in evangelising the people since they are deep rooted in their traditional beliefs and worship. Crowther responded that there would be enough room to exercise patience if they would even make a beginning. The Ifa priest responded that the people are watching the missionaries, to see if they practice what they preach; then they shall be convinced whether this new way will suit them also. Only that Crowther should have patience.

On 5 January 1853, Crowther travelled from Abeokuta to Ketu land. Arriving at Ketu, he lodged with Asai, the Prime Minister, who gave him a warm welcome. Next day he had an interview with the King in a large room, with holes, as in a pigeon house, perforated in the walls, through which his Majesty looked upon his people when they came to plead their wrongs. He was wearing an old pair of red-carpet slippers, which had been sent from Crowther by the hand of Captain Trotter years before. Over his cotton gown, he had draped himself with a piece of red damask, and on his regal brow he wore a crown studded with coral beads. Presently all his audience humbly prostrated themselves, crying, "reverence, reverence." The King, after closely observing his visitor, his hand shading his eyes, said with cordiality: "Crowther, friend, long known by mutual understanding only, here at last we see each other." He then politely spread a handkerchief for Crowther to sit on by his side, drew attention to his old slippers with graceful remembrance, saying: "This is your doing. I have heard of you for a long time and had almost give up on seeing you".

After exchanging pleasantries and long talk about no specific subject, Crowther held his Bible in his hand and showed it to the inquisitive King, telling him that this was the book which God had sent down from heaven to mankind to teach us His mind and will. Crowther proposed its reception by both King and people. The King was apparently touched and replied with seriousness: "Hitherto I have had no helper; now I have found one, I will hold it fast".

The next day being Sunday, Crowther read a few prayers and the Litany, and preached in the morning from St. Paul's sermon at Athens, and in the evening on the parable of the Prodigal Son. Next day the gratified monarch told him to walk round the town and select a spot for building mission premises. In exchange for these considerations Crowther presented him with a beautiful silk patchwork quilt, made by a lady in England, and two silk and velvet caps decorated with feathers and flowers. The King of Ketu was simply captivated. For a time, he was speechless, and when Crowther put on the quilt and exhibited its rainbow tints in the sunshine, his Majesty clapped his hands with gladness. He told Crowther that "Ketu is entirely left open to you; do whatsoever you like in it and bring whomever you think proper. We will receive them with both hands.

On leaving Ketu several natives came to Crowther and begged for more enlightment about Christianity. He inquired what religion they professed in their country, and they said traditional religion and Islam, but mostly the traditional religion. Crowther told them he is a Christian and showed them his Bible, and explained to them that the Bible points humanity to God and answers all questions concerning Him. God Almighty would want everyone to have it. He asked whether the worshippers of their different deities do not live in peace with each other. They said:"Certainly they do not trouble each other, but each one worships what he thinks good for him." He then told them that when Christianity should be introduced into their country, same tolerance ought to be observed.

The failure of the Government Niger Expedition of 1841 had for the time discouraged further effort, though the Consul (Mr. Beecroft) had made a voyage up the river in 1845. Up to that time all exploration of the river had been attended with great loss of life. But Mr Macgregor Laird could not banish from his mind the belief that the Niger could and must be opened to the influence of Christian civilization. His own expedition of 1832-3 had proved disastrous, both financially and in human life, forty out of the forty-nine Europeans having died. Undismayed, he began in the early 'fifties to make preparations for another attempt. Her Majesty's Government was sympathetic, but not prepared to undertake responsibility.

On his return home from Ketu to Abeokuta Crowther found that another expedition up the Niger had been arranged and Macgregor oversaw the arrangements in England. It was proposed to send a small steamer up the river Nun and follow the mainstream of the Niger to the Confluence, and then explore the Tshadda and go two hundred and fifty miles beyond the limit of any other expedition as far as possible. At Rabba, Baikie and Crowther were to travel overland to visit the great Fula Sultan at Sokoto, the capital of the Fulani Empire. There was also another purpose for the expedition. Dr. Barth, the eminent African traveller, was supposed to be lost in the interior, and it was hoped that the expedition might meet with him and bring him home. The number of Europeans for the expedition was reduced to a minimum and where possible black men were to be employed to do the work formerly done by white men. Mr Beecroft, the veteran European settler on the coast and a former leader of expeditions to the interior, was to command it. But Beecroft died before the expedition reached Fernando Po and Dr J. Baikie, who would have been his deputy, took over the command. Dr. J. Baikie was invited to be part of the expedition for the purpose of making fresh observations and notes of geographical value. Mr. Laird made an offer to the C.M.S of a free passage for Crowther, which was thankfully accepted. On 13 June 1854 Messrs. Townsend, Maser, King, and Dr. Irving, kindly came over to bid Crowther farewell preparatory to his joining the expedition to explore the Tshadda. After Rev. Townsend had offered up a prayer for God's protection and guidance, about eight a.m. Crowther left Abeokuta with Mr. Phillip and his son Samuel, who were also going down to Lagos after bidding his family and friends farewell. He travelled to Fernando Po through Lagos. Many of Crowther's Church members followed him to Agbamaya. He took about seven hundred-weight of clean cotton down with him, to be shipped to Manchester.

On the 15 June, he started early in the morning from Agboyi, where they had a night stop, and arrived at Lagos about half-past eight a.m. Here he heard of the unexpected illness of Mr. Beecroft, and that he was about to leave for Teneriffe by the next mail from Fernando Po.

The planting of the Niger Mission gave Crowther the opportunity of his life, and he made careful preparations for the expedition. His chief helper was an African clergyman, the Rev. J. C. Taylor, a son of liberated Igbo parentage. Simon Jonas a native Christian, who was in the first Niger expedition of 1841 as an Interpreter was also to go, together with a few other catechists from Freetown. The intention was to station these workers at Abo, Iddah, the farm, and elsewhere. But Crowther's plan was to reach other great Moslem areas of the Sudan, Rabba, Bida, Kano, and Sokoto. As no convert from Islam was available, he took a liberated Yoruba slave, still a Moslem, who was a teacher of Arabic and full of gratitude to both the British Government and the C.M,S. for all they had done for him. Crowther believed that such a man will do a lot in softening the bias of men by his persuasion.

On 17 June the BACCHANTE arrived in the morning from Fernando Po with the painful news of Mr. Beecroft's death, but Crowther resigned everything to God's good and unerring providence. The following day, he attended Sunday morning Service in Mr. Gollmer's Church.

The FORERUNNER arrived about one o'clock p.m. on 20 June and Crowther met some of the gentlemen of the expedition who were onboard the vessel and was informed the PLEIAD would not touch at Lagos but proceed direct to Fernando Po.

The following day after FORERUNNER's arrival at about nine a.m., Crowther embarked the vessel, and was very glad to meet Dr. Baikie, Dr. Bleek, and Mr. Dalton, a young zoological assistant, onboard. They kindly brought him letters from England and Sierra Leone, and parcels of books and many useful articles from Lady Buxton and Captain Trotter. There was also onboard, the Rev. J. Diboll, with Mrs. Diboll and daughter, Baptist missionary to Fernando Po. They were all very glad to see him. About half-past eleven a.m. the FORERUNNER weighed anchor, and in a short time they lost sight of Lagos. FORERUNNER arrived off the Bonny river the following day, where a ship was lying at anchor and made for Old Calabar. After crossing the bar, the vessel anchored for the night.

On 25 June Sunday FORERUNNER started as soon as it was light and made for Fernando Po. It rained heavily; in consequence of which no Service could be held. About four p.m. she anchored off Clarence and found to great disappointment that PLEIAD had not yet arrived. The expedition team expressed various thoughts and assumptions, as to the cause of her non-arrival. Crowther landed, and took his lodging at Mr. J. Wilson's, the same house he occupied in 1841 with Rev. Schon.

The people were glad to see Crowther and expressed their regret for the loss of Mr. Beecroft who had made preparation for the expedition and engaged many intelligent natives who had travelled up the Niger before with him. After breakfast, Crowther visited Mr. Beecroft's grave, which is on the point of the cliff of Clarence under a large cotton tree, where he himself had directed he should be buried. The chiefs of Abeokuta had sent salutations and messages to him by Crowther which he did not live to receive.

PLEIAD arrived on the 28 June in the evening, to the great joy of all parties. The FORERUNNER had been detained two days beyond her time, or she would have towed the PLEIAD off the Nun, to save fuel. She sailed away the following evening with their letters for England. Dr. Bleek's state of health being considered by the medical gentlemen to be very unsafe for the voyage, was pronounced unfit to accompany the expedition, and was consequently sent back to England by FORERUNNER.

Crowther embarked PLEIAD 8 July in the afternoon, as she was to set sail in the evening. About nine p.m. she weighed for the Nun, with two large iron canoes laden with coals in tow and hearty cheers from friends a short distance from harbour. As the wind rose, and the swell became heavy, the canoes did not tow well, and there was some fear of their capsizing.

PLEIAD could not go more than half her speed for fear of swamping the canoes. The night was, therefore, spent with some anxiety. They had a few accidents, a breakdown in the machinery about noon when the spindle of the safety valve gave way, and steam could not be kept up, so they could not proceed until it was repaired. This took three hours, and vessel drifted eastward by the westerly current, with heavy swell and rains. Nearly all hands were sea-sick and could not conduct Divine Service. They had a difficult crossing of the bar (A large mass of sand or earth formed and raised above the water surface by the surge of the sea. They are mostly found at the entrances of great rivers, and often render navigation extremely dangerous, but provides tranquillity in the inshore waters by acting as a barrier against strong wave) outside the Nun River. On 11 July, off the mouth of the St. John or Brass river the vessel anchored for the night between it and the mouth of the Nun.

The following day at about two p.m. with the flood tide PLEIAD crossed the bar and was piloted by Mr. Thomas Richards, a Yoruba man, who had made many voyages up the Niger with the late Mr. Beecroft and has a good knowledge of the localities about the coast and the Niger. The water was considerably lower than it had been in 1841, and there was need for more careful navigation. Soundings had to be taken constantly to find the deep channels. When they were in the midst of the bar, the hawser of one of the canoes, in which there were seven Krumen, broke. PLEIAD could not stop to render her any assistance and the canoe was left to make the best of her way through the surf, though not without great anxiety for the men. The surf was tremendous, so much so that it broke once over PLEIAD poop (the aftermost and highest deck of a ship, especially a sailing ship), though the tide was in their favour. Every eye was fixed upon the drifted canoe, and it was no small joy to see her now and then buoyed up from the deep furrow upon the top of the surf, following PLEIAD track, till she got across in safety. About three o'clock they anchored inside the bar very near to Alburka Island when the engineer examined the engine and found that the safety-valve was just gone, and it was providential that vessel got across the bar before this happened.

The next two days were spent in repairing the engine and on the 15 July, about six a.m, the vessel got underway for the Niger with the tide still in their favour but missed the right channel, and ran aground on the point of Sunday Island, the left passage having been taken instead of the right, which was the proper channel.

One feature of the expedition was the care taken to guard against sickness, and quinine was served out to all onboard. Despite the few mishaps, they were least bothered, and Crowther was conducting Divine Service on 16 July with all hand on deck preaching from the text: "Then said they unto him. Who art thou? That we may give an answer to them that sent us. What sayest thou of thyself? "A number of canoes came alongside, asking whether they are slave or oil ship, to which they answered "palm-oil ship".

Soon after the vessel made way and sailed past Sunday Island, Crowther began to make notes of changes and developments along the banks of Niger that had taken place since his last visit in August 1841. There is more cultivation of crops than before along the water edge of the river giving a new appearance to the landscape. The many newly cultivated spots having numerous palm trees, shows evidence of continual industry and development. About three hours from Sunday Island the vessel came to inhabited villages of people of the delta. They invited two canoes to come alongside and learnt from them that the people between Brass and Aboh are called Uru. One of the people who came alongside, and who spoke the Igbo language, volunteered to go with them to Aboh. The people on shore never showed the least sign of opposition but folded their arms and gazed at the steamer as she glided on.

Fewer traces of cultivation were observed during the day till they came to the village of Angiama. Brass people came up here to buy palm oil, with large casks in their canoes. Unlike in 1841 when very few of the people had any decent articles of clothing, many could be seen having English shirts on. This is an evident mark of benefits of legal trade over slave trading. The chief of Angiama, or Anya, came and expressed his regret that the steamer did not wait at his village as Captain Trotter did. He and his people would have preferred the steamer to have stopped in their village so that they could reap all benefits of the trade to themselves instead of people beyond them. It was with some difficulty he could be given a satisfactory excuse. Dr. Baikie gave him a red cap and a looking glass.

Since the vessel entered the Nun, Crowther had been thinking what could have made this river unhealthier than any other, independent of the general harsh climate of the delta region. It occurred to him, that the unhealthiness might have partly originated from the unhealthy vapour created by the raw and green wood for fuel kept in the bunkers for days together mixed with the bark and bilge water. He hinted this idea to Captain Taylor, Dr. Baikie, and Dr. Hutchinson, that a trial might be made of keeping the wood in the canoes, and only calling for it as occasion required. They all at once agreed to take every precaution which might likely improve health condition onboard.

On 21 July 1854, PLEIAD anchored off Aboh, where in 1841 the explorers made some progress with king Obi who had been so friendly and had signed the treaty with Captain Trotter. But the Obi was dead and there was a dispute as to his successor. One of the claimants, Chukwuma, a son of the late Obi, welcomed the visitors with cordiality. A palaver was held in public in the presence of a great crowd of people, the white men and Crowther sitting on mats spread for them. So great was the excitement that even the chief failed to get silence and the business had to proceed amid the loud noise. Dr. Baikie reminded the chief and his councillors of the former visit thirteen years before, and of the treaty then signed. He assured them that the British still adhered to that agreement and that in seeking to fulfil it, PLEIAD had come to trade with them and renew the friendship. Chukwuma, in reply, affirmed that the old Obi, before he died used to watch in vain for the coming ships, and at last told his sons with a sad regret; "The white man has forgotten me and his promise to". He particularly charged them not to deviate from the paths he had trod, and to preserve the friendship of the white man.

Chukwuma who now reigned in his place is weak and the team found that the Aje, a younger and more energetic man, was the real governing power. He was absent when the PLEIAD cast anchor.

On 22 July they had an early breakfast, and about eight a.m. they started for the town of Aboh. The town is thickly populated and is about one mile away along the western bank of the creek. They landed close to Chukwuma's house and met him worshipping his god that morning. The god was in a calabash covered with a white sheet and placed in front of the wall in the square. They waited about ten minutes before Chukwuma made his appearance and warmly welcomed them. In a short time, the little square was crowded, and it was difficult to keep one's seat on the mat spread for their accommodation. Chukwuma used all his efforts to command silence, but to no purpose. Obi's daughter and the chief's wives took their turn to command silence, but it only increased the noise. At last' Chukwuma requested them to frighten the people away, which, of course, they did not do. As it was impossible to obtain perfect silence, Crowther suggested to Dr. Baikie to begin business as they could keep close enough to hear each other despite the noisy atmosphere.

Dr. Baikie informed Chukwuma that the Queen sent him to visit the people of Aboh and convey her condolence. He reminded Chukwuma and his councillors of the former visit thirteen years before, and of the treaty then signed. He assured them that the British still adhered to that agreement and that in seeking to fulfil it, the PLEIAD had come to trade with them and renew the friendship. The Queen hoped his successor would keep to the treaty he had signed with Captain Trotter, who acted in the name of the Queen. Dr. Hutchinson would discuss trade between Aboh country and white man country with him.

Chukwuma replied that he was very glad to see a large ship come to Aboh again, and that he and the other headmen were particularly charged by Obi before his death not to deviate from but adhere to the treaty which he signed with the white men. The failure to trade was not their fault; it was the English who had not fulfilled their side of the treaty to trade. He was glad that they had come at last and pledged that they would act accordingly. Chukwuma expressed a wish that they should wait till Aje return home with some headmen from Igara where they went to settle some matter. He expected them back in three- or four-days' time. At this point, Crowther introduced the subject of a missionary establishment among the natives of Aboh. He told him that they had come to see what could be done to establish a missionary station at Aboh, as in his country at Badagry, Lagos, and Abeokuta, and had been done also at Calabar and the Cameroons.

One of Obi's daughters replied that they could not conceive why white men should build houses in Bonny and Calabar, and not in Aboh.

Crowther told them of earlier plan to send Igbo teachers to teach and reside in Aboh. Chukwuma was happy and hoped that the plan will be realized, and that he would not believe anything until he had seen it done as proposed. He explained that there was no difficulty on their part nor unwillingness to receive those who may be sent to them. He puts the fault on the part of the visitors in not fulfilling what they had planned to do and that when Aje and the other chiefs return back, the matter would be fully discussed. To show his readiness Crowther promised to leave Simon Jonas with Chukwuma to teach the people until the return of the expedition to the sea. He was extremely glad to hear of Crowther's intention to leave Simon Jonas with them.

The response of the people of Aboh to the discussions shows they were ready for learning but because the white man had not kept his word with them in the past. A visit onboard the ship was organised for the chief, his wife, the head wife of Aje, and three of Obi's daughters, with luncheon in the saloon. Dr. Baikie gave gifts to them and the whole party returned home happy. The day following Crowther paid a visit to the chief, in his house to discuss Christian doctrine.

Crowther explained to the chief the all-sufficient sacrifice of Jesus Christ, the Son of God for the sin of the world. He illustrated it to him in this simple way. "What would you think of any persons who in broad daylight like this should light their lamps to assist the brilliant rays of the sun to enable them to see better?" Chukwumah said: "It would be useless; they would be fools to do so." Crowther replied: "Just so." That the sacrifice of Jesus Christ, the Son of God, was sufficient to take away our sins, just as one sun is sufficient to give light to the whole world; that the worship of country fashions and numerous sacrifices which shone like lamps, only on account of the darkness of their ignorance and superstition, though repeated again and again, yet cannot take away our sins; but that the sacrifice of Jesus Christ, once offered, alone can take away the sin of the world. Chukwuma frequently repeated the names " Opara Chukwu! Opara Chukwu! Son of God! Son of God!

But many of Chukwuma's attendants were engaged in asking for and receiving gifts rather than listen to all Crowther was talking about. Crowther gave to Chukwuma a Yoruba primer in which he wrote his name and left some with Simon Jonas to teach the children or any who should feel disposed to learn the alphabet and words of two letters.

The next stage was to visit Iddah, eight days higher up the Niger. On 24 July they proceeded on their journey upward the river passing many Igbo villages and the area showing dense population. As their vessel approached the Confluence, they observed that on the right bank of the Niger, from opposite Adamugu, there is scarcely a village to be seen. On the left-hand bank there are new and extensive towns, which did not exist during Crowther's previous visit in 1841. This is accounted for by the warlike raid of Dasaba, who had swept down with his warriors to avenge the death of Mr. Carr. The Atta of Igalla urged Dasaba to punish the people of the Delta who had, without reason, killed a white man coming to establish trade with the upper country. About a hundred towns and villages were destroyed. As some of the exploring party wished to make sketches and observations from the top of Mount Patteh, they started from the ship early in the morning of 5 August in high spirits, and full of expectations.

Mr. May could not make the sketch of the juncture of the Kowara and Tshadda from the elevation of about twelve hundred feet, because the valley was so overgrown with wood and high grass making it difficult to have a clear view. As they could not go on because of the thick grass and swamps, the team returned to the boat and pulled further up till they came to a landing-place, near a little village of eight or ten huts, a scanty remnant of the once secure villages of Mount Patteh. This village is built on the first cove (inlet), about a third part of the way up Mount Patteh, where very old persons only were living. They asked them the way to the Mount but were told there was no way there at this time, as Dasaba had driven or carried all the inhabitants away. The sight of these villages was pathetic. They pointed to the site of the model farm below, which is now covered with trees and grass, and asked if they were coming to rebuild it. They were told it might be taken up again in due time. They entertained the visitors according to their means, with country beer and clear, cool water, which they fetched from the side of Mount Patteh. The team returned to the ship about 10 a.m. The Natives, fancy they can see a difference in the colour of the two streams, Kowara and Tshadda and call the former "the white water" and the latter "the black water."

Ama-Abokko, the chief, had come early onboard, and Captain Taylor had been talking with him about trading affairs till Mr May, Crowther and others returned. Dr. Baikie called him into the saloon and gave him some presents from Government, with which he was much pleased. They tried to get Ama-Abokko to forward letters to the coast for them through Ilorin, Ijaiye, Ibadan, and Abeokuta. He gave many excuses afraid that people might accuse him of sending a bad book or charm through Ilorin, as Dasaba, their common enemy, has taken refuge there. He consented to send with them some of his canoe men which Crowther and others would pay for. Ama-Abokko styled himself the king of this part of the country. After lunch they went to Igbegbe to collect more information about the country, each one in a different direction except that Mr. Richards and Crowther walked together. Ivory was shown to them, as well as trona (salt packed up in grass bags from the coast), horses, and two slaves. Crowther offered to purchase one of the owners herself instead of the slaves, but she trembled at such an idea. He left her to judge from that whether it is right to trade in our fellowmen. Some slaves were in a canoe alongside the ship that day. Many unfortunately became slaves and suffered because of the war between Dasaba and his brother. They fell prey to the Filatas at the destruction of Panda and are now scattered about the country in all directions by their captors. Fortunately, they remain in the country, as there is no place in the Bight of Biafra for exportation of slaves, the only foreign slave markets being Whydah and Porto Novo, in the Bight of Benin.

They commenced the ascent of the Tshadda on the 7 August. At every point of their journey up the Tshadda inquiries were made of the natives whether they had seen a white man, Dr. Barth. There were rumours in England of his death. Dr Barth was a traveller and a scholar with valuable works on West Africa and hopes were raised when they received information that two white men were not far off in a town called Ksana, four days' journey north. This was one of the reasons for this expedition being promoted. Crowther and his party hurried forward, and met with a native of the place, who said that the white men had been there a month ago. When shown the portraits in the Petermann's Atlas of Central Africa, pointed to that of Dr. Barth and Vogel his companion. A messenger was dispatched immediately with a letter in his hand to Dr. Barth, written by Dr. Baikie, and great was their expectation of his reply. This, however, never came. Dr. Barth was at this time safe and at a considerable distance in the interior. Dr Barth returned to Europe some time afterwards.

Sunday, 27 August after Service Crowther was informed that people were running away from the village of Ojogo. They went there to ascertain the cause and quiet their fears. During two previous nights, Dr. Baikie and Mr. May had been on shore to take lunar observations and had lights with them. The bull's-eye lamp seems to have made them afraid. The chief was previously apprehensive of something when he saw Mr. May measuring the beach and thought that he did this because the white man had it in mind to take his country from him. When they got ashore, they had a discussion with him to explain that lack of information of the depth of the river, made their ship to go aground near his village. They remained there for about two days with Mr May measuring the beach to ascertain the breadth of the river and how much it has risen since they have been here. They also were looking at the moon and stars in the night to ascertain how far they were from their country. They explained to the chief that he must have taken notice that the moon does not remain stationary, but rises higher every day, so by looking at either the moon or stars it is possible to know how far they are from home; that God has commanded them to do good to all men and never to do evil, for if they do them harm God will not be pleased. With this explanation both the chief and his people appeared satisfied.

At Ijogo the people were afraid of coming to the PLEIAD for trade because slaves were still sold in the neighbourhood. Meanwhile, he had difficulties learning the Doma or Arago language of the people because he could not get their attention and cooperation. Some men from the interior came down to the shore, among them was a poor fellow named Asaba, from Rogankoto, one of whose legs had been bitten off by a crocodile; but the wound had since healed. It was pitiable to see the man hobbling about with the aid of a long stout stick. As soon as the two doctors onboard noticed the poor fellow, they set about to find some way of improving his locomotion, and with the assistance of Mr. Guthrie, the chief engineer, a wooden leg was made. At the prospect of such kindness the man hobbled back to his town to tell the people the marvellous news that the white men were going to give him a new foot. A large crowd returned with him, and amid their applauses Mr. Guthrie fixed on the wooden leg, and the man was so happy and proud of his new limb.

When they had pushed on to Abitsi, they found a safe anchorage nearly opposite Mount Ethiope. The river was easily navigated because of absence of islands which earlier on their route posed some navigational hazards. The high hills here are quite close to the water's edge. Small farms and fishing villages are seen on either hand as they passed a little group of huts where the people were busy making pottery. After a time, making headway against a strong current, they reached more open country sparsely populated; for miles not, a village could be seen on the flat land.

At four o'clock they saw a group of houses at a great distance and an hour later anchored off the villages of Gandiko and Gaukera, whose chiefs were Ama and Garike respectively. Before anchoring, intelligence had reached the chiefs of the villages, and all hands were up in arms. Their weapons were bows and arrows, and some men also carried three or four poisoned tipped arrows. Crowther's boat pulled toward shore in search of safe landing-place. There were some plantations of maize and guinea corn along the water's edge, and some of the farmers were near; three women stood close to the bank without fear. They addressed them in Hausa, to which they replied, and asked them for the landing-place. A little way higher up they saw a man on the bank, who drove the women away. They addressed him in Hausa and told him that they were from the white man's country and wanted to see the chief. As soon as he saw the Europeans, he cried out in Hausa: " Bature Anasara maidukia na gode allah! " ("White men, the Nazarenes, men of property, I thank God! ") many times, over. He took the lead through old, cultivated grounds, but overgrown with grass and bushes, through which they had to beat their way to the footpath leading to the town. The escort from excitement, became louder in his cry: " Bature Anasara maidukia na gode allah! " They soon came to a juncture of two paths where the Galadima, a war chief of the first rank, with a small party of about twenty-four men, armed with bows and arrows and spears, were stationed. The escort, with his overexcited cry, introduced them as men of peace and trade. In the meantime, they were lost in the midst of the soldiers; Dr. Baikie was in one direction, Dr. Hutchinson in another, and Mr May in the midst of the soldiers.

They had no weapon on them, but with confidence followed the armed party and Galadima led them to the town. The path was full of soldiers coming out to join Galadima but seeing him return with them they all fell back on both sides of the path which brought them to the entrance to the town. The place was fortified with a wooden fence and a ditch around it. They met chief Ama, also armed with a bow and arrows and about two hundred armed men with him at the centre of the town under a kind of fig or banian tree, planted for the sake of its shade. They were introduced to him by the Galadima, and after shaking hands conversed briefly with him about their visit to the country. He gave warm reception and requested them to return to the ship and wait till tomorrow before discussing the object of their visit.

The open hostility and state of alarm displayed by some of the natives towards any stranger is because of the ethnic and plundering wars. The natives are in constant fear of the treachery of their enemies. This makes them carry their weapons and in readiness for any attack. There is no place in Africa, uncontaminated with European slave dealers. Every chief considers himself highly honoured to have Europeans who have the intention of friendly and genuine trade relations.

Their visit to Zhibu brought them in contact with a suspicious chief, who misunderstood their mission. The chief called the interpreter aside to tell him he had a little boy to sell and asked him to buy the boy. He was informed that the intention of the team was genuine trade and evangelism. The Chief eventually brought ivory and maize to the ship for trading. Here Crowther noticed that the men were so much engaged in plundering expeditions, while the frail male and female slaves tilled the ground. No fruits were cultivated, or eatables hawked about the streets by girls and women, or refreshment places arranged for the sale of food. It was the only town without a market they came across on their journey. One night while anchored off this point the expedition had a narrow escape. They had some sheep as well as wood in the canoe attached to the ship, while Dr. Baikie and Mr. May were standing on shore, taking observations of a star's altitude with their instruments they heard a low growl of a leopard nearby. The big cat was attracted by the smell of the sheep. Some shots were fired to scare off the leopard which was close to the two observers.

The vessel needed constant replenishing of fuel and without it they were helpless to proceed and difficult to hold their position without good place to anchor. The voyage became dangerous at one point when current was running three knots against them. At another time the vessel was surrounded by a submerged herd of hippopotami. Again, they found themselves in a valley where the Tshadda became extremely narrow, the depth not less than five fathoms, and the whole volume of the Benue having to rush through. They had to set up two sails to propel the vessel with wind power, and soon afterwards reached the broad bed of the river. Here, they found nothing but green wood which could not be used as fuel growing in the soft and swampy marshes.

As they were in serious need of fuel, a look-out was kept to collect logs floating down the stream, and these greatly added to their little stock to enable the ship to get to Tshomo. In the meantime, Imoru, the mallam of Zhiru, came onboard with the leg of a buffalo killed previous night for a present to Dr. Baikie. The doctor wanted to buy the head, but the superstition of the people was so strong against selling it. They begged him not to be angry at their denying him that request. They could not be persuaded to sell the skulls of hippopotami which were piled up before the fetish in the town of Zhiru. Imoru very earnestly told Alihebi to ask Crowther if he would pray for his wives, as they had no children. Crowther at once called for his Bible and read Psalm CXXVII, which he tried to explain to Imoru. He showed him his arms and neck to prove that Christians never used charms for any purpose but resign their fate to God, who knows better what is good for them. He was quite satisfied with Crowther's explanation, though disappointed.

Crowther had a great desire to visit Mohammad, the King of Hamaruwa and he sent a message to him of his intended visit. This man was influential and held an independent position under the Sultan of Sokoto. One evening from the masthead of the PLEIAD they could see this town at the foot of the chain of Muri Mountains. When they arrived at Little Isumo they met with a native trader named Ibrahim, who became very friendly. This man promised to be their guide. They landed at Tshomo, where the men get a livelihood by killing hippopotami and the women carrying their children on their backs with the hands of the infants under their arms, by which they were held fast. During the journey Crowther had difficulty with their crewmen, who did not relish the hardships and risks of the expedition.

The creek which divides Tshomo had not enough water for their boat, so they had to pull through the flooded cornfields overgrown with grass and corn-stocks to get into the main creek. Ibrahim had to get one of the canoe-men to take the lead. The Krumen from the ship did not like either the appearance of the guide or the passage he was leading them through. As a hunter of hippopotami the guide had with him five or six harpoons or spears, and pulled through the grass with his narrow canoe like a snake, while the grass was so thick that they could not see him ahead nor perceive the track of his canoe. However, they followed in his direction till they met him under a tree, where he waited for them. The bank being only partially covered with water, the men jumped out and carried the boat across, and the pilot then left them. Crowther called the attention of Friday, the head Krumen, to mark the direction of the tree that they might not miss the way on their return; but Captain Friday and his crew did not seem to relish the idea of returning alone in unsafe environment. They followed the creek, thinking they should soon come to the landing-place, but, contrary to their expectation, they did not land till one o'clock p.m., four hours after leaving the ship. From all the inquiries made Hamaruwa did not appear to be more than six or seven miles from the river. Crowther ordered the boat to be pulled up, and, leaving it and all belonging to it to the care of the headman of the village of Wuza, they started for Hamaruwa. An hour's walk brought them within sight of the first farm village. Another hour brought them to a second farm village, and their way led almost direct west towards the furthest mountains they had left westwards. They found the journey to be unpleasant and the road rough to walk on. About thirty minutes after they left Wuza, Crowther was forced to take off his shoes and roll up the legs of his trousers, as did Mr. Richards, to wade through the continual splash of water and mud they met with more than one third of the way.

They reached the town in good time. It was beautifully situated on a hill, from which a beautiful scenery of the river and vegetation around is obtained. From this vantage position could be seen the stretches of light green grass by the water's edge, then the darker green of the tree foliage, and beyond the blue ranges of Fumbina, with the lofty Mandranu mountain in Adamawa, and the Muri mountain in Hamaruwa near at hand. The houses had conical roofs and long public street, with luxuriant trees, that are characteristic of most African towns. The people had few goats or sheep, and the slaves do all the cultivation of the corn in the lowlands. The travellers received a warm welcome from the King and were well entertained with food.

The King sent five sheep and lambs with a kid, six in all, and a large pot of plum honey for their entertainment. Unfortunately, while carrying the honey pot, it fell and broke with the content spilled on the ground. This was a sad loss to the visitors because the ship had been out of sugar. They had also exhausted the butter and milk onboard the vessel, and a pot of honey would have been a substitute.

Their hosts use no lamps in their houses in the evening. Crowther and the rest therefore remained outside the house where they were lodged, seated in the dark, as their hosts did, till bedtime. A few sticks were kindled, which gave out much smoke and little light, to enable them to ascertain the position of their bed. Before they turned in Ibrahim requested to take care of Crowther's sheep and goat in their (Crowther) room for fear of wild animals, which are many in the country. Crowther told him it was impossible to admit five sheep and a goat into a room already filled with eleven occupants. Ibrahim promised to take care of them until morning. Ibrahim's yard was full of visitors going and coming, to whom he was relating the wonderful news of the Anasara's ship made of iron and moved by fire. They left them to enjoy the story and rested after offering a prayer of thanksgiving to God for their protection. They arrived back to their ship on a Sunday morning.

The river was now ebbing rapidly, and it was felt PLEIAD should be turned homeward, if a safe return was to be counted on. Dr. Baikie and Mr. May took a boat to go three days further up the river to make additional observations. Crowther and the rest were afraid at leaving them in such dangerous situation, among an unknown and perhaps hostile people. PLEIAD sailed faster down the stream and ran aground the next day. It was at that position when loud cheers announced the safe arrival of the boat, with Dr. Baikie and Mr. May whom they had left behind.

On the return journey, Crowther revisited various chiefs and was able to make arrangements for opening mission stations at several points. They reached Aboh on the 31 October and were given land at the entrance to the creek on the bank of the main river for the establishment of mission work. Chief Aje promised that no one would interfere with this claim. At Aboh they met Simon Jonas, who was left there, quite well and much respected by all, both chiefs and people. He moved freely about amongst them, and made several visits up the river, to Ossamare, Onitsha, and Asaba markets, and to an interior town called Oko-Ala, on the back of Aboh, of about a day's journey. The chief of Oko-Ala asked Simon Jonas, why the steamers always stopped at Aboh, and never paid them a visit and Jonas replied, that there will not be left a place unvisited in due time. He was about three days absent from Aboh, when he returned, for fear the steamer might arrive in his absence.

A little lower down the stream Crowther met with a young chief, Agbekun, who, being childless, had been paying a visit to Aeo, where Chukwu, the great god of the Igbos, resides, to make inquiries of a domestic character. Agbekun went through many ceremonies and performed many sacrifices before returning home with a favourable answer communicated to him by the priests. He also brought with him several small representations of the god. He showed these to Crowther to know what the Anasara thought of his Chukwu.

This gave Crowther the opportunity to speak to him about the true God, to whom he endeavoured to turn his attention to look for blessings both temporal and spiritual. Chief Agbekun wanted to know how to pray to the true and Great God. Crowther told him to do so just as a little child would ask his father for what he needed. Agbekun was very shy in speaking much about the Chukwu of the Igbos, as a great mystery is connected even with the place of his residence. Since this young chief's return, he has been going through some ceremonies, and cannot be seen or spoken to much in public till the time allotted has expired, which will be in about two days. In consequence of this he did not attend market, but he was told that as they were from the white man's country his ceremony could not be contaminated by his conversation with them. Crowther explained to him that God teaches all men to love one another and expressed his hope that they should soon be able to teach them this love, which Agbekun was glad to hear.

On 6 November, PLEIAD crossed the bar, and reached Fernando Po following day and Crowther held Divine Service, expressing devout thanks to God for everyone on board for such a good and favourable journey. He preached from Joshua IV. 6, 7 and prayed that: May this singular instance of God's favour and protection drive us nearer to the Throne of Grace, to humble ourselves before our God, whose instruments we are, and who can continue or dispense with our services as it seems good to His unerring wisdom.

This expedition was successful unlike the previous in 1841 and during the voyage of 118 days not a single European died of fever. This was largely due to the fact that quinine was used for the first time in these ventures as a prophylactic. The discovery of its power over malaria gave rise to a wave of optimism in England. In government and missionary circles, it was widely believed that the problem of Europeans surviving in the African interior had been solved. To some extent this was so, but the success of the 1854 expedition was also due to the lessons learnt from past ventures: the number of Europeans was reduced to a minimum; where possible black men were employed to do the work formerly done by white men. The planning was entrusted to able and experienced Niger hands, e.g. MacGregor Laird, the pioneer of the British trade with the Niger, was placed in charge of the arrangements in England; John Beccroft, the veteran European settler on the coast and a former leader of expeditions to the interior, was to command it. The expedition also took the recommendation in Crowther's report to stow away the logs for fuelling the vessel in attendant canoes, and not in the ship's hold. This also reduced the incidence of fever amongst the team. It had occurred to Crowther that the mortality in 1841 might have been due to the noxious vapours generated by the raw and green firewood with which the bunkers had been loaded; and he suggested that it should now be kept in the canoes accompanying the steamer, and only be taken on board when needed. The success of the expedition led to a revival of British interest in this region.

The success of the expedition shows time was ripe for the introduction of Christianity on the banks of the Niger, for the people were evidently willing to receive teachers and eager to trade. They had found that for at least 600 miles up the Niger and Tshadda there was a navigable waterway. Crowther greatly regretted the loss of time since the ill-fated expedition of 1841 had discouraged any ascent of the river for twelve years. The expedition also shows the importance of utilizing native agency and letting such workers go back to their own countrymen as a renewed people, whose walk and conversation would do so much to commend Christ and His Gospel in these regions.

From the standpoint of commerce, the expedition demonstrated great trading opportunities. Crowther took much personal interest in the encouragement of cotton growing, and subsequent development of trade in this direction was largely due to his initiative and persistency. He saw a future trade in palm oil yet untapped and that this trade would in time eliminate the slave traffic, with all its evils. Furthermore, the advantage of the increase of palm oil trade, over that of the slave is so much felt by the people. The aged people in the communities could not help confessing to him that they cannot remembered any time of the slave trade in which so much wealth was brought into their country as has been since the commencement of the palm oil trade. They are now satisfied with legitimate trade.

Crowther pointed out in his report that by pushing up the Niger he might strike those great caravan routes of the interior, and open a new world for investment, both in a business and a spiritual sense. He recommended a visit be paid to Kano, the rich province with its large and prosperous town which is the seat of a most valuable cotton cloth industry.

The success of the expedition led to a revival of British interest in this region. A meeting of the friends of Africa was convened shortly after the return of the PLEIAD, and it was resolved to urge upon the Government the importance of establishing a regular service of trading steamers between Fernando Po and the Confluence of the Niger and Tshadda rivers.

These reports gave hope and the British Government of the day discussed with Mr. Macgregor, the enterprising African merchant, as to what should be done. The Church Missionary Society conferred with Mr. Laird, who again offered Crowther a free passage up the Niger to establish a Niger Mission, where the services of converted Africans from Sierra Leone and elsewhere might be useful. They expressed their intentions in a letter to Crowther, which filled him with joy, and he replied thankfully accepting the position, and giving many valuable suggestions in the matter. He freely discussed the commercial side and says that "the first five years the contract was to last should be the seedtime for introducing Christianity and civilization. When trade and agriculture engage the attention of the people, with the gentle and peaceful teaching of Christianity, the minds of the people will gradually be won from war to peaceful trade and commerce.

Throughout the voyage Crowther had done a great deal of valuable preparatory work on the riverside languages. He had prepared long lists of words and phrases, and with the help of the interpreters (most of whom were C.M.S. teachers from Sierra Leone) he had carefully collected the equivalents in the principal vernaculars. In presenting his report to the Committee, he urged the immediate undertaking of a River Mission, and he enforced it with this irresistible plea:-

"God has provided instruments to begin the work, in the liberated Africans of Sierra Leone, who are natives of the banks of this river. If this time is allowed to pass away, the generation of liberated teachers who are immediately connected with the present generation of the natives of the interior will pass away with it. Many intelligent men who took deep interest in the introduction of trade and Christianity to the Niger, who had been known to the people, have died since; so have many of the chiefs and people of the country, who were no less interested to be brought into connexion with England by seeing their liberated countrymen return. Had not Simon Jonas been with us, who was well known to Obi and his sons, we should have had some difficulty in gaining the confidence of the people at Abo .... It takes great effect when a returning liberated Christian sits down with his heathen countrymen ... and invites them, in his own language, with refined Christian feelings and sympathy, not to be expressed in words but evidenced in an exemplary Christian life".

Everything seemed favourable towards establishing the Niger Mission, and Crowther spent some time in conferring on the subject with his old friend, Bishop Weeks, and missionaries Messrs. Beale and Frey. It was arranged that several native teachers should be sent up the Niger from Sierra Leone. But once more the African climate, with its insatiable toll of human lives, claimed all three as its latest victims.

On the return of the expedition from the Niger, Dr. Baikie wrote to Crowther as follows:—" Your long and intimate acquaintance with native tribes, and your general knowledge of their customs, peculiarly fit you for a journey such as we have now returned from, and I cannot but feel that your advice was always readily granted to me, nor had I ever the smallest reason to repent having followed it. It is nothing more than a simple fact, that no slight portion of the success we met with in our intercourse with the tribes is due to you."

FIRSTFRUITS OF NIGER MISSION

The period from 1842 to 1854 had been indeed a time of severe trial to the faith of God's praying people. their prayers were at last answered, when, in 1857, a beginning was made of a Christian Mission on the banks of the Niger. A great advance had been made in earlier missionary efforts on Niger territories. It was clear that the Niger was navigable, and that the natives were not unwilling to receive the representatives of the Christian faith. The C.M.S. was fully prepared to establish a mission in the Niger. After the earlier two missions up the Niger, the C.M.S decided another expedition should be arranged to establish a Niger Christian Mission. The main difficulty was that of access, for there were no regular steamers plying on the river beyond the delta. Macgregor Laird had lost so much money on the PLEIAD expedition that he did not feel able to undertake another. The British Government had its hands full with the Crimean war, and the general public, even the mercantile public, were uninterested. This time it lay with the C.M.S. to make the move. In 1856, soon after the conclusion of peace, the Committee made an appeal by deputation to Lord Palmerston, and this resulted in an agreement between the Government and Laird to send up the river a small screw steamer, the DAYSPRING. Her total length was only seventy-six feet, and her gross tonnage seventy-seven tons. At her bow she carried the figure of a dove with an olive leaf, a fitting symbol of her task. Again Dr. Baikie was in command with Lieutenant Glover as captain of the vessel. Crowther was to accompany the expedition with a band of African workers to be stationed along the river. This time Crowther had a well-defined commission from the C.M.S. to establish the Niger Mission as a predominantly African enterprise and in 1857 the DAYSPRING started on her way. It was at first intended that six different stations were to be established as the basis of future mission work, and for this purpose half-a-dozen native ministers were to accompany Rev. Crowther and his fellow European missionaries. This, however, was not to be; Bishop Weeks died after a visitation of mission field up the river, and also,

Mr. Frey, one of the hard-working ministers of his diocese. Another heavy loss was occasioned by the death of Mr. Beale, one of the mission staff who had conferred with Crowther about the approaching expedition of the DAYSPRING.

The mantle fell on Reverend Samuel Ajayi Crowther and was sent by C.M.S to open a new mission on the Niger territories. The entire staff was African, mainly from Sierra Leone. Crowther during this mission pioneered an early form of Christian-Muslim dialogue in the middle and upper Niger. He oversaw J.C. Taylor's ground-breaking work in Igboland and directed the evangelization of the Niger Delta, with notable results at some stations as Bonny.

The plans for the new Mission were elaborate. Crowther was to post teachers at Aboh, just above the Delta; at Onitsha, an important Igbo town, on the east bank, 140 miles from the sea; at Iddah, still higher up, among the Igallas; at the Confluence of the two branches, the Kworra and the Tshadda, which is a confluence also of tribes and languages—the Hausa, Nupe, Kakanda, Igara, Igbira, and Yoruba tongues being in use there; at Egan, a great ivory market town on the Kworra, 320 miles from the sea; and at Rabbah, the city of an important Mohammedan chief, 100 miles still higher up; and from thence Crowther himself, with Dr. Baikie (who commanded the expedition, as he had done in 1854), hoped to travel overland some 300 miles to Sokoto, the great capital of that part of Africa, to whose Sultan all the petty Mohammedan kings and chiefs owed allegiance.

On 29 June **1858**, DAYSPRING a small vessel left Fernando Po for the Niger, with Crowther on the deck, amid cheers from ships and ashore. As Rev Crowther stood on the deck, with his Bible clasped to his heart, he saw in the voyage a higher purpose, that of laying with prayer and faith the foundations of that missionary work which should for all time be associated with his name.

His old friend and fellow traveller, Dr. Baikie, was appointed as leader of the expedition. He had with him the Rev. J. C. Taylor, a native clergyman, born in Sierra Leone, but the child of liberated slaves from the Igbo country. In addition, he took with him Simon Jonas a scripture reader, who had already done good work in connection with previous expeditions.

But Crowther had also provided himself with another companion by name Kasumu, besides two or three native catechists which made up the party. The objective of the voyage was the great Foulah kingdom, with its important towns of Kano, Rabbah, and Sokoto. He therefore took precautions to make a favourable impression on the minds of the Mohammedan population through whose country he would have to pass to Sokoto and Ilorin by engaging Kasumu, a Yoruba Mohammedan and liberated African, who has been an Arabic teacher for many years, to accompany him on his travels. Kasumu was a man that would do a vast deal in softening the bias and unfairness of men of his persuasion. The missionary operations in territories under Islamic government was not on disputes about the truth or falsehood of one religion or another, but aimed at toleration, to be permitted to teach their subjects who practice traditional religion the religion the missionaries profess.

This action on the part of Crowther indicates his attitude in his dealings with the Muslims and, created friendly allies where the work might have made bitter foes. He was exceptionally a man of foresight always appraising likely outcomes before undertaking any action. Crowther was not carried away on a mere wave of impulse and never lost his head. His focus and primary objective in all these journeys and toils was the establishment of a native Church in Africa; a native clergy, duly trained and equipped, ministering to their own people. Crowther's attitude was not only the welfare of his country, but the conversion of his people. He had already gained experience from the native Churches of Sierra Leone, Lagos, and Abeokuta and this enabled him to reach decisions as to future possibilities and difficulties. Though there were many disappointments in the course of his duty he had such faith in his people and in his God for them. These, then, were the thoughts which motivated him as he looked once more upon the broad expanse of that lordly Niger, whose hurrying waves seemed to bring with them the cry of Macedonia from afar.

DAYSPRING was now well on her way. She had touched at a village of the Brass country. It was in this neighbourhood that Mr. Carr and his servant mysteriously disappeared. They had no time to visit Nembe, a major town in the country but continued their journey until they reached Angiama. In the meantime, Crowther observed so much overlapping in the sphere of labour by each Church and the evil of competition it is breeding. He was always in brotherly union with the missionaries of other communions.

At Sierra Leone this evil has gone to a great extent, and it has been unhappily introduced into the newly established Yoruba Mission, where it has already begun to cause strife and criticism of one another's Church among the newly-converted natives belonging to the different missionary societies. This does no good in a new mission field either to the new converts or to the unconverted native population.

He was concerned that measures should be adopted by the various Christian denominations to avoid unnecessary competition for converts since their sole and benevolent object is the conversion of the unbelievers to Christianity. This should be done effectively while working separately for the extension of the Church of Christ. Why should not this generous hearted proposal be as applicable to Christian missions as to the settlements of Abraham and Lot? Is not the whole land before thee? Separate thyself, I pray thee, from me. If thou wilt take the left hand, then I will go to the right; or if thou wilt depart to the right hand, then I will go to the left.

He was delighted to see improvements in the social and economic life of the natives of the Delta. The soil was cultivated, and he counted one hundred native canoes, laden with palm oil, evidently for trading purposes. The expedition began with a disappointment at Aboh. Simon Jonas was to be stationed there to carry on the work he had begun in 1841 and 1854. But the young chief, Aje, had become unfriendly and forceful. Aje came onboard the vessel with his twelve spouses and asked for rum, and because it was liberally diluted expressed his dissatisfaction, and his insistence upon having his presents at once was firmly declined. Crowther observed this failing among the Aboh people more than in any other with whom they have had communication in the upper parts of the river. Presents from the people was avoided or refused as much as possible, otherwise they would be placed in the difficult position of an insolvent debtor; if a small gift is received, a bigger gift in response is sure to be required in its stead. It was manifestly wiser to look for alternative station sites elsewhere.

After many subsequent interviews with Aje, Crowther went to the headman of another part of the town and secured land where the new mission premises might be built. Passing on they landed at Ossamare, where they were received with much civility, and here also the site of a mission station was arranged.

When they arrived at the important town of Onitsha, which is about 140 miles up on the eastern side of the Niger and on Igbo territory, the people took sheer fright at the appearance of white men, the first they had ever seen. It took some time to persuade them to lay aside their weapons of defence and agree to a friendly palaver. Eventually one of them acted as guide through groves of bombax, coconut, and palm trees, and some plantations to the town. The cotton, yams, and Indian corn were very well cultivated, and the conduct of king Akazua and his headmen showed no small amount of intelligence. The outlook was more promising. Onitsha was a good-sized town with a population of about 13,000, lying two or three miles from the river, and being about 100 feet above the high-water mark was in no danger of such inundations as Crowther had witnessed at Aboh on his previous visit. It was a prosperous town, and the people manufactured their own clothes, generally plain or fanciful white. European manufactured goods are not so commonly used here as in the lower parts of the river. The visitors were entertained by the king and his councilors, who heard with respect all their proposed plans. Their negotiations with the King and chiefs led to the establishment of British trading posts at Onitsha and the founding of the Mission station. Simon Jonas and Augustus Radillo, both liberated slaves of Igbo descent, from Sierra Leone, acted as interpreters. Dr W. B. Baikie, leader of the expedition spoke for the British Government, while Captain Grant dealt with commercial matters. Dr. Baikie and Captain Grant arranged for a factory to be built, and the King addressed the crowd of people in his courtyard, asking whether they agreed to the proposed trading with the white people. With loud cries and the firing of muskets they signified that the proposal was "carried unanimously," and one man stepped forward to voice the approval of the crowd. As in so many African ethnic nationalities, the rudiments of democracy were not unknown. Here, then, the Niger Mission was founded. Then Crowther leading the missionary group mentioned his own particular mission and introduced Mr. Taylor as the religious teacher who was to live in Onitsha, to show them the Word of God, and to teach the children to read. Afterwards the party returned to the town to search for a house in which Mr. Taylor would live till the mission premises were built. The houses they found were mere oblong hut of mud, some three feet wide, just enough to spread mats on, without rooms or windows, at the price of six pieces of romal handkerchiefs at five shillings a piece.

While Mr Taylor and Mr Simon Jonas were clearing the house to make it habitable, Crowther makes a further tour of the town, to estimate the extent and value of this new sphere of work. The rest took a stroll about the town, to know the extent of it, as well as to make acquaintances. They paid a visit to four groups of houses and the chiefs expressed their great joy at their establishments among them. The town of Onitsha is about one mile in length and is divided into two sections. On either side are groups of houses, a little remote from the high road, ruled by heads of familiar or inferior chiefs. Both sides of the road are either covered with bushes or plantations till you come to an open road leading to a group of houses further back. Some of the groups are close and open to the high road, where also a market is held occasionally. In the afternoon they returned onboard, thankful for the success God had granted them, though fatigued after a few days' exertions. They were for two days busy bringing in goods, materials and bushes cleared for the construction of the factory shed. The botanist and naturalist took their departments in the fields. Some of the sailors pitched their tent in the immediate neighbourhood of the hippopotami, hoping to shoot one of them at the same time making their nautical observations, but the mosquitoes did not leave them unmolested during their night watch.

During their stay at Onitsha, they were treated with great kindness and the people were ready to receive the Gospel, but their old religious practice and superstition had a strong hold upon them. The need for the Christian Gospel was noticeably obvious, even while the expedition was at Onitsha. On one occasion as they were going through the town to their temporary lodging, Crowther noticed a number of people dressed in their best, and in one of the square houses was a crowd of men and women dancing to the beat of drums and firing of muskets. When they reached the door, they asked from a headman reason for the jubilation and were told that it was in honour of the burial of a relative who died six months ago. Simon Jonas, who had remained ashore the night before, had also heard that a human sacrifice was to be made. This provoked the anger of Crowther, and in the presence of a crowd of people he protested against this cruel act. It appeared that the victim, a poor blameless female slave, was already waiting for execution, and she was very surprised at the intervention by the Christian teacher to prevent her death. The headman then proposed that Crowther should buy the woman, and they would kill a bullock instead; but this he refused to do. However, afterwards the slave girl was released.

The mission premises and the factory were built in due time by a number of native workmen. At a solemn council of the King and his headmen, protection was guaranteed to the houses, work, and persons employed. They promised to abolish human sacrifices and to excuse all visitors from the white man's country from the native law which permits no stranger to sit on any mat or seat in the King's court. Crowther then left Mr. Taylor, Simon Jonas, and three young traders from Sierra Leone who elected to make Onitsha their future home, affectionately saying "Good-bye," and praying that the blessing of God might be their joy and stay. This was the first stage in planting a purely native mission as an offshoot of the colony of Sierra Leone. Thus, the Mission began entirely with African effort and an African staff. Rev. Taylor an Igbo ex-slave and a convert from Sierra Leone was placed in charge and given the responsibility of establishing the first Mission in the Igbo country fulfilling Crowther's fervently expressed prayer: "May this be the beginning of a rapid overspread of Christianity in the countries on the banks of the Niger, and in the heart of Africa, through native agents!"

In parting with his colleague Crowther gave him much valuable advice. "Though we are about to separate," says he, "for a season, dear brother, yet you are not alone. "Lo, I am with you always," is the faithful promise of the Lord of the harvest to His disciples. Your ministerial duties will be simple and plain. You will have to teach more by conversation when you visit the people or they visit you, at the beginning, than by direct Service. Be instant in season and out of season. May the Lord give you wisdom to win souls to Himself. You will need much patience to bear and forbear with the ignorance and simplicity of the people, they are like babes. Be not disappointed if you find the people do not act as to their engagement; it is rather a matter of surprise that they do so much. They must be taught the lesson of justice and truth, and that by your own example.

With these and many other admonitions of a very practical character Crowther left Onitsha on 31 July 1857, fully convinced that he could not have selected a better place as the headquarters of the Igbo mission establishments. The location was good for health, goodwill of the people, and facilities for holding communication with the interior.

As the DAYSPRING continued its journey up the Niger and drew near to Iddah they heard that the old Ata was dead, and that two rivals were fighting for the throne. A little difficulty was experienced when the ship drew near the shore.

At dawn Crowther heard the gougon at the landing-place, and the town crier said something about the Oyinbo which he could not understand. At 7 a.m. they landed on English Island and met Ama-Abokko, their old friend, who came from the Confluence. He heard of their arrival at Aboh and had been expecting them. Having entertained them as usual, he was requested to send a messenger to announce the arrival of the expedition to the Ata and their intention to visit him later in the day. Ama-Abokko would not tell them, when asked, whether the old Ata was alive or dead. His reply to that question was, "King never dies." They returned onboard for breakfast. Before noon they landed to pay their respects to Ata, and were conducted by Ama's messenger first to Abeya, where they were kindly received and entertained according to custom. After a considerable delay they were conducted to the house of their old friend Ehemodina, who embraced Crowther and Dr. Baikie with open arms to express his joy at seeing them again. Here they sat and were entertained as usual.

But this hospitality was interrupted by the entrance of the head eunuch, and difficulties were promptly placed in the way of an interview with the King. In like manner Captain Trotter had been treated sixteen years before, and Mr. Beecroft, the consul, fared no better, and on the last occasion Crowther found himself stopped at all points when he desired to see the Ata. The team was not happy with this treatment so the whole party returned to the ship without a word. This had the desired effect. A string of royal notables came onboard next morning to apologize and after much palaver the King was finally visited, a new young Atta in the place of the old Atta. He received them in great state, seated on his throne and dressed in a rich silk-velvet robe of light green tint. The conference was much assisted by the presence and sympathy of Lady Adama, a dowager queen, and a site for mission buildings was secured in a very favourable location. The position of this town, standing on a high cliff, and overlooking the confluence of the Kworra and Tshadda rivers, marked it as a point of great value in the future plan of work. The young Ata promised to follow in his father's footsteps as regards his friendship with white men. Before leaving Iddah a learned mallam, who had been there four years, was introduced to Crowther. He had a full copy of the Koran, and from him some slight information was gathered respecting Sumo Zaki and Dasaba, whom Crowther was hoping to see at the end of the journey. A few days later a number of Muslims were also interviewed, and portions of the Koran were read aloud; one of these men not only read with great fluency, but closing the book he repeated chapter after chapter from memory, to great surprise and admiration of all.

The further they went the more convinced Crowther was of the necessity of introducing the study of Arabic into their institutions at Sierra Leone. What advantage it would give the Christian teachers if they could read some verses out of the Arabic Bible. Such capability would place the teachers of the Anasaras in a more prominent position among these people. Beside this, he believes in this part of Africa, the use of the Arabic character, combined with teaching in Roman or italic characters in the native tongues, would be the means of rapidly spreading the gospel among the rising generation.

In Ghebe, at the confluence of the Kowara and Tshadda rivers, which joined the River Niger, Crowther arranged for mission premises to be erected on the north side of the town, while the site of the factory was to the south.

After Service Crowther went ashore to start public Christian instruction in the town of Ghebe. Mr. Crook interpreted for him in Nupe, for there were a large number who speak the language there. Besides his English Bible, Crowther took an Arabic version and Schon's translations of St. Matthew and St. John into Hausa, and an Igbo primer, out of which to teach the alphabets taking his seat in the Galadima's ante-hall. This is the common resort of all the people, accommodating about forty to fifty persons. Some old and young people of both sexes soon entered, as usual, to observe the event taking place. Having carefully placed his books on the mat, after the custom of the mallams, Mr. Crook sitting on his right, and Kasumu to his left, Crowther commenced his conversation by telling them that today was the Christian Sabbath, on which they rest from their labour, according to the commandment of God. The Galadima came in, and to him Crowther read some verses from the third chapter of St. John in Hausa, in the hearing of the people, which he understood and which, by further explanation, became more intelligible to him. In the meantime, some Muslims walked in and desired to see the Arabic Bible, which Crowther delivered to Kasumu to read and translate to them. The Galadima, who reads Arabic, expressed a wish as soon as the school opened to learn to read Hausa in Roman or italic characters. There was an intelligent young man present who could read Arabic, who was also very anxious to read the translations in the italic character. After a long talk Crowther ran over the alphabet from the Igbo primer several times with the Galadima and the young man, at which they showed much quickness in learning. He then gave an Arabic copy of the Bible as a present to the Galadima. This was so unexpected that the Galadima did not know how sufficiently to express his gratitude in words. At Iddah and Gbebe, Crowther was granted land for the building of Mission stations. He was not able, however, to leave teachers there or to make extensive preparations as at Onitsha.

Throughout Crowther's life and voyages, he reverently kept and observed the Sabbath Day. He was always sad to see the sailors busy with getting and storing fuel and working in other ways which prevented them from observing the Sabbath Day of rest and worship. On Sunday, the 23 August, he preached onboard a practical and fervent sermon on the well-known text, Exodus XX. 8, "Remember the Sabbath Day, to keep it holy".

One Saturday afternoon, when a large number of people gathered Crowther began to address them from Matthew VII. 12: "Therefore all things whatsoever ye would that men should do to you, do ye even so to them, for this is the law and the prophets," to which they paid very great attention. He read the text from the Hausa translations as occasion required; and as the Galadima was present Crowther made Kasumu read the verse from the Arabic Bible, to assure him that the Hausa translations agreed with the Arabic text. Lieutenant Glover took his seat on one side of the raised floor to witness the mode of teaching. Every attention was paid to all that was being said, when a little interruption took place among the listeners. As the people stood thick against the doorway, a respectable looking man who was present wanted a girl of about thirteen years of age to move a little out of the way to give him room, but she abused the man by calling him a dog. The man, being angry at such an insult, proceeded to punish her with his long pipe stick, which caused such a disturbance just at the moment Crowther was telling them of the dying legacy Christ left to His Church, "Peace I leave with you," etc., that he was obliged to stop and pacify the man, while the girl made her escape through the opposite passage. This circumstance directed his discourse to the duty of obedience which children owe their parents and inferiors to their superiors. Crowther kept them long until he perceived they were beginning to be tired, when he ceased speaking and employed the remainder of the time teaching from the Igbo primer till half-past three, when he closed altogether.

At Egga, they found an aged chief who remembered the 1841 expedition and received them very cordially. The town, after a shower of rain was almost impassable with soft mud. His Majesty used high clogs under the circumstances; while his guests, sinking at every step far above the ankles, panted after him in vain. Picking their way through the streets they heard a little boy rehearsing his lesson in Arabic; and further on, seeing what they thought to be a mosque, they found a barber's shop, in which the operators were shaving the head, the eyebrows, the armpits, and the nostrils of their customers with marvellous facility and safety.

While anchored opposite Little Fojo the mate died, and the sorrowful party of the ship's company followed his coffin to the place of burial on a small island near the right bank of the river. They laid their comrade to rest under a little tree, opposite the lower corner of the Rennell Mountains, cutting a cross on the bark with a chisel, together with his initials and the date.

On 9 September they reached the town of Muregi, at the Confluence of the Kowarra and Lafun or Kaduna. As this river appeared to be navigable and seemed to lead towards the great Moslem camp at Bida, the centre of Fulani rule along the

Niger, it was decided to explore it. For a whole day DAYSPRING steamed cautiously up passing the villages of Nupeko and Bajofu on the right bank, and Nku and Abogi on the left. At sunset they anchored off the ruins of Gbara, the former capital of the Nupe country, now reduced to a village of potters, standing at the foot of Mount Barrow, called by the natives Kpate Gbara, or Gbara Hill. This happened to be the old home of Mr. Crook, their Nupe interpreter, who was very excited on visiting the place from which he' had been kidnapped forty-five years before. Like so many other places, it had been laid waste by the Fulani. As they approached Wuyagi, the landing-place for the camp at Bida, Crowther looked forward with keen anticipation to seeing the great Fulani king, Sumo Zaki, and Dasaba. The future of the mission in that district depended on the discussion Crowther would have with them. As an act of courtesy some horses had been sent for their use, and at dawn they entered the huge Muslim camp, hearing all round them the low rhythmic sound of the Arabic prayers, from voices of the faithful at their devotions uttering the " Allahu - akbaru,". As they passed through the camp the craftsmen such as blacksmith, carpenter and whitesmith (a person who makes articles out of metal, especially tin) were busy working. At this point light rain came down and the visitors took refuge in a shed, where several natives were sitting round a fire. The weather clearing up, they crossed to the marketplace, with its slaves, a woman with her infant just being sold for 70,000 cowries, equal to £7.

Finally, pressing through a crowd of princesses, courtiers, and other persons of high rank, they were ushered into the presence of the king, Sumo Zaki, a man about forty years old, and of an exceedingly cordial manner. His Majesty shook hands all round, and courteously asked them to sit on mats prepared for their use. In his profuse expressions of joy, he welcomed the visitors and told them that he believed it was God who directed them to visit him.

After this Crowther introduced himself to Sumo Zaki as a mallam sent by the great mallams from the white man's country to see the state of the traditional worshippers who are his subjects and to know the mind of the rulers, whether they might teach the people the religion of Anasara and at the same time introduce trade among them. To this he at once gave a full consent to teach them, and that he would give the missionaries a place for a station at Rabbah on their return after the rains. He also gave free consent to trade in all parts of the river, with his protection as far as his influence extended. He then entertained them with a large calabash full of kola nuts, some of which he first took himself, and after dividing them gave the parts to Dr. Baikie as a token of great friendship between them. After his presents were given him, with which he was well pleased, he requested the missionaries to visit Dasaba in his section of the camp, which was about half a mile distant from Sumo Zaki. The doctor had tried to get them both together before the interview took place, but it was not practical. Dasaba is half-brother to Sumo Zaki on the father's side, who was Mallam Deudo, but his mother was a Nupe. They met him dressed in a fine white silk robe. He is between forty and fifty years of age and appears to be a person of very lively disposition and humorous in his manner. After the usual salutations they took their seats on the mats and hides spread on the ground for them. When the Doctor repeated the object of his coming to this country, he however, seemed to treat the mission as a huge joke and literally rolled on his mat with glee and laughter in such a jocular manner that it excited them all to laughter. He was quite agreeable to anything which his brother agreed to, as he gave the first place to him and made his brother's wishes his own. After the kola nuts were passed, he presented the Doctor with a cow; but when he had received the Doctor's presents he was so pleased that he added a sheep, lots of yams, and a pot of palm oil.

When leaving Dasaba to their lodging, he escorted them to the street and saw them mount in safety. It had earlier been circulated about the country and believed that as the Anasaras do not belong to the religion of Islam they cannot be friendly with the people of that faith nor bear the sight of a Muslim praying in the name of Mohammed. But the appearance of Abdul Kadu, the Foota Toro interpreter, and Kasumu, Yoruba, both Muslims and knowledgeable Arabic scholars, in their company, excited some inquiries respecting their situation and the treatment they received from the visitors onboard. Sumo Zaki was also curious in this respect. They were surprised to hear from these men of their own persuasion that they were treated with the utmost kindness and were not in the least put in any difficulty in performance of their religious exercises. This was certainly unexpected tidings to them in the interior of the country, having not many interactions with the Christian world. Crowther's policy of having with him the Moslem interpreter justified itself. As they left the camp, Crowther knew that a few false reports and seeds of suspicion is all that it would take to arouse Sumo Zaki and inflame his anger against the Christians. Still, Crowther felt that he had made the most of the opportunity.

On leaving the Fula king, the expedition returned down the Kaduna river and continued its voyage up the Niger to Rabbah which is on the north bank. For a time, it had been the headquarters of Sumo Zaki and Dasaba. Its importance was mainly due to the fact that it was the crossing place for caravans travelling between Kano, the centre of Hausa commerce, and Ilorin, the chief Moslem stronghold south of the Niger. From the ruins of Rabbah, the highlands of Yoruba country were seen. Here at this spot one of the native crew, Joe from the South Sea Islands, going ashore after an illness, ate some roots which he mistook for cassava, which is eatable in this country. In a few days he died, self-poisoned by misadventure, and was buried by Crowther on the high cliff. Next day 6 October they were fortunate enough to meet with some Borgu traders, whose business is with Ashanti, and Dr. Baikie's servant, a Fanti, was able to speak to them. Others of the party, who were Yoruba, were brought onboard to see over the ship, and said they knew the very spot where Mungo Park's boat was wrecked. Their fathers used to tell them the boat was built of brass at the bow and the inside was full of sharp irons and they were cautioned of the danger it poses when diving in that direction. Crowther, therefore, entertained the hope that he might see this place, associated with this great traveller. Steering carefully against a strong rapid between the steep rocks which made a narrow channel of the river beyond Jebba Island, the DAYSPRING struck and drifted, leaking rapidly, broken upon some rocky islets (so called Juju rock) partly under the water. Within a short time the vessel settled down aft on her starboard side and became a total wreck. They had only time to collect what was possible, and carry it safely ashore, with the help of friendly native canoes. They had to pass the night under strong wind and rain sweeping over them, with hardly any shelter, except raincoats and umbrellas. When the day broke, they saw their vessel sinking rapidly and disappearing. The captain, seeing there was no hope, decided to abandon her. It seemed at this time as if another great doom was impending on mission planting on the Niger, from the wreck of the DAYSPRING. To add to the danger of the situation, the native Kroomen were insubordinate, and the headman had to be threatened to save a revolt. The whole party returned by canoes to Rabbah to wait for relief. They were aware that another vessel, the SUNBEAM, was to follow DAYSPRING up the river at an interval of a few months, and hoped that, if all went well with her, she would pick them up and take them back to the coast. Friendly natives again brought them food, and a messenger was sent down to the Confluence to look for the SUNBEAM. A camp was afterwards formed near Rabbah, and there they remained for more than twelve months. Meanwhile the villagers around were quite prepared with an explanation for the disaster. They explained that Ketsa, the god of the peak, had a dislike to red clothes, and having seen that colour among the shipwrecked party, had broken up the ship. This gave an opportunity to obtain considerable information about this deity, whose worship had such a hold upon these people. And then Crowther began to declare unto them the true God. He told them that Soko (In Nupe – It means "the creator or supreme deity that resides in heaven) made all nations of the earth of one blood (taking the hand of Lt. Glover and of the Nupe interpreter, being of different nations). The great God who made these great waters on which they had come in their boat, and also the high hill of Ketsa, which stands in the midst of the great waters, is the God whom Christian worship, fear, honour, and love, and nothing else. The time, however, was not wasted and used to great advantage as Dr Baikie toured the Northern Emirates for places to establish a post. Dr Baikie was given a place in Lokoja in 1859 by King Massaba, who was then Emir of Nupe, where he said the British could stay.

Lieutenant John Glover (afterwards Sir John Glover) surveyed the River and some of its tributaries and took the overland route via Ilorin and Ibadan to Lagos. Crowther was able to make many excursions into the interior and examined the possibilities of the district as a mission centre. Rabbah itself offered fine facilities. He was able to get more information about the Nupe Kingdom, language, and about the caravan route from Kano to Rabbah and on to Ilorin sometimes running risks in dealing with chiefs not too friendly. He began to study the Nupe language. At this point the Niger is passed by the large caravans—sometimes of 3000 people and 1000 head of cattle—between Ilorin, in the north of the Yoruba country, and the interior of the Soudan; and there is a regular tariff of fares at the ferry. The position as a caravan centre presented splendid opportunities. The ferrying of such numbers across the broad water of the Niger necessarily occasioned delay which provided opportunity for mission workers to sow among them the seeds of Christian truth. Frequent conversations were held with merchants and others, mostly Mohammedans, from all parts of West Africa, and even from the shores of the Mediterranean.

One day a strange voice was heard in the crowd of natives, saluting Crowther with "Good morning, sir! " and the speaker, dressed in old hand-me-down and Turkish trousers, was Henry George, a Sunday scholar at Abeokuta. He had a sad story to tell of his experiences in the Nupe country, as one of Dasaba's warriors. He then showed that he had not quite forgotten his reading and writing, and with his finger he scratched his full name on the sand. As Crowther's interpreter had been sent down to the coast with the mail, and his Hausa servant had been promised to Lieutenant Glover, he engaged this young fellow to continue with him. The mail passed through the Yoruba country, and the news of the wreck of the DAYSPRING reached England by this "overland mail" in exactly three months.

On 13 December, an American missionary Rev. M. Clark, from Abeokuta paid them a surprise visit, having heard of their misfortunes, and brought with him a load of sugar, tea, and coffee. These was real comforts to Crowther and his companions, who had been living on parched Indian corn, sweetened with honey, for many weeks past. The visitor also brought them news of the outer world and some old newspapers, which were eagerly scanned. Christmas Day was spent with as much decoration as was possible. The Union Jack flew at the head of the tent and string of ship's flags and some branches of green shrubs were arranged over the doorway. At the proper time in the morning Crowther conducted Service and read the Homily on the Nativity and Birth of our Lord and Saviour Jesus Christ. At twelve o'clock seven guns were fired, echoing along the valley of the Yoruba hills opposite, and the purser, with much ingenuity, made a plum pudding out of Indian flour and a few currants, to follow the fowl which took the place of the usual turkey. The Christmas was spent in a happy mood despite their circumstance. The little lonely group thought of wives and children and loved ones far away.

Kasumu, the Arabic interpreter, having returned, came one night to Crowther with the Futa interpreter, and held a long conversation on the Christian religion until one o'clock in the morning. They had some doubts in their mind which they wished cleared up, whether it was Christ Himself who suffered death upon the Cross, or whether another person was substituted in His place, to save Him from that shameful death. They had been taught to believe God would not suffer Christ to endure such shameful death, out of the great honour put upon Him. Crowther spent considerable time to explain the account of Christ's passion, and put it to them thus: "that if Christ Himself had not died, then we were found false witnesses, because then He had never shed His blood, which is the price of our redemption; that if anything were kept back from Christ's humiliating death from a desire to honour Him, by so doing we deduct from the great dignity He obtained by His sufferings and death." So much were these two inquirers impressed with the truth of Christianity that both of them admitted that their knowledge from the Koran alone was very scanty and weak.

Crowther obtained permission from one of the chiefs to secure a piece of ground for mission premises. Five conical huts after the style of the locality, surrounding them with a fence were to be built there. Purchasing a large dug-out canoe, he fitted it up with seats for half-a-dozen passengers in addition to the canoe men and gave to it the name of Mission Canoe. When finished, this canoe was re-launched in the presence of an admiring crowd, and in it Crowther made visits to numerous villages on both sides of the Niger. He also visited places that lay inland from the river, sometimes making quite considerable journeys and running no small risks from dangers of all kinds, including here and there a village chief or headman who turned out to be greedy or treacherous. Amongst the Muslims, Crowther discovered a keen spirit of inquiry, and scarcely a day passed without some question being put to him, comparing their religion with Christianity.

During the fasting days the constant question was: "Do not the Anasaras fast?" His reply was: "Yes, they do fast; but the fast of the Anasaras is of a more private and painstaking kind than your public one. Thousands of the Anasaras may fast today and their neighbours know nothing of it, but their fast is known to God and to themselves; just so is their prayer in secret, as Christ has taught us."

Crowther encountered several dangers faced by travellers at this time, such as the discovery of a huge snake among the meal bags in the tent; a visit one dark night from a leopard, attracted by some young goats which, sprang upon one of the best milch goats (goat kept for milk). They were without firearms and only shouting and general uproar of the camp frightened the creature away and saved their lives. Sickness began to make its appearance and the good health for which Crowther had been so thankful was no longer the rule. Mr. Howard, the good purser (an officer on a ship who keeps the accounts, especially the head steward on a passenger vessel), who had so deftly prepared the Christmas pudding, died after a few days of dysentery.

As might be expected, the only enemies of the proposed mission were the slave dealers, and they circulated false reports of the aims and conduct of the white men, to poison the minds of the kings and chiefs against them. As a result, Crowther had a great difficulty in dealing with the chief eunuch of the King N'deshi, who had fomented a strife about the building of the mission huts. Crowther realized that these problems especially relating to the holding of land, must be settled before he left, or it would entail endless trouble on the mission afterwards.

The condition of the native women is pathetic. They were the most industrious part of the population but suffered most. A great deal of labour is demanded from the women as the care of the children rests solely on them. They had to feed and clothe the children from childhood until they are able to render them a little assistance if they are females, and the boys assist the fathers in the farms if they be farmers. The women without help, had to labour hard in bearing burdens—for they are the chief carriers of loads. They grind corn upon the millstones many times till late hours of the night, making light this tiresome labour by their mill with songs. Labour is resumed at an early hour of the morning, preparing the flour into meal, retailing the same in the market, or hawking it about the town from house to house, and providing their husbands with provision from it. It is no wonder that they are soon worn out, and a female of thirty years has an appearance of forty. The most distressing part of the whole is that in time of war, when these poor women are unfortunate enough not only to lose their own liberty, but also that of their children, the additional care of procuring a ransom for themselves and their children adds tenfold more to their already heavy burdens. During the war which terminated in bringing Umoru under control, thousands of families had been brought into slavery by it, and this added a lot to their painful toil. Very little is done by the husband to ransom so many wives and children. The consequence is every woman must see after herself and her children the best way she can to prevent their being sold into foreign service. Hence, they have no other means but to have recourse to the system of pawning, as it is done in Yoruba country.

After much waiting, in October 1858, the SUNBEAM, the much awaited for relief vessel arrived, and Crowther, with the other members of the party, were taken onboard. Before leaving this place where he was forced to live for two years, he said farewell to the chiefs, and completed all the arrangements for establishing a post of the mission there. Crowther used the period with the natives to understand the natives better and his name now had influence at a spot where the caravans crossed to and fro. Some native teachers came with SUNBEAM also to strengthen their hands, thus Crowther was enabled to place three readers, Messrs. James Thomas, Edward Klein, and Jacob Newland, to begin at Ghebe.

On his way down the river Crowther stopped at Onitsha and did not return to the coast. In the meantime, Mr. Taylor had been working hard with significant success. He took Crowther to the mission station, introduced him to the converts, and related what wonderful victories had been won at Onitsha. Many of his stories were full of encouragement. Mr. Taylor had found the use of the Igbo tongue a great attraction in his Services. The transformation is extraordinary, and the people seemed quite carried away with the glad tidings. One of Taylor's most important tasks was to open a school. Indeed, a week after his arrival twelve children were brought to him to be educated by their respective parents and guardians. They lost no time to teach them the A.B.C. Attendance at the young school was, however, very irregular as the children had to work on their parents' farms. Crowther was very impressed by the progress made and sent a dozen iron slates and two dozen slate-pencils to aid Mr Romaine, the schoolmaster, in his work. People of all ages attended Mr Romaine's school. News about Taylor's work at Onitsha spread far and wide. Delegations came to see him from many Igbo towns, and all wanted Mission stations opened in their respective towns, but mission expansion was impeded by the lack of men and materials. It brought to mind the prophetic words of Crowther's friend, good Bishop Vidal, who said: "The time will come when Chukwu (the gods) of Aboh and the Igbos in general will fall down before the Gospel as Dagon fell before the ark. Their multifarious shrines shall give way for the full liberation and introduction of the Gospel to the neglected, degraded, long bewitched, but ransomed people of God". On the return of Mr. Taylor and Simon Jonas to the coast, to bring their families to the Mission, Mr. John Smart, associated with Mr. W. Romaine, a Christian trader, whose services were secured as a teacher, were left to work the station in Mr. Taylor's absence.

After a short stay at Onitsha Crowther instead of making for home, again ascended the Niger, this time in a dug-out canoe, a slow, wearying method after a more comfortable voyage by steamboats. He had a plan of his own to work out. His experience had taught him the uncertainty of steamboats on the river. If a mission was to be maintained, some more regular and reliable, if slower method must be found. He resolved to try native canoes on to Rabbah, a distance of 300 miles, with a crew which he found difficult to manage. He was sometimes threatened by the crew for more passage money and used threats to enforce their demands, only to find that Crowther could not be intimidated. It was a relief when after these complications he reached Iddah. Here he found his old friend Ghemodina ill, and Olumene, the owner of the canoe, took the opportunity of begging for almost everything he could lay his hands on. Finding, however, that Crowther's means and intentions gave him no hope, he begged for something as a charm to make people fear and respect him. He was told that Christians never made such things, but trusted in God, and prayed to Him morning and evening to preserve them. Crowther eventually gave him a small piece of Windsor soap, with which he was highly pleased,

This voyage to Rabbah was quite an eventful one, and occasionally dangerous, and Crowther's tact and courage stood him in good stead. At Rabbah he enjoyed the comfort of the mission huts at that place. Sumo Zaki was reputed dead; Dasaba was now King of Nupe and was fighting for his throne against the Gbari. The arrival of the American missionary overland after he was shipwrecked, and the sending of his own messenger to Abeokuta, during his year at Rabbah, had made Crowther resolve to explore that " overland route " for himself, realizing that it might prove the most convenient way from Lagos to the Upper Niger, and therefore important for the future development of the Mission. After a brief rest and some work Crowther started for an overland expedition on foot from Rabbah to Abeokuta, a journey of about 300 miles. He was ill with dysentery due to the long exposure and constant worry in the open canoe on the journey to Rabbah. But he pushed on, not afraid, and reached Ilorin, where the King and chief mallam cordially welcomed him. And at a large public meeting he was requested to address them on the all-important subject of Christ being the Son of God, leaving them afterwards with kind expressions of God's peace and blessing to rest on him. From Ilorin he travelled on foot to Abeokuta and Lagos, in February 1859. After a weary and protracted journey, he came in sight of Abeokuta, and was there welcomed by the Bishop and Dr. Baikie, who had just arrived from Lagos. He was the first member of the C.M.S. to make the overland journey between the coast and the river that afterwards became frequent.

He only spent a short refreshing time with his friends here, for he soon made his way to Lagos, after being absent from his wife and family for two years and a half. But he could no longer regard Lagos or Abeokuta as his post; the Niger was his God-appointed sphere and from that time his life was dedicated to its evangelization. He did not stay very long, however, for in the summer of 1859 he went up the Niger again onboard the RAINBOW sent by Mr. Macgregor Laird. He visited the workers at Onitsha, called at Iddah, and intended to go on to Rabbah but was stopped at the Confluence, a message having been sent down by Dr. Baikie, who was up the river that Rabbah was closed to missionary work for the present. Crowther concluded that his own fears had been realized and that enemies had succeeded in poisoning the minds of the rulers against the messengers of the Gospel. Sumo Zaki was dead; Dasaba, the famous slave raider, the man who had laughed so uproariously at the idea of missionaries, had become King of Nupe, and was building the city of Bida where the great camp had been. It was quite understandable that he had no use for missionaries. He therefore had to return to the coast. The work at the two other stations, Onitsha and Gbebe, however, was hopeful, and at each place there were several candidates for baptism. But the native teachers were now put to a severe test. On its way back to the coast RAINBOW was fired on by some natives at the Delta, and two men onboard were killed. This unfortunate incident closed the Niger for two years and again delayed the establishment of regular steamboat services. It was a long period of seclusion for the native workers at the various mission stations which Crowther had established, and they were left to themselves. He and Taylor stayed at the mouth of the Nun (the principal channel through the Delta) for a long time, waiting in vain for the gunboat which was to be sent by the English Government to accompany the next trading steamer. hoping to go up in it, but they returned baffled to Lagos. Early in the year 1861, Mr. Laird, the pioneer of West African trade died. His various factories on the Niger were closed, and his trading vessels withdrawn. During this period of suspense Crowther was often anxious about the lonely workers up the river, but he was undaunted, Mr. Taylor came to England, and awakened a new interest in the Niger work, and returning, he, in conjunction with Crowther, established an important mission at Akassa, the mouth of the Nun river, which is the navigable entrance to the Niger. It was not until July of the same year that H.M.S. ESPOIR entered the river and destroyed the places from which the firing had come. Crowther was onboard this vessel and took with him two fresh native helpers to replace some on the Niger. The evangelization of the Niger ethnic nationalities was disrupted temporarily during this period. During the following winter Crowther was busily occupied in preparations for a permanent occupation of the Niger on a larger scale; and in August 1862, a missionary party of no less than thirty-three native teachers, including wives and children, with their "belongings," were assembled at Akassa waiting for another gunboat, H.M.S. INVESTIGATOR, to take them up to their stations.

Akassa station was subsequently taken up, at the mouth of the Nun, with a double view, of having a halting-place at the mouth of the river in going up and down from the upper stations. The station was to offer the people an opportunity to accept the Gospel of Christ preached to them. At the first opening of the Sunday-school at Akassa, Rev. Crowther took the first class at the head of the table, and with his venerable silver-bound spectacles on, a pointer in his hands, pointing to the alphabet characters, calling out loudly, "A, B, C, D," while the Akassans stood mute, not knowing what to do. As soon as he could make them understand the words for " repeat together," they at once broke out in hearty laughter, one going out and another coming in, and others coming against the table. Crowther was was a patient teacher and he waited till the uproar ceases, and then commenced again to point out A, B, C, D to them. His heart was full of great and broad plans for the good of all Africa, and yet did not count it waste of time to give his whole mind to the simple work of teaching the alphabet to a rowdy Sunday-School class.

They were taken up by the gunboat, H.M.S. INVESTIGATOR. On its arrival at Onitsha on 5 September 1862 Crowther found, to his extreme disappointment, that the commanding officer H.M.S. INVESTIGATOR had no instructions to convey any to the town; but so much sympathy was awakened onboard the ship on his behalf that ultimately room was found for twenty-seven of the party; and with this goodly reinforcement he joyfully passed up the River. He could not visit the mission station and see the people from whom he had been separated so long. When he reached the Confluence, he went ashore at Ghebe. It was a memorable morning when the Christian converts and traditionalists gathered in the mission Church to meet the kind and faithful minister who had first spoken to them of the Christian faith. He was thankful meeting them as the first fruits of his labours. Crowther always knew how to redeem the time. The few weeks spent at Gbebe were well occupied, not only in preaching, teaching, and organizing, but in improving his Nupe vocabulary and translating into that tongue some chapters from St. Matthew's Gospel. He also established an "industrial institution" for the purchase, cleaning, and packing of cotton for the English market, in hopes of developing a trade in that article.

On 14 Sept. 1862, in obedience to the great commission by Christ to his disciples, "Go ye therefore, and teach all nations, baptizing them in the name of the Father, and of the Son, and of the Holy Ghost," Crowther baptized eight adults and one infant in their new chapel. The congregation of one hundred and ninety-two persons, who all sat still in wonder and amazement at the initiation of some of their friends and companions into a new religion by a singular rite, the form in the name of the Trinity being translated in Nupe and distinctly pronounced as each candidate knelt. These nine persons are the first fruits of the Niger Mission and a testimony of the Word which says that they shall reap in due time if they faint not? It was a significant achievement in that the few baptized persons represent several nationalities of large tracts of countries on the banks of the Niger and Tshadda - Igaru, Igbira, Gbari, Eki, or Bann, and even a scattered Yoruba was amongst them. In his joy Crowther wrote: "Is not this an anticipation of the immense field opened to the Church to occupy for Christ?" Nor was it less notable that the first baptisms took place, not near the mouth of the river but 250 miles upstream, at the confluence, the meeting place not only of the great waters but also of great peoples, the traditionalists of the south and the Moslems of the Sudan, and almost exactly in the geographic centre of the vast area that now comprises the Nigeria Mission of the C. M.S. With his new workers, Crowther was able to staff the station at Gbebe and begin industrial work for the purpose of preparing, cleaning, and packing cotton for export to England.

The newly founded mission was, however, destined to pass through more trials, largely owing to the instability of ruling powers and conflict in the area. As a king or superior chief exercises autocratic sway, it rarely follows that on his decease the same favour which he showed to the mission can be counted on from his successors. Crowther had always been successful in winning the confidence of these native potentates. He always made a point of impressing upon them that the visit of the Christian missionary was not with warlike intent, or from any desire to forcibly appropriate territory, but simply to teach them the truths of Christianity and the benefits of trading relations with the world outside.

While Crowther was staying at Ghebe one of the messengers of King Masaba, who seems to have cherished suspicions of the peaceful intentions of the mission, was entertained by Crowther at the mission station. He was taken round the premises, shown the schoolroom, the cotton gins, and the press and bales which were produced out of it, greatly to the astonishment of the visitors.

Crowther asked him to deliver this message to the King, that the Anasara (Nazarenes); there, pointing to the schoolroom, teach the Christian religion; pointing to the cotton gin, Crowther said this is our gun; and to the clean cotton puffing out of it, that is our powder; and he said the cowries which are the proceeds of the operation are the shots which England, the warmest friend of Africa, earnestly desires she should receive largely. The King was to Judge from the messenger, who had seen the proceeding at the mission, whether the efforts of England were injurious to the prosperity of a nation or favourable to its peace and welfare.

To prove what an excellent impression was made by this tactful treatment of the position, it may be added that when Ama Abokko, the King of Ghebe, was on his deathbed, and was giving charge to his head chiefs about his children and the government of the town after his death, until a successor should be elected, he did not forget Crowther and his fellow helpers in the mission, saying, "Suffer nothing to harm Oyinbos; they are my strangers." But unfortunately, when he had gone the country was thrown into confusion and anarchy, and in the midst of the strife the mission premises were destroyed, and the Confluence station had to be removed to Lokoja.

Crowther led a mission force consisting entirely of Africans from Sierra Leone, as he and Schon had foreseen so long ago and was now evangelizing inland Africa. For nearly half a century that tiny country sent a stream of missionaries, ordained and lay, to the Niger territories. The area was vast and diverse: Muslim emirates in the north, ocean trading city-states in the Delta, the vast Igbo populations in-between.

CONSECRATION AND FOUNDING OF NATIVE EPISCOPACY

The Committee of the C.M.S. was beginning to face a very important question with regard to the Niger Mission. There was only one bishop in West Africa, the Bishop of Sierra Leone, nearly two thousand miles away. This made it very difficult for the Bishop to exercise full control of the Yoruba-Lagos Mission. The best he could do was occasionally visit Lagos and Abeokuta to conduct confirmations and ordinations. He was virtually absentee bishop. It would be utterly impossible for him to take effective charge of the river mission also. If the Niger Mission were to be established and develop, as there appeared every possibility that it would, there must be a bishop in charge. Yet all experience tended to show that Europeans could not, with any degree of safety, live on the Niger.

The new missions on the Niger require episcopal superintendence to consolidate progress made in the field amongst the various countries along the Niger and its hinterland. The challenge of superintendence is further compounded by the problem of communication with mission posts far from the coast due to irregular movements of ships going up and down the Niger and occasional hostility from native kings. Despite the various challenges posed which also include harsh climate, various expeditions clearly demonstrated advantages of utilizing native missionaries in mission field. Native missionaries and workers in the field were used to the harsh climate of West Africa that was still a deadly barrier to European missionaries. The native catechists who have been instrumental in raising up congregations at mission stations such as Onitsha and Ghebe require prompt admission to Holy Orders, that they may duly minister to their congregation and promote their spiritual growth. The Christians on the banks of the Niger need to be as quickly as possible utilized in missionary effort among their countrymen. Although few in number compared with the countless inhabitants of the great continent, yet the first fruits of Africa to Christianity is to a large extent multilingual, and thus could render services to the different tongues of Africa. To delay any longer the native episcopate would be unduly to retard the development of the native Church.

Henry Venn's plan was a purely African Mission, under an African Bishop. For this, surely, the hour had come—and the Man. He who was already the leader of the Mission, who now knew the Niger well, and, moreover, who was the first native clergyman ordained in the Society's West Africa Missions, should be the bishop. It was not difficult to enlist the sympathy of home friends with such a project. Indeed, there had already been representations made to the Archbishop of Canterbury and to the Society that the next Bishop of Sierra Leone ought to be a native. This did not seem feasible, for the English missionaries in West Africa gravely doubted the expediency of Venn's proposal. They feared that a Christianity of forty or fifty years standing could scarcely be expected to supply men for the highest office in a Church whose Christianity was the growth of centuries. The time was now appropriate for the Church in Africa to be empowered to grow into a native episcopate. The question is who among the African clergymen could be entrusted with so great a responsibility? And this question the C.M.S. answered in the affirmative. The Niger Mission had begun as a purely African enterprise, pioneered, staffed, and directed by men of Negro race. It is right to continue so under the guidance of an African bishop, Crowther was found qualified to fill the office of the Bishop of Niger Diocese. The success in the mission field and the foundation of the native Church had been achieved by Crowther's intense efforts. He had been involved in the pioneering work of evangelism up the Niger preparing the ground. Crowther was being called to a diocese which he had himself created. He introduced by his discoveries these places in his country which have since become such familiar names in the missionary field. He had done more. He had in a modest and yet distinctive way proved in himself the latent qualities and capacities of the African and demonstrated it in the native agents he employed at his stations. Therefore, the selection of such a man to the highest honour the Church can give was fully deserved and appreciated, both in Africa and England. It was the peak of a unique career.

While the European missionaries in Sierra Leone appreciated Crowther's own personal worth, they wondered how the continuity of the proposed episcopate was to be kept up. Venn, however, persevered; and when, in March 1864, Crowther came to England to report on his seven years Niger campaign, the Committee went to Lord John Russell, then Foreign Secretary, and to the Archbishop of Canterbury, with their daring proposition. Archbishop Longley warmly pressed the scheme upon the Government; Lord John Russell cordially assented; and the Queen's license was issued to the Primate, empowering him to consecrate "Our trusty and well-beloved Samuel

Ajayi Crowther, clerk in holy orders," to be a bishop of the Church of England in the West African territories beyond the British dominions.

Having secured this, Venn set to work to obtain for the bishop-elect, before his consecration, a D.D. degree from one of the Universities, that nothing might be lacking to give him standing and prestige. On his recommendation, Arch-bishop Longley himself wrote to the Vice-Chancellor of Oxford on behalf of Crowther to ask for it. Crowther's Yoruba Grammar, Yoruba and English Dictionary, and Yoruba versions of many books of the Bible, were submitted as proofs of his linguistic talents, together with evidence of a reasonable standard of ordinary scholarship; and the proposal was submitted to the Convocation of the University. It was strongly opposed by one leading don but was carried almost unanimously; and the Regius Professor of Divinity, Dr. Jacobson (afterwards Bishop of Chester), wrote the Latin speech in which Crowther was presented for the degree.

When the news that he might be consecrated Bishop reached Crowther, he declared himself unfit for the post. The much-revered Rev. Henry Venn, the honorary secretary of the C.M.S found a hard task in persuading Crowther, for whom he had such a personal regard, to accept the office of Bishop. But the C.M.S. knew better and he was dully consecrated Bishop on 29 June 1864, in Canterbury Cathedral.

It was a memorable event in the records of the cathedral at Canterbury on St. Peter's Day, 29 June 1864, when Rev Samuel Ajayi Crowther was consecrated as bishop. Special trains were run from London and elsewhere, and as early as eight o'clock an unusual crowd were present at morning prayer. The cathedral never looked more beautiful and it was a bright sign of the future in missionary enterprise for Africa. Among the thousands filling those seats were many friends of Crowther. One in full naval uniform was Admiral Sir H. Leeke, who was the young captain onboard H.M.S. MYRMIDON to first take in his hands the little rescued slave boy filled with fear, from the stinking hold of the captured Portuguese slave ship off the coast of Lagos. This boy, who was soon to be consecrated as Bishop, had never lost sight of his friend, who now, with many thankful memories, is amongst the congregation.

An elderly lady slowly makes her way to a front seat, where she might easily see and hear; but one of the churchwardens reminds her that this place is reserved for a distinguished lady who had a ticket. She turns round and quietly says in answer: "I think I have a right equally to this seat, because that black minister to be consecrated Bishop this morning was taught the alphabet by me." The Dean and the lady referred to, hearing this, at once begged the visitor to retain her seat. She was the widow of Bishop Weeks, of Sierra Leone. The Negro who is to receive consecration had been first received under her care when liberated from a slave-ship, and kneeling by her side as a young boy, had first learned to pray the Lord's Prayer. She early perceived in him an excellent spirit and gave him the name at his baptism of her own revered pastor, Samuel Crowther, at whose Sunday-school, in the parish of Christ Church Newgate Street, she had once been a teacher. The personal friends of the bishops-elect were accommodated with chairs in the chancel, which approached within a few feet of the communion rails. When the Service began it was an impressive sight to see the Archbishop of Canterbury, attended by five other Bishops, enter the choir; and following them the three Bishops to receive the solemn rite of consecration, viz: the new Bishop of Peterborough, the new Bishop of Tasmania, and the new Bishop of the Niger. Mrs Weeks sat behind the Bishop-elect Samuel Ajayi Crowther.

When the Archbishop and other prelates had taken their places, the Bishop of Lincoln read the Epistle and the Bishop of Winchester the Gospel, and the sermon was preached by the Rev. H. Longueville Mansel, Professor of Philosophy at Oxford, from I Peter V. 2, 3, on being " examples to the flock." Then the choir, with beautiful boyish trebles, sang Mendelssohn's "How lovely are the messengers," while the Bishops-elect walked to the vestry to put on their rochets, and on their return, among the others, was this letter patent read:

"We do by this our licence, under our Royal signet and sign manual, authorize and empower you, the said Samuel Ajayi Crowther, to be Bishop of the United Church of England and Ireland, in the said countries of Western Africa beyond the limits of our dominions." When Samuel Ajayi Crowther was consecrated Bishop of Western Equatorial Africa beyond the Queen's Dominions, his jurisdiction extended over all West Africa with the exception of Bathurst, Freetown, Cape Coast and Lagos.

Crowther was led up to the Communion Table by the Bishop of Winchester to introduce him to the Archbishop. At this point the choir again sang Wise's anthem, "Prepare the way of the Lord," and while the Bishops-elect were kneeling with bowed heads, the "Veni Creator Spiritus" was beautifully sung to Tallis' music. Then, with hands outstretched, the Archbishop, in a clear voice, gave the apostolic charge: "Remember that thou stir up the grace of God which is given thee by this imposition of our hands, for God hath not given us the spirit of fear, but of power and love and soberness." At this solemn moment Crowther took from the hand of the Archbishop his consecration Bible, with the words: "Take heed unto thyself, and to doctrine, and be diligent in doing them: for by so doing them thou shalt both save thyself and them that hear thee. Be to the flock of Christ a shepherd, not a wolf; feed them, devour them not. Hold up the weak, heal the sick, bind up the broken, bring again the outcasts, seek the lost. Be so merciful, that you be not too remiss; so minister discipline, that you forget not mercy: that when the Chief Shepherd shall appear you may receive the never-fading crown of glory; through Jesus Christ our Lord". Crowther was the first man of colour to be advanced to a bishopric.

At the conclusion of the Consecration Service the new Bishops took their places within the altar rails. As the new Bishop was conducted to his elevated seat among the Bishops, the countenance of Mrs. Weeks was the radiant satisfaction of a mother in Israel who receives an answer to many prayers, and the accomplishment of her fondest desires for the Church of Africa. The Communion Service, to which a great number of the congregation stayed, concluded this impressive event. Throughout all this solemn function, the heart of the newly consecrated Bishop Samuel Ajayi Crowther was turned to the little flock of his African brethren in spiritual chains for whom Christ died.

No one could fail to see how God had called forth this native from the degradation of a boyhood of slavery, to become a chosen vessel in His service. He had proved himself as a true-hearted standard-bearer of the Cross in much toil and patient endurance, and it was meet that to him should be committed the spiritual interests of the district in which he had spent hitherto nearly the whole of his life since he became a Christian.

This public event was commented on by the Press as a good and promising step in the right direction; a few thoughtful sentences from a leading article in the "Record" sufficiently represent this:

"We might dwell on the practical refutation afforded by Dr. Crowther's merited elevation to the episcopate to the taunts of certain professors who maintain that the cerebral development of the negro shows that he is disqualified for intellectual pursuits, and that he cannot be lifted out of his congenital dullness; but we pass on to entreat the prayers of our readers for him and his diocese. He will need much wisdom, peculiar grace, and constant strength. Humanly speaking, the future of the native Church depends on the manner in which its first Bishop shall administer its polity and organize its laws. It will be necessary also for him to exercise great discrimination in conferring Holy Orders on his brethren, and to take heed that he magnifies his office in the estimation of all by the exemplary consistency of his life and the holiness of his conversation. That he will do so we are assured of past experience, but the slightest consideration proves how much he needs to be supported by the sympathy and prayers of the Church."

The new Bishop, amid many congratulations from friends, lost no time in getting to his field of labour again. On 19 July, Bishop Crowther took leave of the Committee at farewell event for Africa, and his words on that occasion were thoroughly characteristic of the man: "The more I think of the present position to which I have been called, the greater seems its weight and responsibility. In days past, when I went forth as a West African missionary, it was my duty and my delight to give account to my brethren: my present position is different. I need, therefore, much spiritual support, and without strong confidence in the sympathy and prayers of the Church, I feel it would be impossible to go on. In taking this office upon me, I have not followed my own will, but what I believe is the will of Almighty God". On 24 July he left England and arrived at Sierra Leone on 10 August on his outward voyage, where he met with a most enthusiastic welcome. When the MACGREGOR LAIRD reached the harbour of Freetown crowds were waiting to witness the wonderful spectacle of a liberated African, an Aku man, the trophy of missionary teaching at Sierra Leone, coming as Bishop back to their shores. There was no lavish display of bunting or roar of cannon; the delighted faces of his own people, and the chorus of "God bless you," which met him everywhere, were to Bishop Crowther more than enough.

After a day's rest he was escorted to Fourah Bay College, where all the clergy, catechists, and schoolmasters had assembled in one of the lecture-rooms to give him a joyous reception and express their congratulations. Two addresses were signed and duly handed to him amid applause, one by the whole body of the Church Missionary agents and native pastors, the other by the authorities of the College, upon whose history he had shed such fame by his name. The first, which bore over thirty-six signatures, was full of brotherly love, as the following extract will testify:

"We regard your consecration as a token of God's favour to the Church in Africa, and would unfeignedly rejoice with you in this mark of His distinguishing love, believing it, as we do, to be an earnest of richer blessings which are yet in store. In reviewing your whole past career in this colony, and subsequently at Abeokuta and the Niger, we thank God for the abundant grace bestowed upon you and for the measure of success granted you in your missionary work, and we trust that the same grace may be vouchsafed to guide and comfort, to strengthen and support you through all your future course in the high office to which you have been called.

It will be a source of comfort for you to know that prayer meetings were held in every district in the colony on the day of your leaving England that God would protect you from the dangers of the deep, and you may rest assured that prayer will constantly ascend, that under your wise and judicious culture the thorn and thistle may be uprooted and the Rose of Sharon and the Lily of the Valley may be seen along the whole banks of the Niger. May the Spirit of the Lord rest upon you, the spirit of wisdom and understanding making you as a chief pastor of the flock of Christ in Africa, of quick understanding in the fear of the Lord, so that you will judge not after the sight of your eyes, nor reprove after the hearing of your ears, but ruling and superintending all things according to truth and love."

During the reading of the address Bishop Crowther was obviously filled with emotions, and when he rose to reply his voice overjoyed with feeling. He sincerely thanked them for all their loving expressions and prayers towards him. Reminding them of old times, he said:

"When we look back to the commencement, we find the mission took its beginning among a heterogeneous mass of people, brought together in the providence of God from many tribes of this part of Africa, out of whom, through the zealous, faithful, and persevering labour of the early missionaries, arose devout congregations of faithful and sincere Christians. After a time, the mission produced a native ministry, then a self-supporting native pastorate, and latterly, out of the native ministry, a humble step outward was taken in faith to introduce a native episcopate in missions beyond Her Majesty's dominions. Here we pause and raise our Ebenezer to God's praise. Hitherto the Lord has helped us.

This onward progress seems to be an indication from God, beckoning to us to come forward, put our shoulders to the wheels, and ease our European brethren of the great work which they have so nobly sustained alone from their predecessors for fifty years, many of whom had sealed the testimony of their zeal with their lives. Their graves at the burial grounds are existing monuments of their faithful obedience to their Master's command: "Go, and teach all nations".

Whether called to their rest or whether beaten back from the fields of their labour through ill-health and forced to retire, or whether still labouring among us, it is our bounden duty in gratitude to remember and esteem them highly in love for their work's sake, of which we are the fruits.

We must exhibit a missionary spirit ourselves, and encourage it among our congregations, if we are imitators of missionary enterprises; if, like as Timothy knew Paul, we also have known their zeal, we should endeavour to preach the Gospel in the regions beyond the colony.

To extend our line of usefulness we must seriously impress on our Christian countrymen the necessity of exhibiting a spirit of liberality, after the example of the mother Church, whose spirit we should imbibe, not only to support their own pastors and school teachers, keeping in good repair their churches and other buildings made over into their hands, but also contribute, according to the means God has blessed them with, to send the Gospel into countries beyond them which are yet destitute of the blessings of its light.

But, above all, we must be followers of Christ, the Great Shepherd of His flock and the example of His apostles, in the habit of prayer for help from above. This is the weapon which prevails most in the work of the ministry. When we feel our weakness and insufficiency for the work to which God has called us, we must constantly go to the Throne of Grace for divine aid. We are better fitted when we feel our incompetency to change a sinner's heart. This will drive us to apply to the Fountain Head for a quickening spirit from above, which He has promised to all who ask Him; then we shall be encouraged to go on in this our might. Has He not sent us?"

It was now the turn of his Alma Mater, and the address they presented, signed by principal, tutors, and students, was also not less in cordial appreciation of the honour laid upon the Bishop, in which they also shared. A brief extract from the greeting of his Alma Mater:

"We thank God for the grace bestowed upon you, enabling you to labour so faithfully for the past thirty-five years in His service. This Institution at one time enjoyed the benefit of your instruction, but of late years the Yoruba and the Niger missions have been the fields in which you have laboured. Notwithstanding this, we have not been unmindful of you; your name has been familiar as a "household word" among us, and you have ever been held up as an example to our youth."

When he got up to reply he was received with loud applause from his old college comrades. When quiet was restored the Bishop excused himself from any set speech, seeing that since he landed every moment had been taken up with pressing engagements. But he naturally grew reminiscent and urged them to avoid that spirit of worldliness and self-interest which had so decimated the sixty students of Haensel and Kissling's regime, that scarcely a dozen were now workers in the mission field.

He left the college (he said) in 1841 to join the Timmanee Mission, which was then established under the superintendence of Mr. Kissling but was shortly afterwards detached from that field of labour to join in the Niger Expedition. He then entered into a narrative of bitter taunts and ridicule from his friends. Some of them think it was foolish of him to join the expedition without any guarantee of good pay like the Europeans. His response to all these was that the Society had promised to supply him with necessaries, and consequently he should not want. He subsequently served for ten years with the Yoruba mission, where under God's blessing, he had a very promising and much attached congregation. He dated his service with the Niger from 1854, from which period he had been literally moving to and fro. To a friend inquiring at the same time whether he did not mean to rest, he answered: "I shall only rest when I have no more work to do." It was his firm conviction, from what he had witnessed from travelling to and fro along the coast, that the difficulties, adversities, and deprivations of missionaries are nothing in comparison with what many a merchant suffers for a paltry gain. A missionary should be jack-of-all-trades, one ready to put his hands to work and to do in a legitimate way anything that might tend to advance the cause of Christ. In conclusion, he called the attention of the students who were all present, to the fact that though they were but six in the reopening, yet that number was greater by two than what they were when the college was first established in 1827. They had all the brethren before them as an encouragement, whereas he and his fellow-students then had none to look up to.

He trusted that he had succeeded in his attempt to deepen their hearts in the work and prayed that everyone enlisted under the banner of Christ should never fail to prove himself a good soldier of the Cross.

The Bishop then recommended in prayer his brethren and pronounced the Benediction. Soon afterwards he travelled to and reached Lagos on 22 August 1864. Every respect was paid to "the black bishop" by the Governors at Sierra Leone, the Gold Coast, and Lagos. At the latter place he performed his first episcopal function, not for his own Mission, but at the request of the Bishop of Sierra Leone, by admitting to priest's orders the colonial chaplain at Cape Coast Castle. At Lagos Bishop Crowther took up his permanent abode. Then he proceeded to the Niger in H.M.S. INVESTIGATOR, which was taking stores to Dr. Baikie, who was now established at Lokoja as consul. He visited the stations, ordained a catechist deacon, confirmed some converts, and returned to Lagos. There were then no regular steamers; there was no Royal Niger Company; and the Bishop was dependent upon the occasional visits of government vessels until trade, already active in the Delta, began to move up the river. Gradually he was able to enlarge his mission staff, obtaining native catechists and schoolmasters from Sierra Leone, posting them at different stations, and ordaining those who seemed most promising. One outstanding joy came in 1870 when Crowther ordained to the ministry his own son Dandeson, an event of unique interest, it being the first time an African bishop had ordained his African son. By 1871 he had ordained eight of this class of men, in addition to his son Dandeson, who had been an Islington student. The work, as before his consecration, was principally up the river inland, at Onitsha and the Confluence; and the agents, therefore, were very isolated, which was not a favourable condition for their personal spiritual life. Still, the reports in those earlier years of Crowther's Episcopate were in the main encouraging. From now on it became his custom to work from Lagos and to pay annual visits of some months to the Niger stations as transport allowed. Bishop Crowther was a man full of activity, and a born traveller. This was one of the qualifications which marked him out as the Bishop of the Niger. The wide extent of his diocese from coast to wide expanse inland, through which Niger and its tributaries flowed, demanded a man of almost inexhaustible energy. This was a difficult task to a European missionary for the environment was not conducive but harsh. Devoted missionaries with grand ideals had found themselves overwhelmed by the growing need of the work and they are weighed down physically not able to do anything. Either they died in the field with a vision of what could have been achieved before their closing eyes, or returned sick and unfit, with a haunting sense of unaccomplished dreams. But not so with Bishop Crowther. He was a little man, with a determined heart that the harsh environment of the delta could not deter and whom ceaseless work did not seem to deteriorate. He was intellectually alert and creative, spiritually so optimistic, and full of hopeful faith. He was always on the move to achieve new heights and very humble in his dealings. On reaching Onitsha he held another ordination service which excited much interest amongst the natives, by the strange event when an African knelt before an African bishop to receive the laying on of hands. The people gazed in wonder as the event was never seen before or thought to be possible. They were so much amazed and moved by the unique soberness of the Service. The place of ordination, the congregation among whom it took place, the candidate for ordination, the assisting priest, and the officiating bishop, presented such a novel scene taking place in Africa.

But the shadow behind all this was native customs which had a strong hold upon Onitsha. They were still held captive by a cruel tradition, for on the death of Prince Odiri human sacrifices were made. The native missionary tried his best to stop this, and offered with money to redeem the victims, but without success. Amongst others who were buried alive in the grave of this dead prince was a little innocent girl of eight years of age, with a knapsack hung over her shoulder, containing a piece of mutton, some kola nuts, and a snuffbox for the use of the spirit of the dead prince in the next world. The Christian converts in their anger and at the risk of their lives hurried into the King's presence and condemned these cruel practices, as unacceptable to the Christian standards of justice and the belief in the inviolability of human dignity and rights. Despite the novelty of the Christian message the old religion held its own, and beliefs associated with it, such as twin murder, the casting away of infants who cut the upper tooth first, the burial of slaves alive with their dead masters and many other superstitions persisted.

A few days later when the Bishop reached Ghebe he held a confirmation of five settlers from Sierra Leone and sixteen native converts. This again was a new ceremony in this far away outpost and next day Bishop took the Sunday-school. He was always such a favourite with the children and after dismissal had a serious talk with teachers about their work. Then he made his way up the river to Iddah to see the Ata, despite opposition of the chiefs or greedy demands of canoe men.

When he arrived, Abokko, a high chief, was glad to see him, and told him that he, the Bishop, was a true man, because he kept his promise to come and see the king. The Bishop came with presents and gifts that would have a gratifying and profitable effect on the king. He intended to convince the people and the King how superior civilized nations are through knowledge and the reception of Christianity, and how low and inferior the condition of those who are without the Gospel.

The Bishop had a fruitful discussion with the Ata, after many excuses on the part of Abokko to keep them apart. The reason for this was found to be a feeling of terror lest the white man should take Ata's photograph, with severe consequences. To avoid the deceptions of the officials in the palace the Bishop took pains to specify the objects of his visit and informed other people during his forced delay, so that the King might be fully impressed and prepared to consider them. One objective of the visit is that he intends establishing a mission at Iddah. Also, he would be glad if Ata would take the ruinous state of a large portion of his town into consideration and act as a king ought to do, by calling together the elders of his country and consulting to put an end to the quarrel between him and the Abokko's family. The Bishop advised them to rebuild their houses for sake of posterity and for God's sake, who might never forgive us if He were to keep His anger for ever.

During the visit by the Bishop, the Ata entertained these important requests for favour, and at once gave every facility for the building of mission premises and the continuance of Christian work among his people. The Bishop was able to succeed in his endeavours with the natives being a negro like them and having good understanding of their custom. The inevitable present also had its share in keeping the royal mind in a good and peaceable humour. In his turn he gave the Bishop gifts of kola nuts, yams, and a sheep and goat, which were gladly accepted and were expression of friendly disposition.

The Bishop was thankful for the Lord had given success as to enable him to see and gain the confidence of the Ata and his people. But the King had been told that he had the sun (i.e. the watch) about him, which he should like to see. The Bishop got up and opened the watch, which he held to his ears that he might hear it ticking plainly. The Bishop then opened the case that he might see the working of the spring. The Ata had also been told of his glass lantern, and he would be very glad if the Bishop would order one like it for him, also a pair of long boots, with a pair of spurs, and a large umbrella. The Bishop wanted to see the size of his foot and the Attah immediately took off his sandal. The Bishop promised to order for him all the articles.

On his arrival back at Ghebe, the Bishop preached to the people, and afterwards administered the Sacrament, also baptized ten adults and seven children. The journey over, the Bishop visited Bonny, in the Bight of Biafra, and founded the first Delta station there. It was an important opening and destined to become one of the most flourishing stations of delta countries. He recognized the great necessity of dealing with that large and scattered population inhabiting the swampy and malarial region of the Delta. Here the great river Niger loses itself in twenty-six branches, spread out like a network, and intersected continually by other smaller streams stretching from the lagoons of Lagos at one end to the mouth of the Old Calabar River on the other. This territory of dark superstition, with its one hundred and twenty miles of sea front, and a depth landward of one hundred and forty miles was to be the immense parish of the Delta Mission.

The town of Grand Bonny is a typical delta town, built amid dense forests and mangrove swamps, on the banks of a muddy creek not far from the sea. It is situated on the east side or left bank of the river which bears its name, Ubain, on a triangular point of a creek running eastward from the main river. The chief part of the town is built on the bank of the creek for the convenience of working and securing their canoes. Here the surge of the waves is not so much felt as on the beach of the main river; but the creek is very muddy. The town being almost on a level with the flow tide, is seldom free from mud and slush, and when it rains is quickly saturated. All the ships lay as near the point of the town creek as possible, and consequently the chief scene of business. The swamps around were the lurking places of alligators and pythons, and it was a veritable inferno of mosquitoes. The town was infested with huge crawling lizards (iguanas) many of which were six feet in length. They were believed to be the protectors of the town and lay about at their pleasure. Even if they lashed savagely with their long, serrated tails, wounding the bare legs of passers-by, they were not under any circumstances to be molested. There was no end of a to-do if you wound or kill one of them. You were assaulted or robbed by the natives, scolded by the consul on board of a man-of-war, and possibly fined into the bargain. The belief was not that the lizards themselves were divine, but that they were indwelt by the spirits of the departed; any harm done to them, or insult offered to them, was therefore an injury to the spirits of the dead. The dark bush around was the secret abode of "juju" with its evil priests and rites. The juju temples were paved and decorated with the skulls and bones of their victims and the people had good cause to shun the "juju" bush. Human sacrifices were freely offered on the death of a chief.

Bonny's location near the coast gave it natural advantages for trade in palm oil. Being so easily accessible from the sea, Bonny long had a shameful history as a slave market. For many years Bonny was visited by European oil traders, who lived in their ships or hulks anchored in the river, the town itself having no attraction for them. But beyond the mere matter of trade Bonny remained practically untouched by either civilization or Christianity. Commerce alone cannot civilize. A degraded pagan in his squalid hut by the mangrove swamp may don a European shirt and hat and remain pagan. Hence the purpose of various expedition planned since the 1841 Niger Expedition, which is the close co-operation of Government, commerce, and missions.

However, the light of the Gospel was to come and set free those held in bondage by the evil practices in this region. King William Pepple of Bonny had a misunderstanding with his chiefs, which made him go to Fernando Po and thereafter to the island of Ascension, and from here to London in June, 1856. He lived in London till June 1861 when he set sail for his native land, arriving in Bonny in August, and by God's grace again ascended his rightful throne. He had the desire to bring the missionaries to his dominion having seen England. In 1864 King William Pepple wrote to the Bishop of

London asking that missionaries be sent to preach to his people. This letter was passed on in London to Bishop Crowther. He was not a man to miss any possible opening for the Gospel. One of his first acts after his consecration was to establish the Mission station at Bonny - the first outpost of Christianity in the Niger Delta. This made him visit Bonny in 1864 and special attention was given to the Delta in response to King Pepple's request.

The Bishop was cordially received by King William Pepple and his chiefs. In Bonny there are a few good houses owned by the chiefs. The Bishop had to walk over the town many times to find an open dry space for a temporary schoolroom between three choices. After a little acquaintance with the localities, he selected the most suitable place good for his purposes. Here the temporary schoolroom, fifty feet by twenty feet, is put up of native materials. Near the schoolroom a house was hired for the use of the mission agents, and thus the preliminary arrangements to commence their operations are completed till they can erect a permanent mission station outside the town. About ten minutes' walk from the town of Bonny the Bishop found a nice dry, sandy land, overgrown with woods, four feet elevation above the spring tide. Here he has chosen for the building of a permanent mission station, where there is sufficient room, sea breeze, the comforts of dry and healthy ground, and of being separated from the population.

He obtained signed agreements for the establishment of the mission and the king and chiefs also promised £150 a year towards the mission and school. After a short absence, visiting other places, the Bishop came back to Bonny, bringing with him two lay agents, who were lodged in an old hulk. The Bishop was offered two houses for his residence by an old chief known as the "Admiral" which were promptly cleared of rubbish, cleaned, and made suitable for habitation. The next step was to build a big mud and wattle school-chapel, capable of holding two hundred people, and finally the Bishop discovered a good place for mission premises to be permanently erected and obtained the needful permission. But the fear-stricken natives were horrified at the choice and exclaimed that it was "a bad juju bush". A place which had been used for the bodies of victims killed for sacrifice and the rubbish heap where twins were, according to their custom, flung away to die. Cries were accordingly raised that if the missionaries took this place the gods would be angry. "The spirits must not be disturbed", said the priests. "The Christians will die if they go there," echoed the people. The Bishop, however, was not the man to be frightened away by these superstitions. The people allowed him to have the land, at his own risk, and that they would not guarantee the consequences.

"Give us the ground," the Bishop said, "and leave us and juju to settle the remaining palaver."

It was difficult convincing the inhabitants to get the evil place cleared. The horrified people would have nothing to do with this sacred and yet notorious place. King William Pepple sent his son George, who had been educated in England, with ten slaves who could be trusted to cut the bush. When the young prince arrived at the spot, he felt nervous and asked to have a portion of Scripture read, and somebody to kindly pray, as there were so many evil spirits about to be disturbed. After some hesitations, they commenced to cut down the branches, and meeting nothing of a supernatural sort, grew bolder, and the place was soon made fit for building purposes. The place was indeed "very bad juju bush," scattered with skulls and bones of the bodies of human sacrifices and twin babies thrown there and left to decompose. When the vegetation and all traces of man's wickedness had been cleared, a mud and thatch school-chapel was built and opened with prayer and thanksgiving, on the site of that once repulsive fetish grove. Attention was drawn to a large copper bell, three and a half feet in diameter, which for many years had been lying on the ground in Bonny town. It has an inscription which the Bishop deciphered as follows: " William Dobson, founder, Downham, Norfolk, England. This bell was cast for Opooboo Foobra, King of Grand Bonny, in the year 1824." This old bell was used for the service of the newly constructed school-chapel for worship of the true God. Chief Oko Jumbo, at his own expense, in English twenty-four pounds, transferred it from its resting-place in the mud to the roof of the mission chapel.

As a direct result of preaching of the Gospel in Bonny, on Easter Day, 1867, the worship of the lizard or iguana was formally and for ever renounced by King George Pepple and the people. The Bishop wrote the news home with a gladdened heart. These had a firm hold upon the superstitious fears of the natives. The worship of the lizard was so real at this time that the British authorities on the Oil Rivers were compelled to afford it a certain recognition.

At Bonny the monitor lizards became a terrible irritation. For its effectual abolishment, which has been of the greatest benefit to the well-being of the town, it was due to the quiet, unceasing labours of the agents of the C.M.S.

After the mutual consent of the Bishop and chiefs, the geedee or iguana, Bonny juju was declared to be no longer Bonny juju. No sooner was this rejection made and orders given to clear the town of them than many persons turned out in pursuit of these poor reptiles, which had been so long idolized, and now killed them as if it were in revenge. Their remains were littered all about in open places and in the markets. The carcases were exposed to public view as a proof of the people's conviction and former error, and that they were determined to change in this respect. There was another decision made in respect of the removal of the iguanas, lest any should hereafter say he had not had some share in the extinction of the sacred reptile. It was decided that some of the blood should be sprinkled into all the wells in Bonny town to indicate that they had agreed not only in its destruction, but also in its use as food. Many soon after began to feed upon the flesh, roasted with fire. This brings to remembrance the passage: "And he took the calf which they had made, and burnt it in the fire, and ground it to powder, and strawed it upon the water, and made the children of Israel drink of it " (Exodus xxxii. 20).

The people did not have the same courage and resolution as the King and his chiefs. Superstition die hard, and after this, the wells of water were avoided from a superstitious fear rather than disgust. The water girls were sent to the mission premises for supplies of water from the only well unpolluted, and they came in large numbers, their water jugs upon their heads, and many in a state of nudity. The Bishop protested the habits of the people in this respect and refused to allow any to draw water unless decently clothed, and this had the desired effect. Many people suffered by these reptiles killing their chickens and were beaten or even put to death for destroying these creatures. For so many years, these lizards had become quite tame, and treated as domestic creatures, and it was, of course, believed that any injury done to them would incur the wrath of the gods. Had it not been by the command of the King and chiefs, the rejection of the juju worship would have been almost impossible. It was the desire of the old King, William Pepple, to carry out this drastic measure of reform in favour of Christianity, but he did not live to accomplish it. His son, a worthy successor, was not slow in fulfilling his father's wishes. After the old King's death his son wrote to the Bishop to acquaint him of his sad loss. This drastic reformation was effected within three years of Bishop Crowther's first visit to Bonny, and it shows the power of an African chief when influenced in the right direction. It is doubtful if such a change could have been brought about in so short a time had it not been decreed by the chief and his council.

The natives show great aptitude for acquiring knowledge. They study intelligently, have retentive memories, and will often aspire to superior attainments. King William Pepple and his son George had been to England and this motivated others to seek the advantages of a European education for their children. Some of the chiefs, therefore, sent their sons to England for this purpose, but the experiment was hardly a success.

A school was established at Bonny by the Bishop, where good education might be imparted without the necessity for expensive voyages abroad. It was a step in the right direction, and in some cases the pupils, after being well grounded there, were sent to England, where their intelligence and their parents' means warranted this course. The rage for education increased. So anxious were the parents that their children should learn quickly, that they would bring them to the mission school with instructions that the poor child should be kept at study day and night. It was difficult to make them see reason that relaxation and sleep were necessary to young people. Sometimes the Bishop was frankly told that all that was wanted was that the children should be able to gauge palm oil and add up the books correctly. But in other cases, ambition and vanity formed the driving power to get these girls and boys to bring shine upon their name by displaying superior attainments in the presence of less fortunate families.

In 1867, Bishop Crowther took up a new enterprise. At the mouth of another inlet of the Niger delta, between Bonny and the Nun, is the port of Brass, called Brass-Tuwon to distinguish it from the more important town of Brass-Nembe some miles higher up the river. The king Chief Ockiya, welcomed Bishop Crowther and was at once favourably disposed to Christianity, and begged for ministers and teachers to be sent to Brass to give the same blessings to his people as he had heard had come to his neighbours at Bonny, further up the stream. He gave permission for the opening of a mission, and even agreed to bear half the expense of a house and school for a native teacher at his port, Brass-Tuwon. Subsequently the mission was extended to his chief town, Brass-Nembe, thirty miles up the river. The people here were just as superstitious as at Bonny, and the chief "juju" was the boa-constrictor. It was the chief object of devotion, under the belief that the reptiles were possessed by spirits. A treaty made with the Brass people in 1856 by Mr. T. J. Hutchinson, H.B.M. Consul at Fernando Po, contained a clause fining any Englishman who killed a boa-constrictor a puncheon of palm-oil. Slavery, gin, and other baser elements of "civilization" had negatively affected the social life and wellbeing of the people in Brass. Here, then, Bishop Crowther laboured hard, and as a result many were added to the Church; and so prosperously did Christianity win its way among the people that the Juju priests, like those of Ephesus, soon began to realise that their gains were gone. By the influence of the mission, a leading chief called Spiff' was baptized on Whit Sunday, 1875; his son was trained as a mission agent; another chief, who was a violent persecutor, came under instruction. When in 1877 King Ockiya decided to make a solemn and public profession of Christianity, he paid a visit to Tuwon village to be baptized. This rite was administered by Archdeacon Crowther on the first Sunday in Advent, 1879, the king receiving the name of Josiah Constantine. For many years, this native potentate had shown himself very friendly to the introduction and progress of Christianity in his dominions. Despite his juju men, he utterly gave up his idols to the bishop, and the principal of these are to be seen in the Mission House, Salisbury Square. King Ockiya was enabled by the grace of God to give up polygamy, a great sacrifice for a royal African to make; and his example as a Christian led to the conversion of several of his heathen priests, who are now baptised believers in the Saviour's name.

Thus, the Delta Mission was progressing, not without anxieties, but with manifest blessing from God. The converts were weak and ignorant, and liable to yield to old temptations or fall back into old superstitions. Bonny should not be compared with some ideal Christian town, but with what it actually had once been; and then can be appreciated what even a fair profession of Christianity can do, though it may be with but a small nucleus of truly converted souls. Meanwhile, up the river, new stations were occupied from time to time, at Osamare and Asaba, and at a place called Kipo Hill, 350 miles inland, in the territory of the Emir of Nupe. The older stations, Onitsha and Lokoja, sometimes seemed hopeful, and there were many nominal converts; but the agents did not all prove satisfactory, and some sad failures took place. The position was a difficult one. Negroes from Sierra Leone, some of them young and with little experience, were placed in towns in the delta region amid wickedness of every kind. Their isolation was great; and the Bishop could only visit them at certain times of the year when the river was full enough to allow the trading steamers to go up. Even then he was dependent upon their movements. Sometimes they only stopped a few hours where he wished to stay for weeks; and sometimes he would be detained some days at a place where the Mission had no work. In 1877 he came to England and appealed to his friends for a steamer of light draught for the use of the Mission—a most reasonable demand, which might well have been made twenty years before.

The little Mission Church of St. Stephens was opened on the 1 January 1872, and from time-to-time converts were baptized, and the little assembly of believers increased. But the superstition of the priests and their devoted followers constantly made the little Church the object of their persecuting hatred. Because of this, members were compelled to meet in the secrecy of the forest for prayer. The hour of martyrdom had come; some few could not stand the test, but very many gloriously held faithful to their Lord.

One instance of this is the case of Isiah Bara and Jonathan Apiafe, who were important persons in their country before they embraced Christianity. From that moment, they were bitterly persecuted, and publicly impeached by the Juju priests, for the crime of carrying the body of a poor Christian slave to burial. They were offered meat sacrificed to idols, but preferred death to such dishonour of their Lord. Then they were bound with chains and put in a shed in the bush to die of starvation; but in secret some of their brethren conveyed to them a little food at the risk of their own lives. When tempted, first by offers of honourable and influential positions among the chiefs, and then by threats of horrible punishment, they refused to renounce their new faith. For twelve months these faithful ones endured this painful bondage, until relieved at last by the urgent appeal of some English traders; and they looked on emerging out of their captivity, more like wasted skeletons than men.

Under such circumstances Bishop Crowther and his son, Archdeacon Dandeson Crowther, appealed to the Christians everywhere to aid the suffering mission with their prayers, and from all parts of the world letters of sympathy reached them. A special prayer-meeting was held, too, at the Delta; and, after it, the Archdeacon hastened to the chiefs to ask them to withdraw the persecuting hand against the Christians.

Three years afterwards the wife of a chief called Captain Hart, died. She had been at the head of the persecution and had urged her husband to kill many Christians. Crowther tried without success to get access to her on her deathbed, the juju priests prevented this. When she had breathed her last, her husband Captain Hart, was heartbroken, grieving that his Juju idol had failed to save her. Crowther found him and tried to comfort the broken-hearted man. After Crowther expressed his sympathy and explained to the Chief; "we who are believers in Jesus Christ have a balm which heals such wounds; there is a Physician, above every earthly physician, who administers it into our hearts, and a change takes place for good". Crowther asked if the Chief would like to be told of that balm for his broken heart; He answered; "Yes, tell me, and I will listen to you". After reading from the book of Samuel, of the punishment of David's sin, Bishop Crowther turned to Psalm 11, and carefully read the whole to him. The Bishop concluded by pointing him to Jesus Christ, who has shed His blood for us all, and he that believeth in His name shall be saved. The Bishop closed his Bible, and Chief Hart asked him to come at another time and tell him more about the Word of God which is true and good.

The death of his wife, the failure of his gods and priests to deliver him in his trouble, had such an effect on the chief that when, in his turn to await death, he renounced his faith in idols in a remarkable manner. He ordered them to be thrown into the river. This was done on the day of his funeral, and the people broke them into fragments and threw into the river. Thus, his household gods were scattered abroad.

After the passing away of Captain Hart and his persecuting wife, there came to the infant church at Bonny another season of peace and prosperity. The native schoolmaster sent to Bishop Crowther a joyful report, thanking God that Bonny has become a Bethel. The destruction of Captain Hart s idols made a beneficial impact on his friends and neighbours. Members of his household came with great joy and open hands to the house of God.

The influence of the Christian religion was gaining grounds, and the gospel of salvation reaching further up the country. About thirty miles from Bonny is the town of Okrika, where there is an important market. Here people, who had been to Bonny, carried the good news of what God was doing amongst the people there. Though the chiefs and natives of Okrika had never seen a missionary, built for themselves a makeshift Church, which would hold at least three hundred worshippers. They got a schoolboy from Brass to come and read the Church Service to them. They sent a pressing invitation to Bishop Crowther to come and visit them. His son, the Archdeacon, however, came in his place, and was received with enthusiasm, and preached to them in the Igbo language. A few days after he was shown over the town and having brought a brick-mould from Bonny he got some clay and explained to them the process of making bricks.

After a while, the opposition and intrigue of the chiefs, who disliked the support which King George Pepple gave Christianity, caused serious trouble once more in Bonny. In 1883 a letter of complaint against the Mission was signed by many of the chiefs, and shortly afterwards this was followed up by open revolt, and the king was dethroned and exiled. The Churches were ordered to be shut up and burned down, and the severest punishment was inflicted on those who refused to sacrifice to the jujus or idols.

Such a persecution soon displayed the martyr heroism of the Christians of Bonny. Six women who would not recant, were put into a canoe and left helpless in the middle of the river, and several others were banished or murdered. Archdeacon Crowther was warned off from Okrika under pretence of a coming war, and it seemed for the time as though satan had retarded progress made at Bonny. But light appeared at the end of the dark tunnel, and in answer to many prayers, relief came. Her Majesty s Consul, E. H. Hewitt, Esq., arrived at Bonny in August 1884, with a commercial treaty signed by the chiefs of the oil rivers in the Gulf of Biafra, and in this was a clause giving absolute freedom to missionaries to establish stations free from molestation. This was signed by the chiefs of Bonny; and afterwards, at the suggestion of the English representative, a council of chiefs was established, which led to the unanimous reinstatement of King George Pepple as their rightful ruler.

The most important clause in the constitutional memorandum, drawn up and signed by the chiefs on the accession of their king, was that he should be "exempted from taking part personally in any ceremony that may be contrary to his religion". Thus, there was peace once more in Bonny, and the kingdom of Christ continued to extend its gracious power among the people.

Not only is there a great spiritual quickening among the people, but their material prosperity is evident. When Bishop Crowther visited one of the chiefs, Samuel Sambo, he found his house beautifully and luxuriously furnished in European style. There was one apartment, however, more elegantly decorated, in which a table and several forms were seen. This was the praying-room, where, twice a day, the chief gathers his large household for family prayer. This, too, in a land where at the time of Bishop Crowther s first visit, human sacrifice and rituals of the vilest sort reigned supreme. The natives who so lately possessed with cruel practices, are now a wonder of the power of the grace of God.

Few men have been at the head of a tougher missionary operation than Bishop Samuel Crowther. Few have in the face of hindrances and trials shown so resolute a determination. He had endured a long and difficult life so blameless a personal reputation and hard-working Christian in His vineyard. He suffered greatly by the errors of others. In the midst of the challenges in the mission field came Bishop Crowther and his co-workers, bearing the light of the Gospel, and in due time many believed and were saved.

CHALLENGES IN MISSION FIELD

The early soldiers of Christ in the Christian enterprise of evangelising West Africa experienced several challenges, some arising from factors outside their control. The problems and dangers faced by them are numerous as they go into the hinterland of West Africa and make disciples of the nations there. It at times seems as though the toil of years was all in vain. The Church suffered many setbacks and Bishop Samuel Ajayi Crowther faced many of the difficulties and dangers confronted by Christian missionaries of his time.

Unforeseen events begin to emerge to impede the progress of the Niger Mission and it entered an exceedingly difficult period that was to continue for more than a decade. It is so with most missions in all parts of the world; after the early triumphs there comes a period of reaction. In the early stages many of the converts are men and women whose strength of character enables them to stand for Christ almost alone and amid persecution. They are succeeded by larger numbers, too many of whom lack the devotion of the earlier converts. As time passes, some find the restraints of Christian moral law tedious and slackness creeps in. Life in mission field is a life of earnest prayer for support in time of trial and temptation, that the missionary may not be found wanting.

Persecution and Threat to Life.

The twenty-seven years of Bishop Crowther's episcopate witnessed rapid expansion in the work of the Niger Mission. But this expansion was accompanied by many trials and anxieties and often its brave bishop had to drink the cup of sorrow as well as sing the psalm of praise. Many of the challenges arose out of the unsettled state of the country. In the sixties and seventies of the nineteenth century the African communities in the Niger basin began to view the European invasion of their territories with suspicion.

In their attack against the foreigners the natives saw little difference between British trading posts, consular establishments, or missionary stations.

But the trials and persecutions were not solely due to native hostility towards the foreigner. Africans also warred against themselves and inter-ethnic strife was rampant. As an instance is the state of insecurity in the area around Iddah caused by the rivalry between the warring factions of the Mohammedan Emirate of Nupe. In 1866 a civil war resulted from this dynastic quarrel and, as a result, work of the mission station at Gbebe virtually came to a standstill and the mission house was destroyed by the warring parties. Ghebe from its position near the Confluence of Nigeria's two great waterways was a convenient meeting place for traders from all parts up the Niger and likely to make a useful place for mission work. This town was also a veritable confluence of languages. The ethnic nationalities from all parts met here; in its streets and markets might be heard Igalla, Igbira, Nupe, Kakanda, Yoruba, Idoma, and Jukun. The people of this flourishing town were ready to hear the Gospel. But the town of Ghebe and its mission premises was destroyed during those fierce ethnic wars, which break out often. The British Consul, Mr. Fell, hastened to protect the Christians, and saved their lives. Some managed to get into the canoes which he sent to them for crossing to Lokoja while others ran into the bush for safety in the surrounding country. Everything was plundered leaving Ghebe a ruinous heap, and an important town swept away from the face of the earth. The Bishop lost no time in visiting this scene of desolation, noting how the natives had plundered whatever the fire had spared. He confronted the two rival chiefs in turn and protested very strongly explaining to them the consequence of the war to the people at large. That by warring they have deprived Ghebe, the first Christian missionary station at the Confluence, of all the advantages it had above all other places—the privilege of a place of worship, of civilization, and industry and trade. All these were introduced at great expense for the general good and development of the country, but they failed to appreciate the cost of the damage done. This disaster led him to transfer the work of the mission to Lokoja, which from that time took the place of Gbebe.

September 1867 was to be marked by yet another tragedy for while the flock suffered the shepherd was not to go unharmed. In September, while travelling up the river by canoe, accompanied by his son Dandeson and a band of canoe men, the bishop was kidnapped by the Abokko of Oko-Okien (one of the chiefs of the Atta of Iddah), deprived of everything save his clothes, and held a prisoner for ten days. The man had in past encounter appeared to be friendly and Crowther was at first puzzled by this unexpected change of attitude. Ultimately his action was driven by greed and jealousy. The chief had observed that for twenty-five years Crowther had been onboard almost every ship that came to Iddah whether man-of-war or merchant vessels. He had wrongly concluded from this that the bishop owned all the ships and was a man of great substance. He was bitter and felt not fairly treated that this great man, who directed so much trade in the Niger countries, had not given him dues commensurate with his status. He was now determined to force payment. The bishop tried in vain to explain to him that the allegations were not correct and that his main business on the Niger was evangelization. The greedy chief would not be put off and demanded £1,000 ransom for Crowther and another £1,000 for his son.

Meanwhile, he treated the bishop and his team with great harshness and humiliation, making them to sleep on damp ground in an open shed. They were denied access to their clothing and other luggage and provisions. The bishop at last engineered to get a message to Lokoja, and the consul came to his assistance. But the Abokko refused to release the bishop to the consul until the ransom was paid. The consul absolutely refused to pay, knowing full well that it would encourage other chiefs to play the same game. Finding matters at a deadlock, Fell called to Crowther and the others to make a dash for liberty, and the whole party ran to the boat followed by musket shots and a flight of barbed arrows. As the boat was pushing off a poisoned arrow struck the consul; and despite all Crowther could do Fell died before the boat reached Lokoja. The bishop was grieved by the loss of the man who sacrificed his life to save him.

The Bishop's activities were not confined to the Niger valley. As in the Niger valley, progress in the Delta was followed by persecution of converts. Often it was necessary for the bishop to support and advise converts and even teachers who were being persecuted. Usually these were isolated cases, but at times a more general persecution broke out in some towns or villages. Such an instance occurred at Bonny after the work had been 'established there for nearly a dozen years. On Christmas Day, 1873, the baptism of nine converts stirred the juju priests to anger, and they succeeded in rousing the chiefs to believe that their slaves, when they become Christians, would no longer obey them. The root of the matter was Sunday work and worship, and some leading chiefs forbade their slaves to attend Church or school. But the poor slaves could not give up the strength and comfort of Christian worship, and they met secretly under cover of night in the forest. As soon as possible Crowther went to Bonny and reasoned with the chiefs on the value of a day of rest and on God's claims. He admitted that the bodies of the slaves belonged to the chiefs but maintained that both body and soul belonged to God. But the chiefs would not yield, and the slaves had no redress.

A baptismal service held the following year was the cause for another and more violent outburst of persecution. This time the crucial point was that of eating meat that had been presented to idols, a subject that reminds us of apostolic times. One of the converts was a slave of a chief called Captain Hart. As the slave took the baptismal name of Joshua, he became known as Joshua Hart. Nothing would induce him to eat things offered to idols, and he regularly attended Church. No other charges seem to have been made against him. Punishment did not deter him, and his brutal master resorted to harsher measures. Time after time he was flung high in the air and allowed to fall heavily on the ground. Arguments and threats were only met by the brave and calm answer: "If my master requires me to do work for him, however hard, I will try my best to do it. But if he requires me to partake of things sacrificed to the gods, I will never do it." In wrath, the master had his slave bound hand and foot, and taken out in a canoe to be drowned. During those awful moments, while his very life hung in the balance, Joshua prayed aloud that the Lord Jesus would forgive his persecutors. This still more angered Captain Hart. "You be praying again! " he yelled, and the next moment flung poor Joshua into the water. Bound as he was, he did not drown, and his master had him pulled into the canoe again and gave him a last chance. But Joshua Hart would not deny Christ. He was again thrown into the river, and as he rose to the surface he was beaten on the head with a paddle and prodded with a sharp-pointed pole until he was dead. He became the first martyr of Bonny.

The persecution being experienced did not impede the spread of Christianity to the towns of Brass, New Calabar, Okrika and Opobo. Encouraged by the heroism of Joshua, other Christians stood firmly for their faith. There were many other martyrs, not always suffering such an open and violent death, for some members of the persecuting party began to fear that the English might interfere. Therefore, when they caught their Christian prisoners, they secretly hurried them away into the lonely bush, far from any chance of their cries being heard, and left them, stripped naked, exposed to the torment of the sand flies and mosquitoes which infested the place. In some instances, it was slow starvation.

The converts were closely watched, and it was felt even a risk to be seen too much in the company of their own Bishop. One day the latter was going to preach at St. Clement's Church when he overtook some young men going same direction. One of them was formerly a soldier in the Ashanti War, and the Bishop asked him to give his compliments to his master on his return home. The young fellow answered cautiously and in a low voice, "No, I no fit." He was asked why. He replied: "If I deliver your message, I report myself, because my master will say, ' Where did you see the Bishop? Ah, you have been to Church!' therefore I must get punishment."

The Bishop's reaction was prompt and courageous in interceding for the liberty and safety of his flock, and on one occasion waited for hours under an old tree until the chiefs could or would assemble, so that he might lay before them the case of these poor suffering converts. When they did meet at last the chiefs were evasive and claimed that the converts were disobedient to their masters and were therefore punished accordingly. But they were not going to put off the Bishop with these unjustifiable excuses. Despite the threats from the chiefs, he faced and challenged them forcefully, which scared them. They thought with their powers he would be subdued, but God was on his side.

In spite of the cruel edicts against the Christians, the Services were attended with regularity, and the persecuting party could not understand how it was that whippings and irons, starvation, and even death itself, to say nothing of the allurements of worldly inducements, held out by the masters to their slaves, could not stamp out the faith. Converts were being baptized, and the Church roll increased. It was by the blood of such men that the early Church was built up and their steadfastness demonstrated that Africans are not incapable of living for ideals.

The fortunes of the Mission at Onitsha reached their lowest ebb in 1879, when rioting broke out and a mob destroyed the British trading factories and plundered the mission station even while a gunboat with the consul onboard was anchored off the town to intercede. The chiefs were reluctant to negotiate, and during the night H.M.S. PIONEER was fired upon and her captain wounded. Next morning, after giving time for the populace to leave the town, the British Government took reprisals and the gunboat, H.M.S. PIONEER, removed £50,000 worth of British trade goods at Onitsha and then subjected the town to naval bombardment for three days. The native town was nearly razed to the ground and the greater part of the mission premises was destroyed. After the bombardment, the mission at Onitsha was transferred to Asaba on the opposite side of the river. A few of the Onitsha Christians stood firm, and despite the wreck of their sanctuary carried on their worship, a schoolboy reading the Service and explaining the Scriptures as best he could. Thus, Crowther had to contend with sorrow upon sorrow, trial upon trial. Added to theses troubles was burden of daily care of all the Churches.

Despite these setbacks the report on the Niger Mission for 1880 spoke of eleven stations in occupation with over 1,000 Christian adherents. The entire mission was under the control of Bishop Crowther, assisted by nine native clergymen and many native teachers. Whatever his critics may say, within a period of forty years (Crowther first came to the Niger with the expedition of 1841) he had laid firmly the foundations of the Niger Mission. That Mission had shown itself capable of withstanding persecution, whether it came from the traditionalists and Mohammedan communities of the Niger basin or from the less reputable of the European merchants on the river. This is no small achievement when we remember that Crowther and his team achieved all these at a time when no order or Government (in the modern sense) existed in all Nigeria, and when his supervision of the work of the Mission was seriously handicapped by lack of regular transportation. It was not until 1877 that the Mission was able to possess a vessel of its own.

From the earliest beginnings of the Niger Mission, its history is marked with periods of fluctuating fortunes of seeming expansion and consolidation, followed by periods of persecution and a falling away of converts. The early Christian Church had its martyrs, and indeed gathered strength from persecution. So, it was with the Niger Mission. Persecution strengthened rather than weakened it. In the sixties and seventies when native attacks compelled the Government and the commercial firms to abandon their posts and desert the Niger, only the missionaries remained. Obstacles that overwhelmed other groups inspired the Church to greater efforts, and, as if by a miracle, the Gospel message struck deeper roots with persecution.

The Christians were bound to be prepared for the persecutions from the very fact that they were the aggressors and not the natives. They demanded in the name of Jesus Christ that the natives set aside the gods of their fathers and some traditional practices. They preached to them repentance towards God and faith towards Jesus Christ and called upon them to forsake their sins and lead, by the help of God's grace, a life of holiness. The Christians were the aggressors, and it was not natural that satan, whose kingdom was attacked, should sit still, and make no struggle to regain what he had lost. The position of the Bishop was that although Christians were "persecuted," yet they were not "cast down." In connection with the persecution he used the opportunity to vindicate the Christian character, the zeal, the energy, and the courage of the missionaries who were then labouring in the Lord's vineyard.

Polygamy

One of the most serious problems of the African mission field was the universal system of polygamy. The practice has a strong hold and is deep rooted upon the African culture. It was prohibited by Christianity while monogamy was encouraged and upheld. The natives saw polygamy as an integral part of traditional heritage and a source of strength for their farming activities as agrarian people. To them it was indeed a beneficial arrangement of family life in the community. Traditional title holders and wealthy ones take it as a matter of prestige. English missionaries have been confronted with this difficulty whether things might be left undisturbed. To insist upon a man having one wife and dismissing a dozen as an essential qualification for Church membership was a difficult decision that would disrupt the family as it already existed and it meant mountains of failure. The principle of more wives than one is so clearly at variance with Christian teaching and doctrine that no Church would venture upon a compromise to circumstances, however difficult, or practice, however ancient.

The Bishop fearlessly grappling with the subject instructed his pastors what to think and do. He honestly viewed this subject in its various bearings and inquire into the lawfulness and unlawfulness of the system from God's own Word and acts from its effect upon our social state and happiness. He took his listening clergy step by step through the teaching of Holy Scripture on the subject, showing that from the beginning, when God put the first man into Eden and gave him a helpmeet, right along to the Christian teaching of the New Testament, it is the Divine law that a man shall have one wife, and that to her he should cleave without rivalry or dishonour. The bishop tells the naked truth about its evil effects on his countrywomen:

"It has enslaved the female population of the countries where it prevails and made many to be miserable victims to the cruel lust and depraved appetite of one man. It has wrenched from them the right of nature which God has implanted in each for her own social happiness. Let us stand above the level and take a view of this social evil. It is impossible for every polygamist in this country to support from two to half a dozen wives out of his own scanty resources, and when this is the case there is no alternative but that every wife must enter into a life of labour and drudgery and shift for herself the best way she can. Hence to earn her own livelihood she must become a carrier of loads from one market town to another, or she must be a trader to neighbouring towns and tribes, which involves an absence of days and weeks from home, and on her return it has not unfrequently happened that she provides for the husband out of her earnings in addition to providing for herself and her children, if she has any, for the chief care of the children devolves on the mother and her relatives. The occasional gift of a few cowries from the father to the children for their morning gruel, and perhaps occasional share of yams to the mother, constitute mainly the support of the father. It has been often remarked by the men themselves that when a man had but one wife there was that degree of love and affection between them as might be observed in a married state in civilized countries—they were one in everything. But no sooner was a second wife added than the cord of union and affection was broken, and domestic evils immediately showed themselves. Hence arose this memorable proverb among the Yoruba females : Obirin ko rubo ko ni orogun ("No woman would ever undergo the expenses of a sacrifice to procure a rival "); that is, that her husband may have an additional wife. These are the feelings of the female population on the subject. The proverb is their own; it is their watchword, howling the repugnance of their feelings against the system, and may be heard among them today; but it is generally suppressed like their other proper rights, which they forego for fear of being reproached with jealousy".

The Bishop strikes at the roots of the evil of polygamy as consisting nothing of value or any useful purpose, but as an instrument of sin. These was his position on the subject of polygamy at a time when the system had found defenders in England.

Superstition

One of the great obstacles in the way of Christianity in the mission field is the dark and superstitious customs which are part and parcel of the lives of the people. It invests the old men and priests with power by which to rule, govern, and keep the population in awe under their control. The priests in particular, through whom the gods speak as their oracles, whose word must not and cannot be denied, are, in fact, the chief ruling power among many superstitious ethnic nations in the Niger Delta; through them sacrifices, human and animal, are made to appease the gods; through them oaths are administered to bind the keeping of an agreement made between two parties in all matters of importance, commercial or political. For generations, these practices have taken hold on the consciences of the natives, who are priest ridden and live in daily mortal fear. In some instances, as regards animal sacrifices, there is much that is similar to the Levitical usage among the ancient Jews, and the Bishop notices this fact as a foundation to work upon in preaching the doctrine of sacrifice and substitution "through the precious blood of Christ as of a lamb without blemish and without spot." He refers to this in giving his clergy some valuable advice in his first charge.

But it may be said of some of their customs that they have no relation whatever to such a sacred principle but are merely the outgrowth of cruel ideas and disastrous to human life and happiness.

The Killing of Twin Babies

The treatment of twins caused Crowther constant anxiety. To the mind of the natives, the birth of twins has always appeared something unnatural and the work of an evil spirit. Their unfounded fear of impending disaster has overcome the natural love that normal African parents have for their offspring. The destruction of twin children, however, varies in different localities, from the Brass and Izon districts, where it is usual to spare the firstborn and destroy the second; the Bonny and Igbo districts, where both children are killed, and the district of Old Calabar, where not only are both children destroyed, but the mother is banished from her native village, and never allowed to return.

At each mission station efforts were made to dismiss the dark superstitions that lay behind these practices. After making effort at preaching against the practice the crusade against the custom began naturally first among the Christians, in whose hearts the light of the knowledge of God was slowly breaking. As their trust in an Almighty Father increased, their dread of spirits diminished. They abandoned the cruel custom for themselves and began to help the mission staff in their efforts to overthrow it in the town or the village where they lived. Everywhere, in meetings, visitations, prayers, pulpit, social talks, this evil was forcefully condemned. At last, in answer to many fervent and effectual prayers to God, a great event occurred in Bonny. The King and chiefs one day held a solemn council upon the question, and passed a law that as the national constitution will never recognize the existence of twins in the town, anyone hereafter happening to be so unfortunate should call the missionaries to take the children away to the mission station, about a quarter of a mile distance, where they shall make themselves solely responsible for the vengeance of the offended gods. This amiable piece of legislation kept the custom, but transferred the penalty for its disregard, to the missionaries. The missionaries did not mind any consequence and were not scared of these deities. They gladly sent for their watchers to be on the spot and ready. People began to bring their new-born twins to the mission house, and the Christians were vigilant in looking out and reporting such births when the double blessing visited any house. In this way not a few baby lives were saved. The juju priest, however, disagreeing with the enactment, had his pickets posted too, and managed to achieve a massacre of the innocents like Herod before the rescuers came. It was with great difficulty that this legal act of mercy could be made operative. The evil practice died slowly, but it died.

This change of attitude to new-born twins was satisfactory and gaining ground with positive influence on Bonny society. In due time the thing once condemned became a popular privilege, and no home or clan was held captive in fear by the old superstition concerning birth of twins.

Charms

The belief of the people in charms in Soudan and the Upper Niger Mission is so great that they continually ask the Bishop for scraps of the Bible to wear as a means of preventing sickness. He tells a curious story of an old chief who paid him a visit while at Bida, bringing with him a present of two fowls; but it soon transpired that this generosity was only to get from him in return a few sheets of the white man's paper. On being pressed to disclose what use he intended to make of it, the chief admitted that he had lost twelve horses, and was anxious to keep the remaining one by tying protective charms about its body. The Bishop, however, reasoned with him, telling him that bits of paper with scraps of writing, from any holy book, could never charm away evil. He told him, moreover, that for twelve years he had ridden the same horse in his missionary journeys, without wearing a single charm. What he did was to wash and currycomb the horse regularly, never expose him to the sun at midday, and always feed him well. This chief being open-minded man, for he thanked the Bishop for his good advice, and said he would not want any paper after that.

Traditional Practice

A lot of traditional practices were declared taboos and irreverent by Christian missionaries. Christian doctrines frowned upon meticulous traditional practices such as blood pacts, oath swearing, oracles, vows, divination, and secret societies amongst others. Many traditional practices which were integral parts of African culture were stopped.

As regards Igbo people in the Niger Delta Mission and some of their superstitious practices, if a child should happen to cut its top teeth first the poor infant is killed. Cutting of the top teeth is considered to indicate that if the child was allowed to live, would become a very bad person. To say to any person, you cut your top teeth first, is, therefore, as much as to say nothing good can be expected from you; you are born to do evil, it is impossible for you to act otherwise.

Human Sacrifice

Another very serious social evil, that constantly brought sorrow to the bishop and his helpers, was the practice of human sacrifice. All the ethnic nationalities of the delta and up the river practised it. At the newly opened stations of Ossamare (1871) and Alenso (1877) the Mission had to fight this practice. In his report for 1877 Bishop Crowther stated that at Alenso a "living slave was dressed up, and ordered down the grave, at the bottom of which he was commanded to lie on his back with his face upwards, with both his arms stretched open; in this position the corpse of his master was let down and placed on his breast, which he embraced with both arms, when the grave was covered up with earth."

Crowther related similar occurrence in Onitsha that "the King (of Onitsha) does not step out of his house into the town, unless a human sacrifice is made to propitiate the gods: on this account he never goes out beyond the precincts of his own premises." Taylor recorded that every year a girl is put to death to propitiate for the sins of Onitsha people. Despite the work of the Missions the practice persisted, for in 1880 Adolphe Burdo, a French traveller, visited Onitsha and described this annual human sacrifice which he witnessed. According to Burdo, Onitsha girls who were to be sacrificed accepted their fate with resignation and were dragged to the river singing and dancing on the way to death. These customs were undoubtedly cruel.

Lack of Funds.

Almost all the missions in West Africa including the Niger Delta Mission faced financial problems in the early stages of their missionary work. They relied very much on their home Churches for their funds. But the funds and other needed materials even when available could not reach their station in time. This was because all the ships that came to the coast at that time were owned by trading firms and companies whose interest were basically on trade. In such a situation, provisions and other things had to be sent into the country not in large quantities as would have been desired by the missionaries.

CMS supported the work in Niger Mission with a small grant but urged Crowther to make the Church self-supporting. In 1864 he came to England to be consecrated Bishop of the Niger Territories, with eventual responsibility for the whole area from the Nupe country in the north to the Delta nationalities in the south. A special endowment fund was set up to support the bishopric. It was difficult for Crowther to run the various missions in the Niger countries for the work swiftly grew and there was no increased support from CMS either in money or men.

Poor Communication/Supervision

One major handicap to the mission work in planting the banner of the Cross among the vast nationalities and communities of the Niger countries and hinterland has been a want of regular communication and supplies. Annual visitation to various stations that are far from one another was difficult for the Bishop to undertake. The effect of this on the work of the Niger Mission can be imagined. Since the Mission was too poor to provide its own river steamers the Bishop depended upon an annual trip of a trading ship or gunboat to visit the stations, so that when either one or the other of the ships appears, he is seen onboard. This made the natives to believe that he owns the ships and the goods carried by the vessels. It was difficult to dissuade the natives from the belief that he had no interest in those ships. To avoid this, he tried to sever himself from trading ships as much as possible, to be independent, quietly moving to and fro, revisiting the stations in own boat. This option is not without its danger as the Bishop is exposed unprotected to bandits and dangerous attack as it happened when he was kidnapped by covetous Chief Abokko. Of two evils he must choose the least for safety's sake. He must either move in a trading steamer or in a gunboat whenever an opportunity presents itself though he does not own any of them.

In 1861, when MacGregor Laird died, nearly all the trading posts were closed. Crowther saw very clearly that unless the Mission could stand on its own feet its future would remain uncertain. Writing to the C.M.S. on the challenge after the death of MacGregor Laird he stated, "If the Niger Mission is to be taken up by the Society it must be done independently of the trading factories. The natives will never believe that we are sincere until we go to work among them with earnestness and zeal." Crowther asked for more staff and materials, pleading that the existing resources were inadequate.

Lack of Superintendence/ Administration.

The slow but steady growth of the Mission raised urgent problems of administration. The teachers and catechists were men of very limited education and Christian experience, and though earnest and devoted, were not strong enough to deal with difficult situations and the pastoral problems that constantly arose. Because of lack of superintendence these agents, isolated in river stations for long periods, were exposed to moral perils to which some succumbed. The Bishop was himself seriously disturbed by the indiscipline and poor quality of most of the mission workers. But he could do little to alter the situation. To begin with, most of his subordinates on the Niger were appointed by a Board in Sierra Leone. Crowther himself complained a good deal about many of these appointments. Crowther was far from being blind to this. He tried to rectify matters by improving the quality of his pastors through better training at Lagos, Freetown and Islington and later at the Mission's own training college at Eggan; and secondly by dividing the Mission into two, under resident archdeacons, and himself living more in the mission field as transport facilities improved. But progress in these directions was handicapped by lack of funds. It became evident that a mission steamer was needed to enable the now ageing bishop to travel quickly from place to place. He needed "to be everywhere at once," yet he was entirely dependent upon canoes and chance ships, with the result that it was becoming increasingly difficult for him to exercise the oversight that was necessary. The Niger Mission depended less than other missions on the C.M.S. as it was developing just at the time that C.M.S. funds were not increasing and when India and later East Africa occupied the centre of the stage. A good proportion of the funds came from dues collected in the Oil Rivers; and the West African Native Bishopric Fund, collected all over the world from advertising the all-African nature of the Mission, was also subject to fluctuations. This meant that stipends were low and that not only was it difficult to persuade Sierra Leonians of the right calibre to go to the Niger but that those who went were strongly tempted to trade. In the eighties and nineties the situation in the Mission gave cause for serious concern. Special enquiries were instituted by the C.M.S. and drastic steps taken to discipline the agents.

To fix this pressing problem the C.M.S. decided to modify the basis of the Niger

Mission from being an all-African agency to make it, as elsewhere, a partnership between African and European. Following this decision, the Mission was divided in 1890 into the Sudan and Upper Niger Mission and the Delta and Lower Niger Mission. Lokoja became the headquarters of the northern section and European recruits were appointed for work on the Niger. These innovations and the disciplinary actions against African leaders which followed did not make for peace in the Mission. Africans, not only on the Niger but in Lagos and Sierra Leone, looked upon the changes as a declaration of non-confidence in African leadership. A sequel to this was the decision to establish a Niger Delta Pastorate, centred at Bonny and under the leadership of Archdeacon D. C. Crowther, the Bishop's son. This new body was to be independent of the Society. Bishop Crowther did not live to see this separation as he died before it happened.

Misconception of European Missionaries

In 1861 Townsend, Hinderer, and other white CMS clergy had petitioned Venn objecting to the consecration of Crowther. They and other European missionaries working in Yorubaland, including, were strongly against Bishop Samuel Ajayi Crowther diocesan jurisdiction being extended to their area. In 1864 Crowther's new diocese was vaguely defined as being along the River Niger. It was financially weak, poor in physical and human resources, and mainly confined to missionary work. Venn, as Adrian Hastings says, failed to firmly implement his principles and was left with "an arrangement which led to ineffectiveness upon the one side and dissatisfaction on the other." By 1873 his erstwhile white opponents (Townsend and Hinderer inclusive) had considerably changed their views and come to accept the value of Africans as clergy and also Crowther as bishop.

Less than 20 years after Crowther's consecration, European missionaries' attitude towards educated Africans changed. From the 1880s onwards, racist views on the capacities of Africans were expressed more frequently and prominently. Venn was dead and Crowther now old no longer had support from Salisbury Square. Hutchinson, who had taken over Venn's responsibility for the Niger Mission, tried to introduce European supervision and sent out young missionaries to report on the state of the mission. Years of controversy followed and confidence between Crowther and CMS was lost and his mission was dismantled: by financial controls, by young Europeans taking over, by dismissing, suspending, or transferring the African staff.

In 1887 J A Robinson was appointed secretary of the Niger mission which was by then administered by a committee at Onitsha of which Bishop Crowther was chairman. At a meeting in 1890, two European missionaries accused a number of

African pastors of fraud, ignorance and immorality and held Crowther responsible for their alleged behaviour. At the meeting Robinson attempted to usurp the Chairman's power over the clergy. Troubles arose and the venerable Bishop strove with tact and patience to restore unity between the native and European clergy in his diocese. The attempt came as a shock for educated Africans. His son Dandeson, Archdeacon of the Delta, removed his churches from CMS control and established the Niger Delta Pastorate Church still within the Anglican Communion.

At least one of the European missionaries, H.H. Dobinson, repented of earlier hasty judgments. The estrangement between the Society and the Delta Church was to continue for more than thirty years, although the first signs of reconciliation were to come in 1897 with formal approval of its constitution as an independent Church. The formation of such independent Churches reflected growing ideas amongst Africans about self-determination and African leadership.

Church Hierarchy and Battle for Control

As the Church grew and became established, the quest for hierarchy became divided between the white missionaries and the black leaders in the Church. After 1870, there was a change in European relations with Africans which affected their relations in the Church as well as elsewhere. Whites increasingly took top positions and placed a ceiling on those available to Africans. Within the missionary societies, people like Venn Henry were replaced by lesser statesmen and the balance was tipped against African leadership. As it happened to Bishop Crowther (though the CMS tried to protect his impeccable records), Africans were attacked without justice or mercy in the effort to assert European control. At other times, the takeover was achieved by less heavy-handed methods through the increase of white personnel.

The Europeans had their way in eliminating African leadership from the Niger pastorate and in preventing the formation of a Delta pastorate under an African Bishop succeeding Crowther. In the Nigeria Pastorate, of the fifteen ordained African who worked on the Niger between 1880 and 1890, only one remained in the C.M.S. employ in 1895. Yet in the end only one agent died while all the others were re-employed in either Sierra Leone or the Delta. Meanwhile, of the eight Europeans who came to the Niger in 1891, by 1894 only one remained.

Inconsistency of White Traders.

The inconsistency of European traders was a stumbling-block in the way of the Gospel among the natives. The natives having seen the white traders so busily engaged about their trade, and never attending or taking part in religious services, have drawn the conclusion that getting money must be the most important part of his religion but that preaching and teaching, and generally the spreading of his religion, being matters of minor importance. Their conduct bring discredit on the religion because they make no profession of it and thus Christianity is dragged in the dust.

It became therefore necessary to distinguish between nominal and ungodly Christians and those who are real Christians, whose walk was consistent with their profession. It was no easy matter to make these distinctions, and to make natives believe that characters could exist in Christian countries who are not regarded as true Christians. It was not a pleasant subject, but to protect the new Church it was most necessary. The Bishop had to expose the ungodly conduct of some as most inconsistent with the religion they profess, by which they cast a stumbling-block before the natives, and so weaken the faith of the new converts to Christianity.

Isolation and loneliness

Many missionaries had to endure isolation and loneliness. This to a large extent worsened all the other hardships of missionary life. One of the greatest hazards of isolation for a missionary and his family in mission field is lack of a resident doctor and the distance from qualified medical attention when a family member was sick.

One therapy for isolation was the writing of letters and using it as a means of inducing response from recipients to alleviate loneliness. To the lonely and isolated missionary, the letter was his sole point of contact with the outside world. Missionary archives are so voluminous, and the material is a formidable mass of first-hand evidence of record of events. The letter was a means of contact with civilization and to a home left far away and long ago and to which the writer might never return. Though it might take months for a letter to reach London and months more for a reply to return, the mails were a vital psychological link with the mother country, a reminder that they had not been forgotten. The letters were published in the official publications of the missionary society to exploit both the hardships endured and the spectacular results achieved by them in the field in order to encourage financial contributions by their supporters.

Family Life Under Strain

Another challenge faced by the Bishop like most missionaries of his time was being torn between family welfare and mission work in the field. The Bishop wrote a letter by the bedside of his sick wife, lying before him in Lagos in 1880, to his friend Lord Venn:

"Give an account of thy stewardship, for thou mayest be no longer steward. Whether we are willing or reluctant to hear, the truth stands unchangeable; every day's occurrences which we are called to witness, by the removal of our companions and friends to give their accounts, are solemn proofs of the fact of the shortness of time. This night our souls may be required of us; may we learn to redeem the remaining days of our life.

During the last eighteen months my mind has been more or less exercised in these ways at the bedside of my dear sick wife. How watchful I had been for her speedy restoration to health, that I might be able to go out in my annual visitation to the Niger Mission; but the favourable change was long and tardy in coming. As the time for my preparation was rapidly approaching, I could neither hasten the one nor retard the other, till I was obliged to give in under the circumstances. Mental struggles, to choose the preference between two great responsibilities, are weighty; it was a natural duty to attend my sick wife, apparently in a dying state, which could not be avoided; and the cares of the mission, especially at a time when it was disorganized in various ways which threatened its prosperity, could not be easily quitted; so I was obliged to perform the first duty of charity at its proper place, for "charity begins at home." But God, in whose hand our life is, has not seemed to be ready to relieve the patient sufferer, but rather to continue to use the application as a rod in the Father's hand to correct and cure the soul. To Him be all the praise."

Exhaustion and fatigue

This was another challenge to the mission work. The mission had invitations from several native and Islamic authorities from various parts of the country to go and establish among their people. The Bishop is of the view that it is better to wear out in running to and fro in conveying the Gospel invitation to such people, rough handed, than to spend one's days in weeping and lamenting over unwilling people to accept the message of the Gospel. In a letter on 12 January 1885 written from Onitsha he stated: "Better to wear out".

Death

Life was undoubtedly hard, and death was a common feature of missionary work. From Yorubaland, Henry Townsend reported to CMS headquarters, 'it is not unusual for us to see our friends die around us'. The first Bishop of Sierra Leone, Owen Vidal, left England in December 1852 and died exactly two years later. His successor, Bishop John Bowen, died of fever at the age of 44 in May 1859 after only eighteen months in post. Dr Joseph Hill, Samuel Crowther's successor as Bishop of Western Equatorial Africa, survived less than one month, both he and Mrs Hill dying within a few hours of each other in January 1894, a month in which seven European missionaries in his diocese died of malaria or dysentery.

In his visitations to different stations on the Niger the Bishop Crowther frequently experienced that the prevalence of sickness was a serious check to the mission prosperity and the superstition of the people add to the problem. During his stay at Onitsha in 1874 a plague of smallpox carried off some of the most promising converts. Several of the children of the native missionaries also died, and the sorrow which visited the town was shared by the Christian teachers. But the native doctors and juju priests made the most of the disaster to advance their own ends, and claimed the tragedy was due to the anger of offended gods. The people in their fashion started a theory, and explained that the disease had come because a well had been dug on the mission compound fourteen fathoms deep, and the displeased deities would only be satisfied by a human sacrifice being made, and the body thrown into the well. This was averted by argument and persuasion; then the chiefs expressed themselves willing to negotiate, if a sort of indemnity be paid by the missionaries by being permitted to charge them with goods which they had never received. A young convert, however, stood up between the parties, and said to his people: "My friends, I have listened to all that you have been saying about the well at the mission compound. I will join you in filling it up, if you can promise me that, after it is done, there shall be no more death at Onitsha." This challenge they could not accept, and so happily the question of the well was dropped. But they turned their attention from the mission to the elderly women in the town, whom they accused of witchcraft and bringing the sickness among them. They seized upon twenty of these poor old women and made them prove their innocence by drinking mouthfuls of poison, with the sad result that half their number died in agony. This dreadful ordeal by drinking dangerous liquids was a common test among the natives.

In spite, however, of these measures, the sickness did not abate, and even the sudden destruction of their sheep and pigs did not prevent the spread of the disease. The meetings for worship were deserted and after a while the plague was stayed and the public services were soon full to overflowing, but its ravages were great.

Challenge in Malaria Endemic Region

One of the chief arguments used for support of native missionary services in the early 19th century was that Africans can best evangelize Africa. The argument is supported by the European's difficulty in surviving malaria which is the greatest health hazards faced by them and until the discovery of quinine and other curative medicines in the late 19th century.

To a large extent than is realized the work of evangelism in the Niger country in particular and generally West Africa was due to indigenous first-generation Christians rather than foreign missionaries.

The missionary work of evangelizing the natives was done with distinction by some outstanding black leaders until the Europeans scrambled for Africa. The missions were kept alive by black leadership when no white was on the field. Later black and white served together to create a much greater sense of equality than prevailed in the later period.

Language Problems

The early missionaries in the Niger were faced with the problems of the many languages and dialects hence efforts were made to have these languages in written form. It was difficult for the European missionaries to communicate freely with the local people. They had to speak through few interpreters who did not have sufficient education to interpret correctly. In such situations, the message sometimes appealed to the local people depending on the efficiency of the interpreter. Moreover, speaking through interpreters is a defective means of communicating one's thoughts to one's audience.

Insufficient Christian Literature

Another difficulty that the early missionaries faced in the spread of Christianity was insufficient Christian literature at that time. There were no Bibles in local languages, so the missionaries had to spend time learning local languages and translated the Bible and wrote series of grammar books. In Nigeria, one of the lasting works of the C.M.S. missionaries was the development of literature in Yoruba. Among several others, Bishop Ajayi Crowther produced the first translation of the Bible in Yoruba. In 1859, the first newspaper in Yoruba, called the Iwe-Irohin, was published by the missionaries. Similar developments were carried out by the missionaries in other Nigerian languages, Efik, Kanuri, Igbo, etc.

Alcohol

The Niger had now become a highway of commerce. But what commerce? Its exports were legitimate and useful, especially the palm-oil which was the staple of trade in the Delta. But the imports— in the main were ardent spirits, cheap, and specially manufactured for the African market.

Missionaries had to condemn the negative social effects of the alcoholic drink exported from England to communities in the Niger countries. When the barrel has gone before the Bible, or after it, the work of teaching the precious truths of the Christian faith becomes exceedingly difficult. This practice is against the wish of the native rulers and is abundantly shown by the letter from a Mohammedan king which is transcribed. The original is in the Hausa language, written by Maliki, Emir of Nupe, on the Niger, addressed to the Rev. C. Paul, a native missionary, to be handed to Bishop Crowther. The translation runs as follows:

"Salute Crowther, the great Christian minister. After salutation, please tell him he is a father to us in this land; anything he sees will injure us in all this land, he would not like it. This we know perfectly well.

"; The matter about which I am speaking with my mouth, write it as if it is done by my hand, it is not a long matter, it is about Barasa (rum or gin). Barasa, Barasa, Barasa! my God, it has ruined our country, it has ruined our people very much, it has made our people become mad. I have given a law that no one dares buy or sell it; and anyone who is found selling it, his house is to be eaten up (plundered); anyone found drunk will be killed. I have told all the Christian traders that I agree to anything for trade except Barasa. I have told Mr. McIntosh's people today, the Barasa remaining with them must be returned down the river. Tell Crowther, the great Christian minister, that he is our father. I beg you, Malam Kipo (Rev. C. Paul, native missionary), don't forget this writing, because we all beg that he (Bishop Crowther) should beg the great priests (Committee C.M.S.) that they should beg the English Queen to prevent bringing Barasa into this land.

For God and the prophet s sake, and the prophet His messenger s sake, he (Crowther) must help us in this matter, that of Barasa. We all have confidence in him, he must not leave our country to become spoiled by Barasa. Tell him may God bless him in his work. This is the mouth-word from Maliki, the Emir of Nupe".

Back Sliding

The beliefs of most of the natives in the Niger is that religion is a matter of offering sacrifices, performing ceremonies, and observing taboos. Wrongdoing are not regarded as sins against the gods or spirits, but merely as social offences against one's neighbours. A man's standing with his god is not thought to be impaired by the fact that he practises immorality or dishonesty, though such things may put him in trouble with his fellow men.

Brought up with such ideas, it is easy to see how very difficult it is for the convert from traditional religion to grasp the new conception of a God Who demands purity of heart and life. "Ye shall be holy, for I the Lord your God am holy," is to the African an absolutely revolutionary proposition. This requires time and careful training to enable him to adjust to the demands of his new and exacting religion.

Training, not merely telling, but training in the new life, is what is required. To teach these converts to repeat the Commandments is not enough. Just as our own children, in spite of repeated telling, sometimes err, and have to be corrected and patiently trained in what is right, so those who turn to God from traditional religious practice need to be patiently and lovingly trained in this holy way. To them the ancient prayer: " Teach me to do Thy will for Thou art my God" should have a new and deep significance.

Unfortunately, in too many instances, this all-important task of training the converts has to be left in the hands of the workers least fitted to give it. This is one of the greatest weaknesses in a mission field. While many of these subordinate workers are men of experience and established Christian character, others, though earnest, are painfully ill-equipped for their task and sometimes fail disastrously, and occasionally fall into open sin and have to be dismissed.

Such dangers and difficulties of pioneer missionary effort can only be guarded against by constant supervision and training of the catechists.

Unsuitable Climatic Conditions

The tropical climatic condition in the country was not favourable to the early missionaries who came to the shores of West Africa. The high temperatures coupled with high rainfall patterns in some parts of the Delta country, made the missionaries stay indoors, which slowed down their activities.

Food

Lastly, the missionaries were not used to eating our local foods. This made it difficult for the early missionaries to stay in the country for long. However, with time, they brought some crops, which they cultivated, and it sustained them.

Summary

Throughout the last ten years of his episcopate, Crowther was painfully aware of the evils that assailed the Mission from within. It may be that as a leader he was too gentle, too soft for a pioneer, relying as he did on guiding his staff by persuasion and example rather than by strict disciplinary measures. But as already indicated he was working against heavy odds, and it is against the background of his immense difficulties that he must ultimately be judged. Looking back the historian is impressed not by the Bishop's failures but by his successes. Had Crowther been given the tools required for the job, most of the short-comings of his mission could have been avoided. The great things he achieved for God in the Niger basin are triumphs for his own saintly character. Perhaps the most convincing proof that Crowther built the Niger Mission on sound and solid foundations was the fact that after his death the Mission survived the weaknesses that afflicted it from within.

Sun Set

The sun was beginning to set on the grand old bishop during the closing era of his career. He was already old and much over seventy years of age. He was growing a little weary with the heavy burdens he was carrying although no one could detect any dwindling in his never-ending labours and selfless zeal. Yet his responsibilities continued to increase. The African clergy, catechists, and teachers of his immense diocese were established so far apart at great distances that it was difficult to exercise sufficient oversight. To aid him in this work, two African archdeacons had been appointed to share with him the burdens of office; one was his own son, the Rev. Dandeson C. Crowther, and the other the Rev. Henry Johnson, who was in charge of a Church in Lagos. The former was appointed to the charge of the Delta region, and the latter of the Niger from Onitsha to Lokoja and beyond. The aged bishop received still further help from Mr. J. H. Ashcroft, the English lay missionary in charge of the HENRY VENN, who assisted in the business affairs of the Mission.

Before the little steamer, HENRY VENN, was dispatched from England for his service, the Bishop could only reach these places at such intervals as the passing trading ships would allow. This opportunity was occasional and far between. When there is an outrage because of an accident, war, or unusual high fatalities, these would cause a political isolation of the river for a considerable time. And even with the advantage of this little mission craft, which had to carry freight to pay expenses, the Bishop found the work of supervision very difficult with all his labours. He however was patient and never complained about these pains and difficulties. Very few men could have undergone the trials and difficulties that he faced while evangelizing the Niger country. He was literally on the move often, in perils of waters and from hostile natives. The troubles were many that came daily upon him in caring for all the Churches and many unpleasant things happened during the last ten years of the life of the the first indigenous African Bishop and this has often raised some mixed feelings.

The passing away of Mrs. Crowther, at Lagos on 19 October 1880 was one of the most painful moments of his life. She had been a strong support to Bishop Samuel Ajayi Crowther during the period of their marriage. A missionary's wife is full of sacrifices in support of her husband's call to mission work. During their marriage whenever Bishop Crowther was on his long journeys as explorer and away from home, Mrs. Crowther felt her part was to spare him, and faithfully fulfil the not less sacred ministry of virtuous woman keeping the home and children. After celebrating their golden wedding anniversary, she was taken ill during one of the Bishop's six months' visits in the HENRY VENN to the Upper Niger. When he returned to Lagos it was to find his faithful helpmeet at the point of death. It was her earnest wishes, during her long illness, that she might die in her husband arms. The Lord graciously granted her, her wish though she never knew it, for she lay unconscious till her death. The Bishop mourned her loss with secret tears and went about his work again with his heart in heaven.

A few years later another wind of sorrow blew the way of the Bishop when his mother died at Lagos. The summons at last came at an advanced age of ninety-seven and she had lived with her son in these later years. The Bishop was absent when her call came, but she died in a happy condition full of joy to go to her Saviour. The Bishop have much cause to be thankful that she was spared in the midst of so many adverse changes in her course of life and circumstances and at last brought to know the Saviour in whom she placed her trust as her Good Shepherd to the end of her life.

When after twenty-five years of separation through the violence of slave war, they were brought together again through God's good providence at Abeokuta in 1846, Bishop Crowther told his mother not expect him to be at home as other members of the family would do, because he was a travelling public servant. Her reply was: "You are no longer my son, but the servant of God, whose work you must attend unto without any anxiety for me; it is enough that I am permitted to see you once more in this world." She kept to this resolution even unto her last breath.

When she was on her dying bed at Lagos in October 1883, she told Mrs. Macaulay, her granddaughter, who was attending to her not to write to her son Bishop Samuel Ajayi Crowther of her state of deteriorating health for fear that it would take his attention away from his missionary work. She told her granddaughter not to be afraid but to tell him afterwards what took place as she was as good as her father being at home. This aged saint passed to that land where partings, sorrowing, burden of age, and the misery of slavery never vex again.

In 1889 Rev J.F Schon the Bishop old friend and fellow traveller died. To him the Bishop owed his first recommendation to missionary work. He had been as a father to the young African when his friends were few. When Frederick Schon passed on, the C.M.S. placed on record that "he was called away in the very midst of his labours, having been occupied within a few days of his death in the correction of proof sheets of his own translation in Hausa, of the Book of Common Prayer."

Besides these personal losses there lay upon the Bishop's heart the shadow of increasing care and anxiety about the state of his diocese, as the ineffectiveness of native agents on the Niger at this time became a topic of sufficient importance to demand an inquiry. New troubles constantly occurred at the duty posts. In the Delta, things were going well, and progress was made, but up the river difficulties arose with some of the catechists. Traders and other Europeans brought reports of ineffectiveness and failure in their ethical conduct. Probably some of these reports were untrue and others greatly exaggerated by those who were unsympathetic or even hostile to the Mission, but there was enough ground in them to cause Bishop Crowther and the C.M.S. Committee grave anxiety.

There can be no doubt that at some places the workers, left for long periods without oversight or encouragement, had grown slack. They were either through inefficiency or human imperfection arising from lack of supervisory time due to communication problems fell short of expectation of their callings in being a good shepherd of the flock. In their eagerness to show evidence of progress they were bringing forward for baptism or confirmation, men and women who were not ready for so important a decision in life. They were laid-back in their duties to the congregation, and this led inevitably, in some places, to Churches being more or less filled with people whose manner of life proved them to be ignorant of the principles of the Gospel. Some of the catechists themselves were overcome by the temptations around them.

Drunkenness was one of the counts of the indictment brought against these native Christians. Some Europeans failed to set a good example in this regard, and the character and fair name of Christianity is damaged by the contradictions of lives of men, who, make the natives feel that the white man in some respects is quite as much a heathen as themselves.

Another injurious element affecting the Niger Mission, was the inordinate love of trading, which became indeed a passion with the native coming fresh in touch with the world market. With wise foresight the Church Missionary Society bound over all their agents and preachers not to engage in trading of any sort. This stipulation requires more than moral courage to respect for the temptation of doing it secretly was great. In this direction the Bishop was able to keep his clergy well in check. Any infraction of this rule would clearly be injurious to the true interests of the work and provoke reaction from the trading community as an unfair competition.

Under the conditions obtaining- the stations scattered over so large an area, the uncertainty of travel, and the general difficulties of oversight – it was not easy to discover slackness and failure at any given place until things had reached a very serious pitch and could no longer be concealed. For every missionary and African clergyman, it was exceedingly difficult to be sure of what is actually going on at his outposts, unless he is able constantly to visit them and maintain close personal touch with workers and people. When an outpost is so far away that it can only be visited once or twice a year, and then only for a few hours, it is impossible to see below the surface. A visit from the bishop or archdeacon naturally draws a large congregation; the Church is full, the responses satisfactory, the singing good, and the attention all that can be desired: everything appears to be going well. A week's residence in the place, or even a monthly visit, might reveal a different situation.

These, then, were some of the challenges which beset the Niger Mission, and in varying degrees of complicity during this unhappy period. Despite the challenges the old bishop strove to restore discipline in his huge diocese, and he was well supported by his archdeacons and clergy. But it soon became evident that a crisis had arisen, and these became so serious that it was impossible to disregard them. The CMS therefore arranged that a committee, composed of the Bishop, three European missionaries, the two native Archdeacons, and others, should meet to discuss the situation. Their report, written by the Rev. J. B. Wood, a missionary of experience and judgment, showed an unfavourable state of affairs, and soon after its receipt in London it was naturally referred back to the Bishop for his consideration and comments. It was quite an unforeseen and pathetic coincidence that it reached Lagos at the time of Mrs. Crowther's death in October 1880.

Crowther was on the island of Madeira in the Atlantic Ocean west of Morocco for a conference. He was accompanied by his son, Dandeson, an archdeacon, on Church business in March 1881. The Lay Secretary of the Society and the Rev. J. Bradford Whiting were sent out to Madeira to meet the Bishop and others there and the various allegations against the native agents were carefully discussed. It was resolved then that it was necessary either to limit the sphere of operations or to strengthen the staff. The latter course was decided upon with the concurrence of Bishop Crowther that it would be a great advantage if the work on the Niger is reinforced by a few European missionaries to assist him as secretary to the mission. The first European to be appointed to the Niger in that capacity was Rev. Thomas Phillips, an Irish businessman, who took theological course at Islington and was ordained priest by Bishop Crowther. He was the first European to receive ordination at the hands of an African. But in nine months Rev. T. Phillips returned home and upon his recommendation several of the native agents on the Niger were dismissed. Rev, Phillips was succeeded by the Rev. James Hamilton. A medical mission was planned for Lokoja, but Dr. Percy Brown, who was sent out to take charge, died before the work was established. Three lay missionaries, sent out to run the HENRY VENN, did useful service. All these changes and acts of necessary discipline of the native agents upset the mind of the Bishop, especially since it reflected upon the supervision which he, had struggled so hard to maintain. He had done his best, but he was conscious that it was a physical impossibility for him to visit the stations of the Upper Niger more frequently.

The trouble which was exercising the minds of the Bishop, his workers and supporters, both at home and on the Niger, was greatly worsened at this juncture by the publication in English journals, copied from native sources, of a shocking scandal—nothing short of murder, under brutal circumstances, of a girl by two native agents of the Society at Onitsha. The Central Secretary, Mr. Sutton, wrote immediately a public disclaimer, explaining that the persons implicated were not then connected with the work, one having been dismissed by the Bishop three years before, and the other had since withdrawn. As a matter of fact, the offence, grave as it was, had been committed five years before, and its reappearance at this time was due to the firm action of the Rev. J. B. Wood, who having discovered the offence insisted, at any cost, upon the guilty parties being punished. A wave of criticism and blame had, however, been evoked at home, and the opportunity well served some individuals to make an attack upon missions generally, and the Niger Mission in particular. The Secretary, however, put the case effectively in the following words, which deserve quotation, as they refer to the difficulties on the Niger, apart from the specific charge:

"A case like this, we need hardly say, is in reality no argument against missions. On the contrary, it is an additional proof, if proof were needed, of the necessity of missions and of working them vigorously and without stint. Christianity at home does not prevent crime, nor is Christianity in Africa likely to do so in the present dispensation. But individuals may be saved from falling, and if the means at the Committee's disposal had enabled them to give more support to Bishop Crowther in his arduous undertaking, and in particular if the HENRY VENN steamer, which has made frequent inspection of the stations so much easier, had been provided some years earlier, it may be that individual agents might have been rescued in time from the temptations with which the great enemy has so persistently beset them".

While these criticism and allegations of gross misconduct were giving so much anxiety in Britain, it was equally distressing at the scene of operations on the banks of the Niger. The Bishop had been in England the year before, conferring with the Committee and labouring hard to find a satisfactory and sustainable solution to the difficult problems of his diocese. Back again at his work with a burdened heart, but renewed vigour, he hurried from station to station, to admonish and put things right with his little flock. Archdeacon Henry Johnson meanwhile was hard at work on the Upper Niger, sometimes at Lokoja preaching to a crowd of mixed nationalities, with four different interpreters at his side. His remarkable facility in mastering the various languages proved a great advantage to the mission.

It was felt that his hands would be much strengthened if a medical mission could be established at or near Lokoja, and a young, qualified man, Dr. Percy Brown, came out from England and started a dispensary, doing good service in this direction. But the healing ministry of this young missionary of so much promise was short-lived by the African fever. His own patients, watched with pity and wondering why the white man, who could heal others, is unable to heal himself.

He was lifted onboard the next vessel sailing for England, but died on his way home, and was committed to the watery deep until that great day when the sea shall give up its dead. This pathetic failure of a brave attempt to start a needed branch of the mission was a misfortune to workers and natives alike.

The Bishop was much cheered when the Rev. James Hamilton consented, under these difficult situations, to go out to the Niger and act in place of Rev. Phillips, who had been invalided home. The new secretary was an old and valued Sierra Leone missionary, who understood the nature of the native work, and had retired for a time, working as Association Secretary in England. He performed his duties with tact and delicacy of feeling, travelled with his old friend the Bishop from place to place, holding courts of inquiry, and, where necessary, dismissing any agents against whom the evidence was sufficient to warrant such acts of discipline. He seems to have grasped the difficulties and found the Bishop always ready to agree to any suggestion for improvement of the work in the field. For a time, all things were working well; a new HENRY VENN was built and sent out to take the place of the old vessel, which had ceased to be of any value.

Archdeacon Henry Johnson being in England in 1885, the University of Cambridge conferred upon him the honorary degree of M.A., in recognition of his linguistic attainments. Before returning to his work on the Niger he confirmed a report he had sent on the state of things there, pointing out how very difficult it was to conduct its operations with any measure of success with such a weakened and diminished staff of workers. Still he said he was optimistic of the ultimate result.

The work in Niger mission was divided into two distinct parts, the Upper Niger and Soudan and the Lower Niger, represented by the Delta. Very drastic measures of reform adopted by the local committee at Lokoja involved the dismissal of several native agents, and the continual anxiety by these events began to tell upon the strength and patient endurance, of the old Bishop. The condition of the work fully justified prompt and efficient action to enforce discipline and remove the reproach which the inconsistency of some agents had brought upon the mission. At the same time, no blame was attached to the Bishop personally, for he had done his best to keep his under-shepherds and their flocks in order, and with great fairness and judgment he presided over these committees, whose function it was to deal with such matters. But his feelings were much wounded by what he felt was a lack of consideration and even interference with his proper province as Bishop of the diocese. He never objected to the introduction of European missionaries; indeed, he always felt that their co-operation and help were most valuable; but he was quite naturally jealous of that native ministry which had been created by his labours and prayers during a lifetime, and which he firmly believed to be a necessity for mission work in Niger countries. As the first African Bishop he honoured and loved his native clergy. He was no fanatic on the subject of a native ministry, but he was patriotic to the core, and rejoiced to see his own country being evangelized by her own sons. It must also be borne in mind that the great ideal of a native Church with a native ministry, self-supporting, was first advocated by that venerable and honoured Secretary of the Church Missionary Society, the Rev. Henry Venn, for whom the Bishop had the greatest respect and affection.

As regards the inconsistency of the members of these native Churches, which had been so strongly, and in some cases justifiably criticized, it is only just to take into consideration that they had emerged from heathenism but a few years before, and had not had the advantage, as is the case with the converts in England, of a Christian parentage and a favourable environment. They could not fairly be measured by European standards, and their backslidings, regrettable as they were, might be largely due to the pressure of peculiar temptations and of surroundings of which they recently formed a part, and might easily entangle them again. The native Christians, however, knew how to suffer for the faith, and endured with patience and fidelity trials which would be impossible for the white man to bear. The slaves who had trusted in Christ were the prey of their masters and made to suffer indignities and penalties which would not have been their portion if they had not chosen the Gospel brought by the missionary. Some had suffered the pains of slavery, but their liberty had been assured under the British flag. Now, however, as the willing slaves of Jesus Christ, they, like St. Paul, were ready to endure all things. When a leading chief passed through their towns and villages these poor people were the specially selected victims of their hate and brutality.

One instance that occurred at Lokoja will suffice. One of the relatives of a passing chief exercised their privilege of robbing these hapless natives, and if they dared to resist, they were made to suffer for their protest. One of the Christian converts having tried to draw attention to the simple fact that his sheep was stolen, was tied up, together with his wife, and exposed to the heat of the burning sun, while three thieves went to his house and barn and carried away everything they could lay their hands on. Even then the suffering was not over, for the chief fined the poor man fifty bags of cowries, and slavery for three of his household. Utterly ruined and half dead, he had to escape into the bush, and after hiding for three days, crossed over to Ghebe, and waited patiently till this tyranny was over. Disappointed of their victim, these ruffians fell upon the house of his neighbour, and carried off some of its inmates to be sold as slaves. This incident will give some idea of the lawlessness of a town which had a certain importance as a trading station, and what the Christian converts had to bear.

Picture of Bishop Samuel Ajayi Crowther and Archdeacon
Dandeson C Crowther - Wikipedia

Every missionary has a peculiar love for his converts. They have seen the horror of great darkness which preceded their conversion, and now that the Divine light shines on them, there is joy as of a battle won. For this reason, the backsliding of his flock was more keenly felt by the Bishop. He was not afraid to exercise discipline, and was vigilant to detect its necessity, as far as human discernment could allow. He did not shut his eyes to the faults of the agents of the Niger Mission during a period of now over twenty-five years.

The Bishop in the course of his work always firmly demand and insist upon entire separation of all Christian converts from having a hand or voice in any such acts of violence, injustice, or brutality. But when such stand is made it should not be overbearing in the punishment for what has been done against the will of those who were involved in such acts, who would have willingly got out of it if they could find a way to do so, they being under the influence of the native authorities, whom they could not contradict. In cases of these severe punishment to maintain Christian discipline it was moderated with sympathy and guided by due allowance for the measure of knowledge and experienced Christian principle which the converts possessed to guide and govern them under such confusing circumstances, they having scarcely emerged out of these rooted barbarous practices of their forefathers.

Through all these trials of the mission the Bishop never hesitated in his confidence in the value of native agency. To his mind the lesson to be learned from these painful experiences was that the selection and the training of agents should be more carefully considered and safeguarded. The Bishop however made use and had the co-operation of agents whose education was slight, but being of ripe Christian experience, and having the spirit and perseverance of pioneers. These adequately equipped them for the needs of that time. They were superior to the chiefs by having a knowledge of the Christian religion, and able to hold their own in argument. As an instance of this, old King Ockiya once asked for a teacher, adding, " I do not want a boy, but a man," meaning not age, but the capacity to discuss and take a superior stand among the chiefs and headmen. These agents were not from an intellectual standpoint ideal teacher, but they performed their duty. The Bishop is so anxious that the character of the native agents should be maintained and all-round, capable men of God.

His one absorbing thought was his work; while under Divine guidance he could be of any service he was ready and willing to go on; but if any better way or wiser worker could be found, the Bishop was quite willing to stand aside. At times the old man grew sad and depressed; worry began to wear even where hard work had told little as yet.

He was ready to yield place to others to act as leading managers of the Niger Mission if the authorities felt he was incompetent in the superintendence of the Mission. He was willing, if his health permit, to labour as a pioneer in opening fresh grounds, while the already established stations can be worked by superior intellects and better managers. The work is a public one and of great importance and should by no means be allowed to suffer for want of proper management, strictness of discipline, and firmness of principles.

The Society, true to its great traditions, would not consent to the step suggested by the Bishop. Amid all the clamour and criticism of their own administration, with its conflicting reports, resignations, personalities, and misunderstandings. The Committee did their utmost to hold blameless that venerable figure. To his labours, life, and unique personality the work on the Niger had owed its very existence. His stainless name was associated with every step of its advancement, and when the storm of trial came, and it seemed as if shipwreck was inevitable, his courage and loyalty were not counted on in vain. When the Niger Delta Mission had been purged and agents adjudged unsatisfactory dismissed it was reorganised with additional European staff strength diocese. One of the first fruits was the expressed desire of the native Churches of the Delta to form themselves into a separate and self-supporting mission. The idea was not a new one. So far back as 1881 the Bishop drew attention to a plan whereby the chiefs (and particularly when in 1864, after King Pepple's death) might subscribe and share at any rate a part of the expense of establishing a Christian mission in the Delta. The subject did not at the time receive much attention, but the native Churches were constantly encouraged to do their utmost for the support of the work. Consequent upon the reorganisation of the Niger Delta Mission, it was not surprising that the converts felt the time had arrived when they should make an effort to put in practice that hope expressed by the late Henry Venn, "that in course of time the Churches in the Niger Mission shall become self-supporting, as those in the Colonies are." After a consensus on the matter by members of the Churches, a formal application was placed in the hands of the Bishop, who sent it to Salisbury Square, with his personal approval and support. His closing words were:

"When the extensive openings in the oil rivers in God's good providence are taken into consideration, and the unhealthiness of the muddy Delta region as a natural impediment to European health and life is weighed, I feel convinced that the suggestion of the Churches of the native pastorates of Lagos and Sierra Leone is providential that the Delta district should be made a native pastorate to be worked entirely through native agency, towards the expenses of which they resolved to contribute a supplement".

And now at last the Bishop broke down. He had always been so uncomplaining, and his energy never failed him, for he had a constitution which carried him through toils and hardships to which others succumbed. Nobody expected him to fall; even those who were with him, and knew him best, marvelled that he kept up so bravely, despite constant toil and anxiety. But it came at last. In a letter written to Salisbury Square in August 1891, came tidings of sudden indisposition, which made his many English friends greatly grieved. Still, in his quiet, cheerful way he made light of it, said the trouble was only the result of a cold after enduring the excessive rains of two months wet season, but it was much more serious. In a letter addressed to General Hutchinson, dated 16 October 1891, and thanking him for some words of sympathy, he gives some details:

"I was laid aside by a sudden attack of paralysis, as I got up from my desk, which paralyzed my right hand and leg and affected my speech for many days, so that I could not speak audibly. The doctor thought a change of place would improve me, and therefore ordered me to this place, for which I left Bonny on the 25th September and got here on the 28ᵗʰ. I am thankful to say that I am improving, hoping to be all right again in a few weeks. I sincerely thank the many kind friends who sympathize with me in my affliction, from which I never suffered before. Wishing soon to recover my health, to spend the remainder of my days in the service of our Divine Master, I remain.

Sincerely yours,
Samuel A. Crowther."

When Archdeacon Hamilton landed at Lagos on one of the last days of December, he spent an hour with the Bishop, and afterwards both attended a graduation ceremony of seven schoolmasters going out from the training institution. At the close of the event he stood up and gave his blessing, tenderly, fatherly, with slow and faltering speech. This was his last act of public service. So much had he brightened up with the change of air and scene that he spent a good part of the next day in diocesan business with his visitors, at which time, with evident effort, he rallied his forces of memory and mind to the important matters under discussion. He even spoke of leaving for Bonny the first week of January, and sent a letter to Major Macdonald, the Consul from the Oil Rivers, who happened to be at Lagos, asking if he could give him a passage in his steamer. On Christmas morning he walked to Christ Church, and this was his last attendance at the house of God. A week passed, and the last day of the old year was reached. It was his custom to write out in draft form any correspondence of importance, and in an old Letts's Diary there is a feebly written letter which he had attempted to compose in acknowledgment of a kindly expressed letter from Salisbury Square. This letter was never sent and has a very pathetic interest as being scrawled by a dying hand. It was possibly the very last writing he penned before he died. There is a pencil note to the effect that the doctor in attendance on the Bishop forbade him to write any more:

"My dear Sir,—You will see by my handwriting that I had been sick since these four weeks, sick by—on my right hand and foot and affecting my speech, so the doctor forbid my doing anything, but I am getting better.

But, sir, your two accompanying documents brought to my memory my visit to the Archbishop of Canterbury about two archdeacons. It is possible I was accompanied by a secretary, by whom (explained) the matter to the Archbishop, to which he gave his assent, or he assented to the secretary. I thought it was right, I being a novice and not knowing the difference. I apologize for my ignorance. Your memorandum of my character before (and after) my call to the ministry in 1843, and after my call to the episcopacy in 1864, to this day was in answer to my prayer that the God who called me first from among my people to the important post in His service, may give me grace to set a good example for others to follow.

Since my appointment to the superintendent of the Niger Mission in 1857 to the

152

present I never refuse any suggestion made by the Committee for the improvement of the Niger Mission. Though I am single-handed, I like to be improved by the ideas of others".

On the final day before his death, the Bishop was up as usual on the morning of the 31 Dec, dressed, and went through the morning devotions as he did every day; then had his tea after seven o'clock. About eight o'clock he sent for his daughter (Mrs Macaulay) in whose house he was now staying to read a letter to him. She took the letter and read it, and said: "Father, I have read this letter to you several times." The Bishop replied: "I have read it too." (This was the last letter he got from the Secretary of the C.M.S., Salisbury Square.)

Mrs Macaulay now told the Bishop if he wants any more letters read to him to call Charles (a grandson of his) who will read them to him as she is busy with his breakfast. The Bishop smiled, and she left him sitting at the table, with his Prayer book and hymnbook and some papers.

About nine o'clock or so an old Christian woman, Emma Taiwo, called to see the Bishop. Mrs Macaulay told her she could go and have a chat with Bishop as he is not busy and will be leaving in a day or two for Bonny. She went into the parlour and returned in haste and told Mrs Macaulay that the Bishop's head was not properly on the sofa. She ran in just in time to take hold of him, to save him from dropping from the sofa, and called: "Father! father!"

He answered her and she inquired and said: "What is the matter?" He made no reply, but when asked if he was cold, he nodded, and said: "Yes." She ran for some brandy and water, which he drank, and sent for Dr. I. Baudle, as Dr. O. Johnson was away from home.

After the attack he did not speak much but answered when spoken to. At two o'clock in the afternoon the doctor said he should go into his bedroom, as the wind was blowing cold. He walked to the room supported. His daughter had not the least thought there was anything serious, although she kept all the time with him. The doctor was in and out constantly; his last visit was at seven o'clock. He took the medicine patiently, sitting. she said something about his coughing, and he replied, "No pain."

At midnight when she came in to give him his medicine he sat up and said he hoped it was the last dose. He lay down, and as she covered him and said, "Good night, father," and he said, "Good night." Half an hour later she heard movements in his room and saw her father just lying down, and she jumped on the bed, for she saw he was dying. "Father! father!" she cried. He heaved a sigh, and all was over. The grand old bishop passed into the presence of his Lord at a quarter to one in the morning of the new year.

Thus, the sky was cloudy as his sun went down in the west. But he had fought a good fight, and his purity of life and loyalty to Christ and His Church, had given him, cause for thankfulness and peace. He was active almost to the last days of his career, though for some time his health had been failing.

He was buried 1 January 1892, honoured and loved on every hand. The funeral service was held at Christ Church, and a solemn address given by the Rev. James Johnson (later Bishop) to a large congregation, including the Governor and most of the chief European officials. Ten clergymen, European and native, including his two nephews, preceded the coffin, strewn with ferns and frangipani, to the grave, the Rev. E. Pearse taking the first part of the service, and Archdeacon Hamilton the committal. He was laid by the side of his wife and mother at Ajele Cemetry in Lagos, and the mourners sang together, " Hush, blessed are the dead."

Something, however, more enduring than these sweet but fading flowers was destined to mark the resting-place of the late Bishop. His many friends in England and West Africa gladly subscribed, and as a result a beautiful monument in white marble was erected, and this was unveiled with much ceremony on 4 August 1898. A large crowd of people of all classes gathered in the cemetery. On every hand there were signs of the deepest respect for the one whose memory they came to honour. Several hymns were sung, and prayer offered by the clergy. His Excellency the Governor then spoke of the virtues of the Bishop and unveiled the monument. An address was afterwards delivered in Yoruba by the Rev. James (later Bishop) Johnson, and after the choir had sung the recessional hymn following the Benediction, a large number of the spectators lingered behind to read the inscription, which is as follows:

Sacred to the Memory of
The Right Rev. Samuel Ajayi Crowther, D.D,
A NATIVE OF OSOGUN, IN THE YORUBA COUNTRY;
A RECAPTURED AND LIBERATED SLAVE;
THE FIRST STUDENT IN THE CHURCH MISSIONARY SOCIETY'S COLLEGE, AT FOURAH BAY, SIERRA LEONE;
ORDAINED IN ENGLAND BY THE BISHOP OF LONDON, JUNE 11TH, 1843;
THE FIRST NATIVE CLERGYMAN OF THE CHURCH OF ENGLAND IN WEST AFRICA, CONSECRATED BISHOP JUNE 29TH, 1864.
A FAITHFUL, EARNEST AND DEVOTED MISSIONARY IN CONNECTION WITH THE CHURCH MISSIONARY SOCIETY FOR 62 YEARS, AT SIERRA LEONE, IN THE TIMINI AND YORUBA COUNTRIES, AND IN THE NIGER TERRITORY; HE ACCOMPANIED THE FIRST ROYAL NIGER EXPEDITION IN 1841; WAS A JOINT Founder with others of the Yoruba

Mission in 1845, AND Founder of the Niger Mission in 1857; AND OF THE SELF-SUPPORTING NIGER DELTA PASTORATE IN 1891; HE FELL ASLEEP IN JESUS AT LAGOS, ON THE 31ST DECEMBER, 1891, AGED ABOUT 89 YEARS.
"Well done, thou good and faithful servant...... Enter thou into the joy of thy Lord."—Matt. XXV. 21.
"REDEEMED BY HIS BLOOD."

The Church Missionary Society, to which he owed so much, and for which he had laboured so faithfully, have placed on record that: "As regards the world, it is the poorer for his removal. From his earliest years, in the providence of God, Samuel Crowther's lot was cast amidst some of the saddest manifestations of its wickedness and of the depravity of the human heart; and in this environment he patiently and consistently carried on the battle against evil, maintaining throughout an unblemished reputation. As regards the Church, he has most courageously fulfilled for nearly thirty years, to the best of his abilities (and they were of no mean order), and with unremitting diligence and devotion, the duties of a Bishop under circumstances of almost unexampled difficulty, and in face of very exceptional discouragements and disappointments. As regards himself, we may justly say that his life is a conspicuous proof of the power of the Gospel, and of the continued presence of the Spirit of God in Christ s Church."

After Bishop Crowther's death a short account of his life was published by the C.M.S. and their own assessment of his character and contribution is stated as follows: "In the annals of evangelisation of West Africa, no name stands higher than his. A boy picked out of heathenism and slavery, with no background and no inheritance save generations of crudest paganism, yet he became a man whose Christian character was an example to everyone, a scholar capable of translation work of high merit, the founder of a great pioneer mission, and the organiser of a large African Church. Where is the parallel to such a life?"

Samuel Ajayi Crowther was probably the most widely known African Christian of the nineteenth century. He embodied the reality that an African Church can be led by Africans. By the time of his death the bright confidence in that reality had dimmed. Though after his death the Niger and Yoruba Missions were united in one diocese, Western Equatorial Africa, under an English bishop J S Hill. Not until 1952 was there an African successor to Crowther.

LEGACIES

The legacy of Samuel Ajayi Crowther, the humble, devout exponent of a Christian faith that was essentially African and missionary, still lingers on. He left indelible marks for up and coming missionaries and Church workers to emulate. Some of the legacies of Bishop (Dr.) Samuel Ajayi Crowther can be categorized as follow:

Education

Perhaps the greatest service of the missionaries was the promotion of western *education* and the development of vernacular literature. Samuel Ajayi Crowther appreciated intellectual culture and frequently pointed out that the spiritual must be allied to the educational and stressed the disadvantage under which the African labours through having no written language, and therefore no literature. He assured his clergy that the Apostles of old found it a great advantage that the age in which Christianity was introduced into the world was that of literature. With an imperishable treasure of writings, the Jews were versed in the oracles of God. The Bishop declares, you could get them to compare one writing with another, to search and prove for themselves, not depending only upon the uttered word of the Apostles. And this, he urges, is the advantage today, where the missionary goes to a people who read for themselves. But the African of his time never had books and is not a reader. With this disadvantage, then, the missionary must make a written language from the lips of the natives, and then teach them the use of it in books. And he shows that by patient effort that in Niger Mission they succeeded in getting over this difficulty.

Through his influence and effort, the CMS Grammar School in the Bariga district of Lagos is the oldest secondary school in Nigeria, founded on 6 June 1859 by the Church Missionary Society and his son-in-law, Thomas Babington Macaulay, became its first principal. Coates Crowther was in the foundation class of CMS Grammar

School, Lagos in 1860. The foolish but prevalent idea, that the African intelligence cannot develop under teaching, is at once debunked by the products of such institutions of learning.

Samuel Crowther always preached a strong anti-slavery message, and his missionary work and attempts to 'civilize' African peoples were part of a broader abolitionist movement taking place among Anglican Protestants and Quakers at the time. Although Crowther cooperated extensively with the British colonial government, he also believed that the education of African peoples was vital to their gaining success. He often persuaded missionary boards to promote education and finance the development of new African schools.

Religion

Samuel Ajayi Crowther saw Christianity not just as a religion but as a way of life. Hence, he did not use his Christianity with all its social as well as political advantages in the colonial era to the detriment of his fellow brothers who are non-believers. Instead, he was tolerant, patient, and amiable to all. No wonder he was accused of being too lenient and soft with people of other religion and even Christians who erred in abiding with the doctrines. However, Samuel Ajayi Crowther was a replica of His Lord and Savior, Jesus Christ, in his incarnational approach to Christianity. He preferred to be like them so that he could win them to Christ.

Nationalism

The Bishop preaches that Christianity has come into the world to abolish and supersede all false religions, to direct mankind to the only way of obtaining peace and reconciliation with their offended God. He recommends virtues as laid down in the Gospel of Christ, the great Lawgiver of the New Covenant. These they must impress upon the minds of converts who are now born-again and point this out to them from the Word of God. But it should be borne in mind that Christianity does not undertake to destroy national assimilation.

The Bishop warned his clergy against losing sight of their nationality, and not taking sufficient heed of the native customs and ideas which, they met on ground. He knew the native pastors would adopt European ideas without stint; their outward dress and their inward thought would be quite soon enough and sufficiently after the pattern of the white man. He warned them against expecting too much from their converts, and not to force them to abandon what is perfectly natural and becoming in their life for a merely artificial imitation of the European.

Patriotization

Samuel Ajayi Crowther's sense of patriotism never diminished even though he was forcefully taken away from his hometown as a slave and deprived of the care and love of his family. He did not allow the trauma of his early life to affect his concern for his country, town, and people. He became a free man in Sierra Leone and was always thinking about the freedom of his people. Like Nehemiah, the immigrant steward in the Bible, he used all his influence, connection, position, and status in a foreign land to pursue the rebuilding of social, economic, physical, and spiritual walls of his nation. Like Esther, the lady immigrant in Persia, he risked his life for the emancipation of his people.

Missions

The mission of the Church is to reach the unreached with the Gospel. Samuel Ajayi Crowther was a dedicated, committed, and passionate missionary to West Africa and especially to Nigeria. He did not hesitate to help his people who were suffering physically, socially, politically, and spiritually. He could have settled down in Sierra Leone or England and began to enjoy with his family. Instead, he believed that the best place to be the light was not among the lights but in the midst of darkness, in Africa. Even though white missionaries were already showing the light to them in Africa, but the difference was clear when a black man like them brought and showed them the light.

Bible Translation and Development of Vernacular Literature

Just as Martin Luther, the German reformer, believed that everybody must have and read the bible in his/her native language, so did Samuel Ajayi Crowther. He was never trained as a linguist or language expert, but he acquired the skill by himself so that he could provide Bibles written in native languages for his own people. And by the grace of God, Crowther began translating the Bible into the Yoruba language and compiling a Yoruba dictionary. In 1843, a grammar book which he started working on during the Niger expedition was published; and a Yoruba version of the Anglican Book of Common Prayer followed later. Crowther also compiled a vocabulary of the Yoruba language, including many local proverbs, published in London in 1852. He also began codifying other languages. Following the Niger Expeditions of 1854 and 1857, Crowther, assisted by a young Igbo interpreter named Simon Jonas, produced a primer for the Igbo language in 1857, another for the Nupe language in 1860, and a full grammar and vocabulary of Nupe in 1864.

Crowther's attention was directed more and more to languages other than Yoruba, but he continued to supervise the translation of the Yoruba Bible (*Bibeli Mimọ*), which was completed in the mid-1880s, a few years before his death.

The Bible written in Yoruba language was not the first translation into an African language but, the first by a native speaker. Early missionary translations naturally relied heavily on native speakers as informants and guides; but in no earlier case was a native speaker able to translate into native language.

Indigenization of the Episcopate

The ordination as a clergy as well as the appointment of Samuel Ajayi Crowther as the Bishop of the Niger marked the beginning of indigenization of Christianity in Africa. Up till this time, Christianity has Christianized Africa but Africa has not indigenized Christianity. With his episcopal and sacerdotal elevation, it was now clear that Africans can head the African Church. It was the policy of Henry Venn, then newly at the helm of the CMS, to strengthen the indigenous ministry. More Africans were ordained and some for the Yoruba mission. Henry Venn also wanted well-educated, well-trained African clergy; such people as Crowther's son Dandeson (who became archdeacon) and his son-in-law T. B. Macaulay (who became principal of Lagos Grammar School) were better educated than many of the homespun English missionaries. Venn sought self-governing, self-supporting, self-propagating Churches with a fully indigenous pastorate. In Anglican terms, this meant indigenous Bishops. The missionary role was a temporary one; once a Church was established, the missionary should move on. The birth of the Church brought the euthanasia of the mission. With the growth of the Yoruba Church, Venn sought to get these principles applied in Yorubaland. Even the best European missionaries thought this impractical.

Gospel and the Plough

Bishop Crowther was a firm believer in "the Gospel and the Plough", in other words, the combination of Christianity and industry. Without denying that prior to the introduction of Christianity in West Africa the people had developed their own crafts, one must admit that it was Christian missionaries who introduced modern forms of crafts such as carpentry and masonry. The early missionaries set up craft centres as part of their educational programmes. Also, the missionaries set up model farms where scientific agriculture was taught and new crops were introduced for the people, to go alongside longstanding indigenous production.

When he arrived at Onitsha, in 1857, the mission introduced the cultivation of the cassava plants and other fruit trees, and one of their pastors took great pains to teach them to raise a second crop of Indian corn, and to make more of their yams.

The Bishop regarded industry as a necessary though a secondary part of missionary labours; it is a direct command of the apostle Paul to the converts at Thessalonica: " For even when we were with you, this we commanded you, that if any would not work, neither should he eat. For we hear that there are some which walk among you disorderly, not working at all, but are busy bodies. Now them that are such we command and exhort by our Lord Jesus Christ, that with quietness they work, and eat their own bread " (2 Thess. iii. 10-12). Those who were already made converts are commanded and urged to habits of industry. This is consistent with the principle of the Gospel and the plough, or Christianity and industry of the C.M.S both the Gospel and plough worked hand in hand—the Gospel primarily, industry as the handmaid to the Gospel.

In a letter written by the Bishop to his dear friend H Venn on 7 March 1860, he gave of an account of a commercial venture at his station at Igbein. It engrossed the time and energies of the mission there, but Crowther was always keenly alive to the material well-being of his country. The letter shows that at the earliest stage of cotton export he took the initiative. He commenced the venture with a deaf and dumb boy whose name is Thomas Craig, who seemed to be delighted in the working of the saw gin, when everyone ran away from it as being too laborious to turn all day, and, being a strong lad, it was he who chiefly worked the 500 lb. of clean cotton which was first produced from Abeokuta in 1851. From this small beginning, with a deaf and dumb boy, the work gained the interest of the chiefs and people of Abeokuta. They were consigning their cotton to merchants in England of their own choice, being taught by the Industrial Institution to develop the resources of their own country, for which a market was shown them. Thus, the secondary part of missionary labours for the Society has been answered.

The Engagement with Islam

Crowther's Niger Mission also represents the first sustained missionary engagement with African Islam in modern times. In the Upper Niger areas in Crowther's time Islam, largely accepted by the chiefs, was working slowly through the population in coexistence with the old religion. From his early experiences in Sierra Leone, Crowther understood how Islamic practice could merge with traditional views of power. He found a demand for Arabic Bibles but was cautious about supplying them unless he could be sure they would not be used for charms. His insight was justified later, when the young European missionaries who succeeded him wrote out passages of Scripture on request, pleased at such a means of Scripture distribution. They stirred up the anger of Muslim clerics not because they were circulating Christian Scriptures, but because they were giving them free, thus undercutting the trade in Qur'anic charms. In discussion with Muslims, Crowther sought common ground and found it at the nexus of Qur'an and Bible: Christ as the great prophet, his miraculous birth, Gabriel as the messenger of God. He enjoyed courteous and friendly relations with Muslim rulers.

Suppressed Slave Trade

Christian missions also took a leading role in the campaign to end the slave trade and to suppress slavery.

Public Enlightenment

Crowther was also a close associate and friend of Captain James Pinson Labulo Davies, an influential politician, mariner, philanthropist and industrialist in colonial Lagos. Both men collaborated on a couple of Lagos social initiatives such as the opening of The Academy (a social and cultural center for public enlightenment) on 24 October 1866 with Crowther as the 1st patron and Captain J.P.L Davies as 1st president.

Bibliography

"The Black Bishop" SAMUEL ADJAI CROWTHER by Jesse Page, F.R.G.S. New York, Chicago: F. H. Revell Company, 1909.

Samuel Crowther, The Slave Boy who became Bishop of The Niger By Jesse Page New York, Chicago: F. H. Revell Company, 1909.

Journals of Rev James Fredrick Schon and Mr Samuel Crowther on the expedition up the Niger by Hatchard and Son, Piccadilly; Nisbet And Co., Berners Street; Seeleys, Fleet Street.

The Legacy of Samuel Ajayi Crowther by Andrew F. Walls Literacy & Evangelism International 1800S Jackson Avenue Tulsa OK 74107.

A charge delivered on the banks of the River Niger in West Africa. Samuel Adjai Crowther, D.D. Oxon, London: Seeley, Jackson, & Halliday, 54, Fleet Street. Printed by C. F. Hodgson & Son, Bough Square, Fleet Street, E.C.

The History of the Church Missionary Society. Its Environment, Its Men and Its Work by, Eugene Stock, Editorial Secretary 1836-1928 in Three Volumes, Printed by Gilbert and Rivington, Ld., St. John's House, Clerkenwell, E.C.

Niger Mission. Bishop Crowther's Report of the Overland Journey from Lokoja to Bida, on the River Niger, and thence to Lagos, On the Sea Coast, from November 10th, 1871, to February 8th, 1872. London: Church Missionary House, Salisbury Square. Seeleys, Jackson, & Halliday, Fleet Street.

Samuel Ajayi Crowther, Black Victorians and the Future of Africa by Katharina Oke a DPhil student in Global History at the University of Oxford.

Abstract from Christian Missionaries and Civilization in Southern Nigeria, 1841-1960: Implications for Contemporary by Christians Kanayo Louis Nwadialor.

Journal of an Expedition Up The Niger And Tshadda Rivers, Undertaken By Macgregor Laird, Esq. In Connection with The British Government, In 1854. By The Rev. Samuel Crowther. With Map And Appendix London: Church Missionary House, Salisbury Square; Seeley, Jackson, And Halliday, Fleet Street.

The Contribution of Henry Venn to Mission Thought by Wilbert R. Shenk Anvil Vol. 2, No. 1, 1985.

Love and Death in the Mission Compound: The Hardships of Life in the Tropics for Victorian Missionaries and their Families by John Darch ANVIL Volume 17 No 1 2000.

Beneath the Wilberforce Oak, 1873 by David Killingray International Bulletin of Missionary Research 1997.

The Romance of the Black River. The Story of the C.M.S. Nigeria Mission by F. Deaville Walker. Made and printed in Great Britain by the Camelot Press Ltd London and Southampton.